MW01707305

HAND IN HAND

VOLUME ONE

A PRACTICAL APPLICATION OF
ART AND PLAY THERAPY

Edited by:

Betty Bedard Bidwell

Published by

GENERAL STORE
PUBLISHING HOUSE

Box 28, 1694B Burnstown, Ontario, Canada K0J 1G0
Telephone (613) 432-7697 or 1-800-465-6072

ISBN 1-894263-38-3
Printed and bound in Canada

Design layout by Derek McEwen

General Store Publishing House
Burnstown, Ontario, Canada

National Library of Canada Cataloguing in Publication Data

Main entry under title:

Hand in hand I

Includes bibliographical references and index
Contents: I. A practical application of art and play therapy / edited by Betty Bedard Bidwell

ISBN 1-894263-38-3

1. Art therapy. 2. Play Therapy. 3. Group psychotherapy for children. I. Bedard Bidwell, Betty, 1951-

RJ504.H354 2001 618.92'891653 C2001-900248-3

DEDICATION

This book is dedicated to three very special women in my life.

Irene Dewdney for her training and sharing her vast knowledge and experience.

Marian Hindmarsh for her past and continuous unconditional support and love.

Gwen Bidwell for always being there to pick up the slack when my life gets overwhelming. She is a wonderful grandmother!

Betty Bedard Bidwell

CONTENTS

Preface vii

Chapter 1 1
The Therapist
Betty Bedard Bidwell

Chapter 2 9
Play Therapy
Bridget Revell

Chapter 3 29
History of Art Therapy in Canada and the United States
Betty Bedard Bidwell and Suzanne Lister

Chapter 4 39
Links between Art and Play Therapy
Margot Sippel

Chapter 5 45
Theraplay
Dr. Evangeline Munns

Chapter 6 59
Art and Playroom Equipment and Observations
Betty Bedard Bidwell

Chapter 7 73
Puppets as Allies in Therapy
Marg McBride

Chapter 8 89
A Systemic Art Therapy Assessment
for Use with Children
Barbara Dorrington

Chapter 9 117
Becoming a Therapeutic Storyteller
Greg Lubimiv

Chapter 10 151
Implementation of Play and Art Therapy
Programs in the Schools
Donna Cuthbertson

Chapter 11 185
An Individual Play/Art Therapy
Assessment Model
Judy Jones, Julie Regan
and Barbara Jones Warrick

Chapter 12 205
Using Play and Art Therapy
to Work with Families
Bridget Revell

Chapter 13 229
Children And Death: Understanding,
Grief Process, and Counselling
Suzanne Lister

Chapter 14 245
Ethics and Professional Practice
Sharron Zweig

PREFACE

This volume is the product of several years of experience in the fields of Art and Play Therapy on the part of the contributors—multi-talented contributors—who represent a diverse number of therapeutic approaches, styles and beliefs, and each of whom has illustrated and tested his or her theories in practice.

It is also the result of a perceived need in the literature for a text on Play and Art Therapy that is "user friendly" and is directed not specifically to theoreticians or academics, but to those working in the field itself. It is our hope that the various contributions will greatly broaden the reader's knowledge and enhance his or her experience in Art and Play Therapy.

The reader will discover that the various authors in this volume may disagree with each other on certain points. Because it is the editor's belief that such diversity is healthy and that the range of conceptual viewpoints has something of significance to say to the reader, no attempt has been made to unify the thoughts expressed here into one integrated whole; rather, it is our hope that through these various systems of beliefs and practice, the reader will perceive a common thread: an overriding belief in, and respect for, the client, and a desire to serve the client in the best way possible.

Special thanks to . . .

Gwen Kiar for her artwork.

Jane Karchmar, for her incredible patience and skill in re-editing this edition.

CHAPTER ONE

THE THERAPIST

Betty Bedard Bidwell

THE THERAPIST

Although this chapter is titled "The Therapist," I am referring to caretakers in general. This chapter speaks to all of us in the social services profession. The term "caretaker" includes social workers, child and youth workers, developmental services workers, occupational therapists, lay counsellors, special education teachers, guidance counsellors, Y.O.A. counsellors, foster parents, and of course concerned parents.

In this chapter, the term "therapist" will be used to cover all of the above caretakers.

I have dedicated this chapter completely to the therapist. The therapist is the main character, the entry force behind the success of therapy.

When a client comes to therapy, he is often at a point in his life where he lacks the energy and internal guidance to deal with his personal issues alone. He comes to you, the therapist, to get that guidance and energy. To help him, you must be solid and grounded yourself, personally and professionally. If you are tired, overworked or frustrated, from lack of professional recognition or professional support, or if you are not taking care of your personal needs, you won't be able to give your client the professional assistance that he expects from you.

Sometimes, as professionals, we think that if we could add to our techniques new skills from different methods of therapy, we would be better therapists.

But techniques such as art therapy, play therapy, strategic therapy, Gestalt therapy, reality therapy, etc., are not magic tools. They can't be effective unless the users of these techniques are also effective engineers of these therapies. A therapist knows the theory and the official techniques of her craft but she is more than just a technician. Like an engineer, she brings reasoned intuition, professional experience and responsibility to her task. A therapist uses more than technique. Without a solid, healthy, well-grounded therapist, the technique itself is useless or ineffective.

So what is a solid, healthy, well-grounded therapist? He is a person who has learned to take care of himself professionally, personally and spiritually.

Taking Care Professionally

The first way that a therapist takes care of herself professionally is to become involved in continual re-education and development by attending workshops, conferences and training programs. This kind of contact with peers and colleagues can serve to rejuvenate, refocus and clarify. Often this professional contact can re-ignite a creative spark or provide the support needed to return to therapy with increased enthusiasm and confidence. Also the professional communication and network building which occurs at these seminars is an effective way to grow professionally.

A therapist who is taking care of himself professionally attends regular team "supervision" sessions. As distinct from formal professional development conferences, these are opportunities to meet more informally with other therapists, or in fact, any small group of like-minded professionals who share his work experience and philosophical approach.

An individual therapist is not all knowing and all-powerful, nor does he have all the answers and direction for all his clients. A small professional group, where members can give each other "supervision" or feedback and suggestions is an invaluable aid in preventing tunnel vision and burnout. Supervision may begin with a mentor who is involved in teaching the therapeutic process. However, it can continue and flourish in a climate of mutual respect, understanding and trust between colleagues who are concerned about their clients and who wish to be objective and as effective as possible in their private practice, agency or institution.

Part of the therapist's ongoing professional care is to continue her own personal therapy. If a therapist respects her profession, then she also recognizes its benefits for her own emotional health. We all struggle with personal crisis, but professional therapists and counsellors are often the last people to seek assistance. Their attitude is that therapy is for the client, not the therapist. But the therapist must also be able to cope. When a therapist avoids working on her own emotional needs, she is in danger of developing an attitude that will cause her to turn off, to become blocked and ineffective to her clients.

In fact, a therapist has a professional obligation to maintain emotional stability if she continues to counsel others who are in stress, in need or in danger. "Practice what you preach" is a good motto for any therapist to keep in mind.

Although a therapist always has to deal with his own stresses and personal issues, in a session with a client the problems and issues of that client are paramount. A therapist should be able to internalize the emotional and physical feelings that a client expresses. And that is what happens when a therapist is alive, effective and involved: the therapist connects with his client. The therapist bears some of the client's burden when he sees that the client's issues and problems are a concern, and the client is not just a number, an appointment or a dollar sign.

A therapist needs to remember to keep her own professional perspective. Balance and effectiveness are professional responsibilities. But a therapist's own life situation or her client's presenting problems may upset this balance. A therapist should recognize her limits. A therapist is not almighty or all-powerful. We all have our saturation levels. A good therapist recognizes when that level is reached. She accepts the problem and does something about it. This is when a therapist must take responsibility to seek formal supervision or professional help, or to refer a client to another therapist, or even to discontinue providing therapy until her own personal issues are sorted out.

It is not a sign of weakness for a therapist to recognize and address his own professional needs. On the contrary, it is a sign of respect for the client and for the self. Continued interest in professional development and ongoing self-evaluation are positive indications that a therapist is involved, active and growing. On the other hand, if the therapist allows himself to remain in a non-stable condition, then he runs the risk of becoming permanently ineffective, a robot in word and action. Even worse, a wounded therapist can seriously damage the psychological or emotional state of a trusting and vulnerable client.

Taking Care Personally
A therapist who is grounded personally is someone who is aware of and looks after her own well-being. Relationships, physical and emotional health, friends and family and outside interests and involvements are all important to a therapist's balance and grounding.

Therapists, social workers, counsellors and other members of the healing professions are notorious for not taking care of themselves. It is a recurring theme that we prefer to look after the needs of others while sometimes ignoring our own.

Too often a therapist's spouse, lover, children, family or friends are the last to receive her energy, time or involvement. A therapist can feel that there just isn't enough to go around after a long day with clients. And sometimes there isn't. If it comes to this point, the therapist should realize that she has lost sight of important priorities—her own personal needs and the needs of her loved ones. If a therapist neglects herself and her family because she is "too busy" and her job is "too important," how can she presume to help a client understand and improve his personal relationship?

Without support from people we love and who love us, our lives become empty. Clients cannot take the place of our family. In fact, there is nothing that can take that place, no matter how much money, prestige and professional acceptance we receive. Without someone to share it all, the rewards or status quickly become meaningless. Healthy relationships with partners, friends or family feed us, nourish us and enrich our lives. These relationships are a source of energy, not a drain.

As a therapist, you need to set priorities to balance your professional and private life. For example, you must make decisions to limit late nights at the office, evening meetings, and the number of clients on your caseload at one time; and also to limit additional responsibilities to ensure that you are not overextended on a personal level. By discussing time schedules with a partner or family members, a therapist can determine what is an appropriate schedule for her lifestyle and her family. When a therapist asks for help in determining signs of over-involvement, anxiety, stress, avoidance or lack of close contact with loved ones, she will maintain a perspective that is based in reality, but tinged with love and concern.

Personal private time is also extremely important in the ongoing personal care of the therapist. This is the time a person needs to relax, revitalize and re-motivate. What you do to recharge is not as important as making sure you enjoy the activity—and that you make and take the time to do it.

For example, some of the things that I do for myself are regular massages, frequent, relaxing hot tubs, facials, and reading at night before I go to bed. I enjoy social activities with my family and good friends, such as going out to dinner or to plays, art exhibits, craft shows, antique shopping and bargain hunting. I love to organize and redecorate rooms, apartments and cabins. I consider it an accomplishment to create a warm, homey and comfortable environment on a budget.

I have to admit that I am not a regular fitness type. I do not have an extensive physical program but I do try to be physically active. Frequent changes of leisure time activities keep me from getting bored. For example, I work in our flower or vegetable gardens, or with the animals at Homestead, our small farm. I enjoy camping, canoeing and walking in the bush. Contact with nature is very important to me.

Physically, I also need to take care of myself. If I am exhausted or ill with assorted aches and pains, then obviously I cannot concentrate on the needs of my clients. I must get the sleep I need, pay attention to my diet, and be aware of my own body's biorhythms. I need to know and understand how different foods affect me and, if necessary, to go on a personalized vitamin program.

Taking periods of time away from your work as a therapist, whether alone or with your family, is another important issue. I believe that in order to deal with the continuous stress of our profession, we need time away to do something totally different. I take most of the summer off from my private practice. I retreat to a beautiful place near water and trees and rocks. I camp, canoe and relax in the shade. I catch up on sleep, sun and inactivity. I also catch up on my professional reading. I find that through the year I cannot do therapy, counselling, supervision, report writing and teaching all day, and then read about it at night. We all need to find a balance for ourselves, and this one works for me. Every therapist needs to find that individual balance that will contribute to her own personal growth, stability and happiness.

Taking Care Spiritually

The area of spirituality is the most difficult to address because spiritual matters are so personal, intense and private. Each person's needs are different in this regard. A therapist in touch with a personal notion of spirituality is usually more grounded and secure than one who hasn't considered this issue.

Spirituality for me is personal grounding. It is not necessarily a structured religion, a philosophical viewpoint, or even specifically Christian. But it is an individual belief that there is a source more powerful than ourselves from whom we can seek support and strength. The desire to be omnipotent, to have all the answers, to wield all the power, or to shoulder all the responsibility, can soon lead to complete exhaustion as well as a sense of failure. No therapist has all the answers. Everyone needs to search outside, as well as inside. This personal search is an ongoing process that contributes to all aspects of our lives.

Conclusion

The professional, personal and spiritual nature of a therapist is intimately connected with the working philosophy that provides the foundation for the therapist's approach. Without a clear understanding of this philosophy and the skills to put it into practice, a therapist can do little. The synthesis of all these aspects is vital to the therapist and client alike.

Various people have written about the qualities that make a good therapist. In his book *Children in Play Therapy*, the American therapist Clark Moustakas discusses three basic attitudes in client-centered therapy: faith that the client can work through the conflict; acceptance of the client's feelings and perceptions; and respect for who the client is and what his issues are in therapy.

In her book *Play Therapy*, Virginia M. Axline, another American therapist, deals with eight basic therapeutic principles, which I have also found to be inspiring for my own work:

1) The therapist develops a warm, friendly relationship with the client.
2) The therapist accepts the client.
3) The therapist develops a permissive atmosphere so that the client is able to express himself completely without fear of rejection.
4) The therapist is able to recognize and work with the client's feelings so that the client gains insight into his own behaviour.
5) The therapist respects the client's ability to solve his own problems, to make appropriate choices for healing himself.
6) The therapist allows the client to lead the way, with the therapist's support and understanding.
7) The therapist places no time limits on how long a client needs to continue in therapy. The client has his own personal time frame for healing, which may be longer or shorter than the therapist's expectations.

8) The therapist uses only the limits necessary to maintain safety and ensure professional, ethical behaviour. (For example, in my therapy room, I enforce only these basic rules: the client cannot physically hurt herself; she can't physically hurt me; and she can't deliberately try to break any furniture or equipment in the room.)

Although Clark Moustakas and Virginia Axline were discussing therapy with children, I believe their principles apply to clients of any age. Adults and adolescents also need faith, acceptance and respect in order to feel comfortable and trusting in the therapeutic relationship. The above principles are guidelines that I use in working with clients of all ages.

By working from a solid, well-integrated philosophical base and by attending to professional, personal and spiritual issues, the therapist is able to clearly focus on the client's needs. The therapist who is able to recognize his own needs and to provide for them is more likely to give top quality therapy for his clients. That therapist will provide the energy, acceptance and support that his clients need to grow and progress.

CHAPTER TWO

PLAY THERAPY

Bridget Revell

PLAY THERAPY

Play Therapy involves using play materials as part of a therapeutic process designed to meet the emotional, social, psychological and developmental needs of clients. However, it must be recognized that "Play therapy consists of a cluster of treatment modalities that include a variety of highly developed theoretical orientations and technical strategies" (O'Connor, 1991, p. 6). The parameters of "play therapy" are marked by:

1) The tools available
2) The deliberate use of the therapeutic aspects of play
3) An underlying theoretical framework
4) A distinct therapeutic relationship

This chapter will explore each of these defining characteristics in depth. Through this process, the reader will gain an appreciation for the range of interventions that are recognized as "play therapy."

The Tools Available

As suggested by the name, play is fundamental to play therapy. As such, the tools of play therapy are the tools of play.

At first glance, looking into a play therapy room is like looking into a child's room, a kindergarten or a toy store. You will find shelves lined with toys, buckets and bins of cars and blocks, dress-up clothes, paper, markers, crayons, art supplies, balls, telephones, a doctor's kit, dolls, and puppets. You might also see a kitchen set, a dollhouse, a sandbox or some musical instruments. Immediately, the room would feel familiar, filled with things you had seen before, as a child, a parent or a teacher.

Despite the apparent familiarity of the toys in the playroom, they have been carefully selected for the purpose of play therapy. Garry Landreth (1991), in his book *Play Therapy: The Art of Relationship*, outlines a number of issues that should be considered by the therapist when choosing toys for the playroom:

1) *Are the toys interesting?*

The toys available in the playroom must be engaging and interesting so that the children will become involved and engrossed in play. A range of toys that are appealing to clients of all ages should be available. Older children will be reluctant to play if they feel that the toys are beneath them and younger children will be unable to play if the toys are too complex.

2) *Is there a choice of materials?*
Having a variety of materials available allows the child to make choices and control their therapeutic direction. Having control is an experience that many children who come to play therapy have not previously had. Providing them with this opportunity is in itself one of the therapeutic aspects of the play therapy process.

3) *Are the toys durable?*
"The toys should be durable and should communicate a message of 'Be yourself in playing' rather than a message of 'Be careful'" (Landreth, 1991, p. 115).

4) *Do the toys facilitate creative expression?*
Play therapy is based on the premise that children communicate through their play; that they will speak to us of their hopes and dreams, pains and sorrows, feelings and needs in the stories and games they create (Axline, 1969; Landreth, 1991). It is expected that the emotions and conflicts the children project onto the toys and reflect in their play will represent issues that are important to them. Thus it is essential to select toys that allow the children to express and explore a variety of issues, in a number of different ways. In keeping with this principle, therapists should limit the use of toys that have a predetermined use. When a child feels that a toy can only be used one way or a character have only one personality, she will not be able to use it as effectively to express herself.

5) *Do the toys encourage emotional expression?*
One of the goals of therapy with children is to help them recognize, differentiate and appropriately express their emotions. As a result, there must be toys available in the playroom that encourage a full range of emotional expression. Garry Landreth (1991) notes that "puppets provide a safe way to express feelings without being threatened since the characters of the puppets are the ones expressing the feelings" (p. 119). This same premise holds true for dolls and miniature figures (people, characters, animals, dinosaurs etc.). Other useful tools for facilitating discussion of emotions are puppets and puzzles that allow children to change the facial expression and thus the reflected emotion of the character.

6) *Do the toys allow exploration of real life situations?*
Toys must be available that allow children to act out and work through real life situations. Having human toy figures (puppets, dolls or miniatures) available will allow the child to play out experiences from his home, school or community. When a medical kit is available, a child can illustrate a visit to the doctor or an experience at the hospital. Kitchen sets, play dishes and play food are other items that allow the child to review his day-to-day experiences.

7) *Do the toys provide an opportunity for success?*
Feeling a sense of accomplishment and of being capable is important to the development of self-esteem. The toys in the playroom should allow the child to create, to feel competent and to experience success. The child should not be thwarted by toys that are either too complicated or that she will need an adult's assistance to use (Landreth, 1991).

8) *Limit the toys that allow the child to isolate himself.*
There are some toys (puzzles, playing cards, books) that allow children to isolate themselves or prevent themselves from engaging in imaginative and creative play. If these toys are getting in the way of the therapeutic relationship or process, they should be removed from the playroom (Lubimiv, 1994).

Lists of suggested toys can be found in some books about play therapy (Axline, 1969; Landreth, 1991; Lubimiv, 1994). While these lists can be useful, each individual therapist will equip her playroom uniquely. The therapist's choice of toys will reflect the therapist's personality, the play space available, the therapeutic goals and the theoretical framework that direct the work in the playroom.

The Deliberate Use of the Therapeutic Aspects of Play
Play therapy involves play. Children can be found creating puppet shows, playing house, drawing, painting, playing in a sandbox, telling stories, playing checkers, setting up a doll house, or building with blocks. Children are not given these opportunities in play therapy merely because play is something that children naturally do. Children are invited to play so that the play therapist can make deliberate use of the therapeutic properties of play. The fact that play is an inherently healing, natural activity is capitalized on during the play therapy process. However, it is important to recognize that "play in itself will not ordinarily produce changes . . . the therapist's

interventions and utilizations of the play are critical" (Chethik, 1989, p. 49).

The therapeutic aspects of play that are used in play therapy are explored further below:

1) *"Play is intrinsically complete; it does not depend on external rewards or other people"* (O'Connor, 1991, p. 4)

Children provided with toys will generally pursue play, whether or not they are rewarded and whether or not other people are present. Children do not have to be coerced or forced into playing as part of a therapy process; for most of them it comes naturally.

2) *Relationship Development*

Anna Freud "advocated using play mainly to build a strong positive relationship between child and therapist" (Gil, 1991, p. 28). Play materials can serve as an icebreaker and increase the child's comfort level, as she gets to know the therapist. While most therapists recognize that play will facilitate the development of their relationship with the child, this is only one of many ways that play is used in play therapy.

3) *Play is the "natural medium of communication" for children* (Axline, 1969; Landreth, 1991, p. 10)

Using toys as their words, children can speak to the therapist about what they have experienced, their reactions to and feelings about their experiences, wishes, wants and needs and their view of themselves (Landreth, 1991, p. 15). Children's inner wishes, fantasies and conflicts are represented in their play (Esman, 1983). Since children are still developing cognitively, socially and emotionally, they are unable to talk about issues that they are able to explore through play (Landreth, 1991).

Children relate to the outer concrete world more readily than to their inner world. This fact is recognized by teachers who give young children blocks to manipulate and count when they are learning basic arithmetic. Play therapy provides children with the tools to make their inner world concrete (Landreth, 1991). When a family of dolls is placed in the dollhouse or a car accident is played out with small cars, the images and thoughts that were inside the child's head are now observable. The child can see, touch and rearrange the toys, playing with alternate endings and different resolutions. Children can show the therapist things that they could never say. “For children to ‘play out’ their experiences and feelings is the most natural dynamic and self-healing process in which children can engage” (Landreth, 1991, p. 10).

Through play, children can release and explore their emotions (Gil, 1991). Anger, sadness, loneliness, fear, happiness and excitement are just some of the emotions that the children playing or the characters of the play experience can express. Helping children to develop an understanding of these emotions and appropriate ways to express them in their lives is often a central goal of play therapy.

4) *Play provides children with an opportunity to manipulate and control objects.*

As noted earlier, many children who come to play therapy have not had the opportunity to be in control of their experiences, their lives or their fate. In the playroom the child is given that control. They are usually allowed to choose the objects they wish to play with and decide how they will play with them. This unique experience can help children recognize that at some level, in some places, they can exert control over their destiny (Landreth, 1991).

Many children who enter the play therapy room have had overwhelming and frightening experiences. When they replay these experiences realistically or metaphorically, children have an opportunity to make the unmanageable become manageable (Landreth, 1991). For example, when a person is in a car accident, he is overwhelmed by emotions, thoughts, concerns and questions. Following the accident an adult will verbally replay aspects of the accident over and over: “Can you imagine what would have happened if the fence hadn’t stopped the car? We would have fallen down that hill. The car might have rolled over and over and you know Jim wasn’t wearing his seat belt. We are so lucky that the fence was strong enough, otherwise it might have been a disaster . . .” A child will engage in the same replay using toys. The child may act out the accident and then act out the accident again as it would have been if the fence had broken. The child can slow the process of the accident down in his play and thus consider issues individually. One week the child may focus on the cars hitting each other, the next on the ambulance coming and the next on the fight he was having with his sister before the accident happened. In slowing the process down and considering alternate endings, the child comes to understand his unbearable experience. Each time the child replays the experience, he is faced again with his emotions. When these anxieties can be tolerated in play, the child gains a sense of mastery over his feelings (Erikson, 1950; Russ, 1995).

5) *Play facilitates children's development* (Piaget, 1962; O'Connor, 1991; Russ, 1995; Schaefer, 1993).

Play therapy can assist children in their overall development as well as in developing basic play skills, self-esteem and social skills (Gil, 1991).

The severe neglect experienced by some children who come to the playroom means that they have not learned to play. For example, a seven-year-old girl, Lynn, came into the playroom and stated that she wanted to paint. She went to the easel and painted one stripe of each colour on the paper. When asked about her picture, Lynn said that it was a monster. The next week she again came in and asked to paint. Again Lynn painted one stripe of each colour on her paper. When she had finished, she described her painting as a house. Lynn repeated this process for several weeks, each time stating that she had painted something different but always painting one stripe of each colour on her paper. It was known that Lynn had been raised in a very neglectful home. One week the therapist sat beside Lynn while she painted and the therapist painted a picture of a simple stick figure and a house on a piece of paper on the floor. Lynn watched the therapist and then began experimenting. She painted a recognizable person. The next week, when she returned to painting, she painted a monster with six legs. Over time, Lynn's paintings developed further and further. Due to her neglect and lack of exposure to painting materials, Lynn seemed to require modelling of how the materials could be used. With an example provided by the therapist, Lynn was quickly able to develop and further her own skills.

When children are involved in a play therapy process they are provided with an opportunity to participate in a valued relationship, speak and be understood (through play), and develop new skills. Together these experiences allow the child to feel special, unique and valued, which in turn allows for growth and development of her self-esteem.

Through play, children can learn how to share toys, take turns, cooperate, introduce ideas for play and develop these ideas with the people around them (O'Connor, 1991). In addition, through play therapy, children participate in an intimate relationship, learn to express and explore emotions and practice ways of relating. Children who have struggled with peers are often able to directly and indirectly develop abilities during therapy sessions that allow them to relate more effectively with others outside the playroom.

The play therapist must be aware of the therapeutic attributes of play and must be alert to their contribution to the play therapy process. Having this knowledge will allow therapists to modify their interventions in the playroom to meet the treatment needs of the children with whom they work. Different therapists will maximize the use of different healing elements of play based on their personality, their style and the theoretical framework that forms the basis for their work.

An Underlying Theoretical Framework

In order to set goals, plan sessions, implement interventions and monitor progress, play therapists must have a theoretical framework that guides their work. This framework will impact the toys the therapist uses, how he uses the play material, the relationship he develops with his clients and the way he intervenes with his clients. A wide range of therapeutic models have been used by therapists using play in their work with children:

1) Psychoanalytic Play Therapy (Bromfield, 1992; Esman, 1983; Freud, 1964; Klein, 1959)
2) Release Play Therapy and Structured Play Therapy (Levy, 1939; Hambridge, 1955; Solomon, 1938)
3) Relationship/Client-Centred Play Therapy (Axline, 1969; Landreth, 1991)
4) Focal Therapy (Chethik, 1989)
5) Behavioural Play Therapy (O'Connor, 1991)
6) Gestalt (Oaklander, 1978)
7) Jungian (Allan, 1988; Kalff, 1980; Weinrib, 1983)
8) Filial Therapy (Guerney, 1964; Landreth, 1991)
9) Theraplay (Jernberg, 1979)

Excellent summaries of the development of the field of play therapy and of the therapeutic models used by therapists in this field have been provided in a number of books and will not be repeated here (Gil, 1991; Landreth, 1991; O'Connor, 1991; Russ, 1995; Schaefer & O'Connor, 1983).

Research conducted by Weisz (1986) has suggested that children's improvement in therapy is unrelated to the therapist's theoretical orientation. However, it must be recognized that "the therapist's theoretical orientation, whatever it may be, is the framework in which she organizes all her thinking about the client's difficulties, the interventions to be used, and the assessment of outcome" (O'Connor, 1991). Without this framework, the child and therapist run a significant risk of becoming lost in the play therapy journey, unsure of their destination and unable to judge if they have met their goals. The beginning therapist is strongly urged to review the available literature and to establish a firm theoretical underpinning for her clinical work.

While therapists should work from a clear theoretical framework, it is equally essential that therapists recognize that each client is individual and every situation is unique. No one therapeutic model, approach or set of techniques can be expected to work for every child that walks into a therapist's office. It is quite likely that "different types of child therapy" that "emphasize different mechanisms of change and different techniques" should be used with "different populations of children" (Russ, 1995, p. 370). The therapist must remain open to adjusting his approach to meet each child's unique needs or to refer some children to other therapists with different skills. One of the greatest mistakes a therapist or agency can make is to arrogantly assume that their way is the only way for everyone.

A Distinct Therapeutic Relationship

The Nature of the Relationship

A therapist's relationship with a child in play therapy is like no other relationship the child has experienced (Landreth, 1991). The relationship is different from that with his parent, teacher, coach, Scoutmaster, or neighbour. "The relationship with the child is a continual prizing of the uniqueness of the child and an empathic experiencing of the moment-by-moment living out of the child's world at a pace of unfolding determined by the inner direction of the emerging child" (Landreth, 1991, p. 72). It has been postulated that this relationship is central to the healing power of therapy (Kottler, 1993; Lubimiv, 1994).

Many of the children that come to play therapy have been hurt at the hands of adults, and have learned that adults are not to be trusted. Our relationship with the child in play therapy is an opportunity to teach her that this is not always so (Gil, 1991). Through their time with us, children can learn that not all men or women inflict hurt and that some adults maintain a deep respect for children. Research has suggested that having "experienced a supportive, close relationship in childhood with a relative, foster parent, or some other significant adult" is one of the factors differentiating mothers who have broken a cycle of abuse from mothers that were unable to break that cycle (Erickson & Egeland, 1991, p. 2). The power of our relationship to have long-standing consequences for the children we meet should never be underestimated.

The theoretical model from which a therapist operates dictates to a large extent the type of relationship she will develop with clients and what the therapist's role will be in that relationship (O'Connor, 1991). However, therapists taking divergent approaches "seem to share the qualities of curiosity and a desire to explore, creativity, respect and awe of children's resiliency and uniqueness, sensitivity and a sense of humour" (Gil, 1994, p. 5).

Despite the varying approaches that play therapists take in working with their clients, they strive to ensure that the playroom is a place of safety and sanctity for the children. Predictability, consistency, respect, a sense of belonging and a belief in the child's tendency to move towards growth and maturity, are conveyed to the child through the therapist's actions (Axline, 1969; Landreth, 1991; Lubimiv, 1994). The child is allowed to come into the playroom, be who she is, and have this self accepted by the therapist. This is a central tenet for many play therapists (Axline, 1969; Landreth, 1991).

One way that play therapists provide safety to and convey their deep respect for the children they work with is through assuring each child that his time in the playroom is confidential. With the exception of information that must be shared in order to guarantee the safety of the child or someone else, the child's actions and words in the playroom are not repeated to the his caregivers, teachers or friends. Children are usually informed of this right in their first session (e.g., "What we play and talk about in here is private. You can tell anyone you want, but I won't tell your parents or your teacher. If I think that you are not safe or someone else is not safe then I will tell someone."). When a therapist wishes to meet with a caregiver, general information about the child's progress and needs can be shared. This is usually reviewed with the child and her permission obtained prior to meeting with the caregivers (e.g., "I am meeting with your foster parents tomorrow. I would like to tell them that sometimes you feel sad and that when you feel sad, an extra hug might help you. Is it all right if I tell them this? Is there anything else you would like me to tell them? Is there anything that you do not want me to tell them?"). With their confidentiality assured, children feel free to become vulnerable and explore deep issues.

"The child standing before the therapist in the playroom is not a problem to be analyzed but a whole person to be related to and understood" (Landreth, 1991, p. 51). Not only are they children we work with people, they are children. In addition to whatever struggles they bring to the playroom, they will bring all the trials and tribulations of growing up. There is a significant danger of pathologizing the children with whom we work, of assuming that every tantrum, tear or smile is somehow related to the issue that brought them to therapy. We must remember that the children are children first; and, as children do, they will scream, cry and laugh.

Garry Landreth (1991) says that "Attempting to describe the almost imperceptible but nevertheless fully present subtle nuances characteristic of a shared relationship with a child is a bit like trying to pick up a small bubble of mercury with your fingers" (p. 73). Through further consideration of the role of the therapist in play therapy it is hoped that the reader will gain a fuller understanding of the unique relationship that develops between therapist and child in the play therapy room.

The Therapist's Role in the Playroom

The role that a play therapist assumes in the playroom is based on the model that inspires her work. A psychoanalytic therapist serves as an interpreter; a child-centred therapist's main role is to develop an environment that facilitates the child's growth and development; the behavioural play therapist makes note of the presence or absence of specific behaviours and provides rewards or consequences in relation to these; and the Theraplay therapist guides the child through a variety of carefully planned interpersonal interactions (O'Connor, 1991).

Degree of Direction.

Every beginning play therapist must decide how "directive" she is going to be in her work. There is a significant division in the field of play therapy between play therapists who call themselves "non-directive" and those who call themselves "directive". The therapist's level of "direction" is determined by how often and to what degree she allows children to make choices in the play therapy room. There are four areas in which a therapist may or may not make decisions for the child in the course of play therapy:

1) To what extent does the child make choices about his activities during play therapy sessions?

Some therapists allow the child to choose which toys to use and how to use them at all times, in all sessions. Other therapists may make suggestions of specific activities for the child to pursue (e.g., "Draw me a picture of your family."). Still other therapists will limit the child's activity by providing only one set of toys or one activity.

2) To what degree does the child determine how her play and stories will proceed?

While some play therapists allow the child to maintain complete control over her play and story lines, others will make suggestions for changing or altering the play that is presented by the child. For example, a therapist may bring an ambulance to an accident scene that was created by the child or create a "safety zone" during a war, where characters may go if they wish to stop fighting.

Therapists will differ in whether or not they allow the child to decide when to start and stop his play or whether they encourage the child to continue to develop his story when he attempts to end it. For example, John was drawing a picture of a fight between two men. When he had finished, he threw the picture on the ground and began playing with the cars. The therapist picked up John's picture and asked him what it was about. From where he was, John said, "A stupid fight." When asked who was fighting, John said, "My dad and his friend." The therapist asked John if he had anything he wanted to say to the men fighting. John started yelling from where he was and then came over and started poking at the picture with his finger. "Stop yelling. I can't sleep. Shut up," John shouted. Then John turned to the therapist and said, "Sometimes they are so loud." Rather than allowing John to end his work with the picture when he threw it on the floor, the therapist encouraged John to explore the issues in the picture further by drawing his attention back to the picture and asking him questions.

3) Who determines what issues and inner conflicts the child will work on?

Most therapists are aware of a wide range of issues that a child may bring with her to play therapy. In many cases, the therapist will observe the child's play to determine which issues appear central. In other therapeutic situations the therapist may decide that a particular issue needs to be addressed during therapy sessions, even though it has not been raised by the child. For example, when working with a child who has been the victim of sexual abuse, therapists may feel that it is important to review who bears responsibility for the abuse even though this issue has not been raised by the child.

4) Who decides what the child's play and words are communicating?

It is believed by some therapists that particular toys convey particular meaning when used by children in play (Norton & Norton, 1992). For example, a list of "Symbolic Meanings of Animals" provides the following associations for a beaver: "stability, persistent, workaholic, eager, structure, compulsive, organized" (Norton & Norton, 1992, p. 5). Others, recognizing that personal associations are affected by individual experiences and cultural influences, feel that the child must be allowed to teach the therapist what a given toy means for her (Barnes, 1995). A therapist who has an established set of assumptions regarding the meanings of the toys used by children in play is obviously more directive in determining the meaning of a child's play.

Garry Landreth (1991) outlines a play scenario in which a child is asking a therapist which colour to paint a frog. At one point the child says, "You're supposed to tell me what colour to use." The therapist responds by saying, "You would like for me to make the decision for you" (p. 87). Yet, the child had not just said that he "would like" the therapist to make the decision, he stated that the therapist was "supposed" to. The therapist could have chosen to respond by saying "You think I am supposed to decide . . ." or "You think it is my job to decide . . ." The response that a therapist makes to a child's statement or play conveys what the therapist has decided the child meant by her words or actions.

Each event in a child's play can point to several different issues and may communicate a number of messages. In the course of their work, therapists make choices about which aspect of the play to emphasize. For example, Axline (1969) provides the following example of an interaction in a play therapy room. A child is playing in the dollhouse. As he arranges the items he says, "This is the back door. We can go in here and go to the icebox and get an orange or a cookie and come out again. See?" The therapist responds by saying, "There is food in this house" (p. 181), choosing to emphasize the child's comments about the icebox and the orange. Another therapist might have responded differently, focusing on the door by saying, "They can use the back door to go in and out." In choosing which aspect of the child's play to emphasize, the therapist is, in effect, determining what the child's play means at that moment.

Some therapists attempt to make assumptions about the meaning of the child's play by asking questions to develop an understanding of what he is trying to say. For example, in one session, a seven-year-old girl, Ann, initiated a game of house, saying that she was the mother and the therapist was the child. Ann then proceeded to cook some food and to give it to the therapist, telling him to eat. The therapist asked, "Do I like the food?" Ann said, "No." The therapist then asked Ann, "What do I say?" Ann responded, "Say, 'I am not going to eat it and you can't make me.'" The therapist then repeated these words. Without these questions, the therapist could have directed the play to have a radically different meaning by eating the food and saying, "Wow, Mom, this food is good. Thank you for cooking it."

As Eliana Gil (1994) points out, "Several play therapists have proposed a rigid separation between the directive and nondirective approaches' (p. 14). Yet, a division between a directive and non-directive therapist is not made simply. Four different areas in which a therapist may be more or less directive have been outlined above. Therapists that are non-directive in one area are often directive in another. Each therapist makes an individual decision about when and to what extent she will be directive during play therapy sessions.

Therapists' Interventions.

When working with a child in the playroom, the therapist intervenes in a number of different ways (Allan, 1988; Axline, 1969; Bromfield, 1992; Gil, 1991; Landreth, 1991; Lubimiv, 1994; O'Connor, 1991).

The tasks that a therapist may be involved in during a play therapy session are outlined briefly below:

1) The play therapist carefully observes the child's play, taking note of the toys that are used and how they are used. The therapist will also watch to see what themes, emotions or problems emerge in the child's play and how difficulties are resolved. Consideration will also be given to the way that the child approaches and interacts with the therapist, in order to assess the progression of the therapeutic relationship. These observations play a vital role during initial sessions when the therapist is getting to know the child and later are an important way for the therapist to gauge the child's growth and development. Through their observations, therapists hope to learn:

a) How the child views himself
b) How the child views the world
c) How the child views the presenting issues
d) How the child expresses emotions
e) How the child's needs are currently met
f) What other interventions are required

2) The therapist may ask a variety of questions during a session to assist him in understanding the child's play and experience:

"I wonder how the cow feels about being left behind?"
"What is happening to the dinosaur?"
"What makes those two guys keep fighting?"
"What could help the girl feel better?"
"What does that boy wish the dad would do?"

If a therapist does not ask questions, clarifying the nature of the child's play, she runs the risk of making incorrect assumptions about the process, dynamics or emotions that are being communicated by the child.

3) During a session, the play therapist may verbally reflect what is happening and the emotions that appear to be expressed in play:

"The truck is pulling into the garage."
"It looks like the car can't get down that road without having an accident."
"The bear seems to be happy to be back with his friends."

When the therapist is making statements about aspects of the play that cannot be directly observed (e.g., character's emotions or motivations), it is helpful if the reflections are tentative, leaving room for the child to contradict or correct the therapist.

4) When observing the child at play, the therapist develops hypotheses and draws conclusions about the meaning of the child's play and the connections between the play, the presenting issues and the child's life. "The child's play is symbolic of his feelings, and whenever the therapist attempts to translate symbolic behaviour into words, she is interpreting because she is saying what she thinks the child has expressed in his actions" (Axline, 1969, p. 98). Whether or not and how these interpretations are shared with the child depends to a great extent on the therapeutic model being followed by the therapist. O'Connor (1991) provides a detailed examination of the use of interpretations in play therapy. Examples of interpretations that may occur in play therapy include:

> "I wonder if you ever feel as angry as that clown?"
>
> "That bear must be very sad that he has no food."
>
> "You want to get your picture just right. When it doesn't look like you want it to, you rip it up."
>
> "When that horse was left shut up in the barn, it reminded me of the time your mom locked you in the room."
>
> "Other girls I have talked to feel worried when they think their mom is being hurt."

Therapists can offer their interpretations in many different ways during play sessions. However, it should be remembered, as Axline (1969) suggests, that we are guessing; only the child truly knows what he is trying to say to us.

5) Play therapists may play during sessions. When and how a play therapist engages in play depends on his theoretical orientation. Some therapists await the child's invitation and direction before becoming involved in play. Other therapists play alongside a child as a way of teaching specific play skills or social skills.

6) Limits are an essential aspect of the play therapy process. Limits allow a child to feel safe and secure in the playroom (Axline, 1969; Landreth, 1991). Generally, limits are kept to a minimum so that the

child has the freedom to express herself (Axline, 1969). Standard limits include not letting the child hurt himself, not letting the child hurt the therapist, and not letting the child wilfully destroy the playroom or the toys. In addition, therapists will often set limits to cope with specific situations in the playroom (e.g., the child wishes to take a toy home, the child tries to undress, the child wants to leave the playroom, the child wants to stay for a longer session). Garry Landreth's (1991) book *Play Therapy: The Art of Relationship* contains a chapter detailing the therapist's role in therapeutic limit setting.

The interventions, involvement and actions of a therapist in a playroom are determined by the therapist's personality, the setting in which the therapist is working, the theory on which the therapist's work is based, the goals of the relationship, the materials available in the playroom and how the therapist chooses to use those materials. Taken together, these factors define the role of the play therapist.

Conclusion

The aim of this chapter has been to introduce the reader in a general way to the wide range of interventions called "play therapy." Play therapy is not a single entity but has emerged as a mode of intervening with clients that is used in different ways and in different settings. Other chapters in this book will explore the specific ways that play therapy can be used with specific client groups.

For simplicity, in this chapter play therapy has been described as an intervention to be used with individual children. However, play therapy has also successfully been used with adults, in groups and with families. Play therapy can be used as a short-term or long-term intervention.

Play therapy is defined by its tools, the way they are used, the theory that is followed and the relationship that is developed thereby. A unique blend of these factors allow each play therapist, in her own unique way, to create a safe place where a client (or group of clients) is free to express himself both verbally and nonverbally. Through this process it is hoped that those who play develop a better understanding of who they are, where they have been and where they want to go.

REFERENCES

Allan, J. (1988). *Inscapes of the child's world: Jungian counselling in schools and clinics*. Dallas, Texas: Spring Publications Inc.

Axline, V. M. (1969). *Play therapy* (2nd. ed.). New York: Ballantine Books.

Barnes, M. (1996). *The healing path with children: An exploration for parent and professional*. Ottawa: Viktoria, Fermoyle and Berrigan Publishing House.

Bromfield, R. (1992). *Playing for real: A child therapist explores the world of play therapy and the inner worlds of children*. New York: Plume.

Chethik, M. (1989). *Techniques of child therapy: Psychodynamic strategies*. New York: Guilford Press.

Erickson, E. (1963). *Childhood and society* (2nd. ed.). New York: W. W. Norton & Co. Inc.

Erickson, M. R. & Egeland, B. (1991). Toward new ways of caring: Lessons from intergenerational research on maltreatment. *The Advisor*, *4*, 1-3.

Esman, A. (1983). Psychoanalytic play therapy. In C. Schaefer & K. O'Connor (Eds.), *Handbook of play therapy*. New York: John Wiley & Sons.

Freud, A. (1964). *The psychoanalytic treatment of children*. New York: Schocken Books.

Gil, E. (1991). *The healing power of play: Working with abused children*. New York: The Guilford Press.

Gil, E. (1994). *Play in family therapy*. New York: The Guilford Press.

Guerney, B. (1964). Filial therapy: Description and rationale. *Journal of Consulting Psychology*, *28*, 304-310.

Hambridge, G. (1955). Structured play therapy. *American Journal of Orthopsychiatry*, *25*, 601-617.

Jernberg, A. M. (1979). *Theraplay: A new treatment using structured play for problem children and their families*. San Francisco: Jossey-Bass Publishers.

Kalff, D. (1980). *Sandplay: A psychotherapeutic approach to the psyche*. Santa Monica: Sigo Press.

Klein, M. (1959). *The psychoanalysis of children* (3rd ed.). London: Hogarth Press.

Kottler, J. A. (1993). *On being a therapist* (Rev. ed). San Francisco: Jossey-Bass Publishers.

Landreth, G. L. (1991). *Play therapy: The art of relationship*. Muncie, Indiana: Accelerated Development Inc., Publishers.

Levy, D. (1939). Release therapy. *American Journal of Orthopsychiatry*, *9*, 713-736.

Lubimiv, G.P. (1994). *Wings for our children: essentials of becoming a play therapist*. Burnstown, Ontario: The General Store Publishing House.

Norton, B. & Norton, C. (1992). "Symbolic meanings of animals." (Handout provided at workshop From Tears to Diamonds: the Metaphors of Childhood," presented at the 1995 Summer Play Therapy Institute).

Norton, B. & Norton, C. (1992). "Symbolic meanings of environments." (Handout provided at workshop From Tears to Diamonds: the Metaphors of Childhood," presented at the 1995 Summer Play Therapy Institute).

Norton, B. & Norton, C. (1992). "Symbolic meanings of toys." (Handout provided at workshop From Tears to Diamonds: the Metaphors of Childhood," presented at the 1995 Summer Play Therapy Institute).

Oaklander, V. (1978). *Windows to our children: A gestalt therapy approach to children and adolescents*. Moab, Utah: Real People Press.

O'Connor, J. (1991). *The play therapy primer: An integration of theories and techniques*. New York: John Wiley & Sons, Inc.

Piaget, J. (1962). *Play, dreams and imitation in childhood*. New York: Norton.

Russ, S. W. (1995). Play psychotherapy research. *Advances in Clinical Child Psychology, 17*, 365-391.

Schaefer, C. E. (Ed.). (1993). *The therapeutic powers of play*. Northvale, N.J.: Jason Aronson.

Schaefer, C. E. & O'Connor, J. (Eds.). (1983). *Handbook of play therapy*. New York: John Wiley & Sons.

Solomon, J. (1938). Active play therapy. *American Journal of Orthopsychiatry, 8*, 479-498.

Weinrib, E. L. (1983). *Images of the self: The sandplay therapy process*. Boston: Sigo Press.

Weisz, J. (1986). Contingency and control beliefs as predictors of psychotherapy outcomes among children and adolescents. *Journal of Consulting and Clinical Psychology, 54*, 789-795.

CHAPTER THREE

HISTORY OF ART THERAPY IN CANADA AND THE UNITED STATES

Betty Bedard Bidwell

HISTORY OF ART THERAPY IN CANADA AND THE UNITED STATES

HISTORY OF ART THERAPY IN CANADA

I have had the privilege of being a student of the "Grand Lady" of Canadian art therapy, Irene Dewdney; she was my trainer, my teacher, my mentor and my supervisor. What I am going to share with you is what Irene Dewdney has explained to me both by personal communication and in lectures.

Art therapy officially started in Canada in 1953 when Irene's late husband Selwyn Dewdney was appointed as a "psychiatric art therapist" for the psychiatric unit of Westminster Hospital in London, Ontario. Westminster was a veteran's hospital where art was used in a rehabilitation program. In 1954 Irene became Selwyn's assistant in this unique program in Canada.

According to Irene's perspective, art therapy and the use of art as therapy grew from a vision to reality through the activity of the pharmaceutical companies. These companies were printing reproductions of paintings and drawings by mentally ill patients. Irene explained that at this particular time a breakthrough had occurred in the development of mood-altering drugs. These reproductions were given to all the mental hospitals in Canada. The head of psychiatry at Westminster Hospital, Dr. Earl Metcalf, had seen these reproductions and had the foresight and the courage to develop the position of psychiatric art therapist.

As a psychiatric art therapist, Selwyn joined the treatment team of nurses, doctors, psychiatrists and psychologists. Selwyn had been under contract to Westminster Hospital since 1947 as an art instructor, with a selected number of psychiatric patients. During the beginning stages, Selwyn and Irene had to deal with the disturbing reality that the treatment of some of the patients by some of the staff was unacceptable. The only treatments available to patients at that time were shock therapy, both by insulin and by electricity, and frontal lobotomy. Freud was known, but not accepted by most of the psychiatrists in the London area. However, Selwyn and Irene's philosophical base was definitely Freudian, which was accepted by their professional colleagues because of their respect for and acknowledgement of Selwyn's vast talents. He was a skilful artist with both pencil and paints, an accomplished sculptor, a mural painter, a writer, a geographer, a teacher and illustrator and, in his final years, achieved the distinction of becoming the first and foremost native rock art researcher in Canada and quite possibly in North America.

Irene often said that her late husband was the history maker, and that she was more his assistant and support. She was and continues to be an insightful and incredibly intuitive therapist and teacher. She used art in a creative, projective, analytical and problem-solving manner. As instructor and trainer she was supportive, yet direct. Her experience and knowledge of life were her gifts of wisdom to everyone with whom she was involved. You couldn't help but feel blessed by being involved with her, whether you were a client, colleague, supervisor or student.

Irene shared the fact that she and Selwyn felt accepted as therapists with Westminster Hospital even though art as therapy was a new concept. The staff were supportive and extremely interested in the patients' artwork. The early fifties and sixties for the Dewdneys were a wonderful experience that not only supported art therapy as a valued therapeutic approach with the London community, but also allowed the concept of art therapy to spread throughout Canada.

The publication of the *American Journal of Art Therapy* occurred in this time frame as well. Through this journal, Irene read about and later became familiar with Elinor Ulman in the United States. Margaret Naumberg's second book, *Psychoneurotic Art: Its Function in Psychotherapy*, published in 1953, was another resource that both Selwyn and Irene used.

Selwyn and Irene Dewdney are well known and acknowledged for developing three specific and unique techniques: The Objective Approach, Memory Retrieval, and Picture Projection. With the Dewdneys' encouragement and creative support, other art therapists have been able to expand upon this base to provide a repertoire of productive interventions for varied populations. In the profession of art therapy, as in other professions, the current generation of practitioners stands on the shoulders of those pioneers who have gone before.

Not only were the Dewdneys able to lay a foundation for how we do art therapy and for the role of the art therapist within the team, but they were able to define the nature of art therapy. One of Irene's definitions of art therapy is, "Art therapy is based on the theory that the graphic expression, whatever the medium, is a valid form of expression. As an expression of our feelings, it has as much or even more credibility than the spoken word."

Irene worked at the London Psychiatric Hospital and St. Joseph's Hospital. As an art therapy consultant, Irene was contracted to work at the Western Ontario Therapeutic Community Hostel in London. In 1979, Irene founded the Ontario Art Therapy Association. Selwyn and Irene published numerous articles in the *American Journal of Art Therapy*. In 1979, Selwyn Dewdney died during heart surgery. After a short break from art therapy, Irene returned to practice as an art therapist, teacher and supervisor. Irene supported the development of the art therapy program at the University of Western Ontario, where she was an instructor and supervisor. Although she says that she has retired, now in her eighties, Irene continues to play a strong role both as an inspiration and mentor in the field of art therapy. Presently, Irene is writing her own book on the history of art therapy in Canada from her unique perspective.

Other important dates and history makers of art therapy in Canada are:

1972	The Toronto Art Therapy Institute became a reality under Dr. Martin A. Fischer.
1977	Dr. Martin Fischer founded the Canadian Art Therapy Association.
1979	Kay Collis brought art therapy to the west coast and initiated programs in British Columbia.
1980s	The University of Montreal developed a Master's of Art Therapy program. A Jungian art therapist, Michael Edwards, developed and directed this program.
Mid-1980s	The University of Western Ontario started an art therapy program. Linda Nicholas developed and directed this program with the strong support of Irene Dewdney.

From this modest beginning in 1953 at Westminster Hospital until now, art therapy continues to grow and be acknowledged as a valuable therapeutic approach for children and adults of all ages and treatment needs.

Today, art therapists practice from a wide theoretical base. This may include psychoanalytic, symbolic, object relations, Jungian, humanistic, Gestalt, behavioural, cognitive, and eclectic. In my opinion, the four art therapy approaches that best fit with play therapy appear to be: the analytical approach, where the art therapist analyzes the client's artwork; projective art therapy, where the client, with the assistance of the therapist, is able to project her own feelings, issues and resolutions into her artwork; the cognitive technique, where the client is able to do his own problem solving through step-by-step art techniques; and art as therapy, where the art product represents the creative expression of the client. These four therapeutic approaches are the result of my training and experience with Irene Dewdney, as well as twenty years of practice. Also these approaches connect strongly with play therapy. As a teacher and a supervisor of both play and art therapy, I need to be able to locate my practice within substantial theoretical frameworks. In 1994, I was able to start the play therapy program at the University of Western Ontario in collaboration with the Canadian Association for Child and Play Therapy (CACPT). At this time, both programs are based on these four therapeutic approaches.

THE HISTORY OF ART THERAPY IN THE UNITED STATES

The emergence of art therapy can be traced to the beginnings of analytical psychology, namely Freud and Jung. It was Freud who brought the concept of the unconscious to mainstream thought and Jung who continued with the concepts of the collective unconscious and archetypes. Jung placed a lot of emphasis on the dream images and on the drawn or painted image. These images, Jung felt, often had symbolic significance because they were stimulated by the unconscious, the seat of creativity. Jung understood that symbols were healing agents. Therefore, the supposition was that in creating symbols and art, the creator moves towards health, psychologically and/or physically. It is this assumption in which much of the power of art therapy resides: through the creation of images, the unconscious manifests itself and the act of creation intrinsically provides release.

Therefore, art therapy can be used in two ways: either focusing on product or focusing on process. These two approaches need not be mutually exclusive and most art therapists will testify that they employ both during the course of therapy; however, for the sake of clarity, these two approaches will be presented separately.

Art Psychotherapy

American pioneer Margaret Naumburg is considered by most to be the first person in the United States to develop the field of art therapy; however, Mary Huntoon worked at the Menninger Clinic in Kansas in the 1930s. As a trained artist, Huntoon came to the attention of Karl Menninger, who asked her to establish an art program for the patients and later the war veterans. It was here that Margaret Naumburg, already developing a reputation in this field, first was introduced to the term "art psychotherapy."

A graduate of Vassar, Naumburg continued by pursuing graduate work at Columbia, at the London School of Economics, and later with Maria Montessori. She was one of the first Americans to undergo psychoanalysis and so was familiar with the psychoanalytic framework of Freud and Jung. Naumburg founded the Walden School in 1914, which was a unique school focusing on the emotional development of the child through creative expression and self-motivated learning. Naumburg's sister, Florence Cane, began teaching the art classes and Naumburg was so taken with the art of the children that she began to conclude that spontaneous art was also basic to psychotherapy. (By spontaneous art, we mean that the picture comes from within, not directed by the teacher or therapist.)

Thus Naumburg was beginning to realize, when looking at her students' pictures, the power of the image. She was beginning to realize that the students' pictures were reflecting their psychological state more accurately than when the students verbally discussed how they were feeling. This demonstrates one of the advantages to art therapy: the bypassing of the censor that we have developed in our verbal communication. It is very natural for us to consciously choose appropriate words, particularly when discussing a topic. We will think of what and how we wish to verbally communicate to someone. However, we have never learned how to censor our art; we do not have the tools at our disposal to regulate the image. We can choose media, topic, or style; however, often what is portrayed in our minds is not what appears on the paper or canvas. Even when we take into account a person's artistic talent and skill, the image still has an independent life. The unconscious can still emerge in the image just as it can in dreams. Therefore, what can emerge is often a truer reflection of the self.

A typical art therapy session for Naumburg would have the therapist introducing the client to art therapy in a variety of ways. The first approach would have the therapist explaining and often demonstrating the media. As with any language, it is important that we have access to the basics; therefore, if we have never used watercolour paints, a demonstration on the various ways we can use the medium will help us express ourselves more fully. A similar occasion occurs when we travel to another country and do not speak the language. To manoeuvre effectively through the land, it is helpful to have a basic understanding of the language, by learning phrases such as, "Where is the hotel/ the bathroom/ the train station/ the hospital?" Otherwise, we can retreat and not derive the full benefit of the experience. Therefore, in both instances, we have some familiarity of the way in which we wish to express ourselves effectively.

The second approach has the therapist and client discussing the client's issues or problems first before venturing into the art. Many clients feel intimidated by launching into the art immediately and need some time to converse in a way that feels more natural to them, and thus empowering. Based on the conversation, the therapist can suggest to the client a specific drawing, thus being directive with her, or the client can choose for herself what to draw. Again, the therapist is flexible to the needs of the client.

The third approach offers the art first and discussion to follow. In this situation, the client begins a spontaneous picture and once he completes it, the therapist and client discuss the picture. In fact, these approaches need not be mutually exclusive. For example, there could be demonstration of the media, followed by a spontaneous picture, and then a discussion of the completed artwork. In any case, the therapist and the client work together as a team. The therapist is active with the client in deciphering the images, both of them trying to elucidate the meaning and significance of the picture. Naumburg felt that as the client grew to decipher her own pictorial images, she gained independence and a narcissistic identification with the pictures. The client could then look at the pictures with a certain detachment so that she could view them more objectively. Thus the pictures provided a mirror to the self.

Naumburg outlined four advantages to art psychotherapy. The first advantage is that the art is a direct expression of dreams, fantasies, and inner experiences that occur naturally as pictures or images. This concept was discussed earlier when referring to the shared language of the image. The second advantage is that the art escapes censorship. As we mentioned earlier, art is a novel form of communication for us; thus we have not established censors and the art is a clearer representation of the unconscious and of the self. The third advantage is that the art is durable and unchanging. Art cannot be erased by forgetting, like the spoken word, and authorship cannot be denied. We often regret things we say and in an attempt to gloss over it, we merely say that we don't remember saying it or that we didn't say it at all. The art is a concrete representation of those communications and despite our discomfort with them, the art is there for us to reconcile and accept as representing aspects of ourselves. The final advantage is that the resolution of transference is easier. Transference occurs in a therapeutic situation when the client displaces feelings and behaviours first experienced with significant individuals in one's past onto the therapist. In a psychoanalytic relationship one of the goals is to resolve the transference through various techniques such as free association. Naumburg felt the transference was more easily resolved because the client was encouraged to associate to his picture independently and thus eventually not rely on the therapist.

Thus, in choosing to use art psychotherapy, the therapist chooses to actively engage the client and be actively engaged with the client and the art. Art psychotherapy not only relies on the art but also on the verbal communication about the art. This is in contrast to the second approach, art as therapy.

Art as Therapy

Art as therapy was first coined by Edith Kramer, who is usually considered to be the pioneer of this approach; however, interestingly enough, Margaret Naumburg's sister, Florence Cane, first saw the intrinsic benefits in this approach. As mentioned earlier, Florence Cane taught art at Margaret's school. Cane also underwent psychoanalysis and was very open to ways of freeing the human soul and body.

Cane's goal was to integrate the person through art and she attempted to do this by activating and unifying our three functions: movement, feeling, and thought. Cane felt that these three functions corresponded to the underlying principles of art. Movement corresponded to rhythm in a picture; feeling paralleled dynamics and harmony; and thought was represented through the balance of the picture. By teaching these principles of art, the person integrates and grows naturally from that experience.

Therefore, Cane laid the groundwork for Edith Kramer to develop her approach. Cane focused on the intrinsic creative nature in the child and tried to develop it through movement, thought, and feeling. Because Cane was first and foremost a teacher, her approach had elements of teaching to it. Kramer's belief was similar to Cane's theory. Kramer uses psychoanalytic theory to understand human growth but she sees her role as art therapist as distinctly different from that of a psychotherapist. Kramer does not see the therapist's role as an interpreter of pictures or of the unconscious. The basic aim of art as therapy is to provide people with the pleasures and satisfactions that creative work can give.

Kramer, an artist, felt that the art therapist must develop her own art skills thus, enabling her to better facilitate the client's process. Therefore, Kramer would help the client maximize his creative skills because she felt that the primary goal of art therapy was sublimation. Sublimation is a defence mechanism whereby drive energy is deflected from its original goal and is displaced onto accomplishment, which is held in high regard by the ego and is usually socially acceptable. Thus, the client can displace sadness or anger onto the art and through the art process. The client can best achieve this when he knows how to best use the art medium and when he has tapped into all his creative skills and energy. When the client's skill or insight fails, the therapist's abilities can assist the client over the hurdle.

In summary, art as therapy focuses on the creative process and the act of making art. Unlike art psychotherapy, it does not rely on verbal discussion before or after the process, but instead relies on the intrinsic benefits of engaging in the creative process.

As mentioned earlier, one approach is not better than the other. Both approaches have their place, and therapists may have a preference for one over the other; or the therapist may adapt the approach to suit the client's needs. As with any form of psychotherapy there are schools of thought and it is important to be aware of the various approaches so as not to develop tunnel vision

CHAPTER FOUR

LINKS BETWEEN ART AND PLAY THERAPY

Margot Sippel

LINKS BETWEEN ART AND PLAY THERAPY

Many practitioners utilize both play and art therapy to enable them to offer clients an optimal therapeutic experience. Each client arrives with her own unique set of needs and preferences, which requires a unique response from the therapist. My initial training was in art therapy and when I began to study play therapy I found myself wondering whether the same principles applied. It seemed to me that there were a number of connections, and in fact much of my art therapy with children had already incorporated aspects of play therapy.

Art therapy is not recommended for children under eight years of age; however, early in my career I made an exception for an exceptional little boy. Paul was very bright, quite verbal, and loved art. His parents were going through a divorce and he had some real concerns about his mother "leaving him." He seemed to be in touch with his emotions and able to put his feelings into words despite a minor speech impediment. We started to work on his feelings of loss and anger using the traditional drawings: self-portrait, colour emotional chart, and family portrait. He was a delight to work with and seemed to be able to utilize the art to create a solid foundation for our work together.

As the weeks went by it seemed to me that he was experiencing an increasing amount of anger. During sessions he began to chew the ends off pencils and spit them out. The magic markers we used were kept in a plastic case and while we were chatting about the drawings he would absent-mindedly begin poking holes in the case with a sharp pencil. He started to destroy his drawings at the end of each session and his speech was deteriorating. I realized that talking was not going to provide him with the therapeutic opportunity he required, but I was hampered by the fact that we worked in a friend's upscale office with a beige carpet and had no access to any toys.

We began to discuss anger and I asked him if he thought he might be angry about what was happening in his family. He said he didn't know, but if I thought he was, then maybe he was! I told him that I noticed he had been poking a lot of holes and asked him if he knew why. "No, all of a sudden I just like poking holes," was his response. We went to the kitchen and I took a stack of paper serviettes about an inch-and-a-half deep and set a piece of paper over the top. I gave him a sharp pencil and told him to poke holes. For the next twenty minutes he poked that piece of paper (and a few others) right down into the serviettes. The next week I brought in some nails, a hammer and some soft cedar boards. Whenever he or I had the sense that what we were talking about was too much for him, out came the cedar and nails. His mother had heard the pounding from the waiting room and arrived one day with some playdough they had made together. This little fellow had a deep reverence for all living things, including plants and trees, and made it clear to me that he could never hurt a living being but it sure felt good to pound something made of playdough!

Despite the fact that we were doing art therapy and didn't have access to a playroom or toys, we were able to move ahead and so he could do the symbolic work he needed. He would easily slip back and forth between art and play. As my training in play therapy progressed I realized that play and art therapy are connected in a number of fundamental ways.

Access To the Inner World

The unconscious holds the key to many of our issues in daily life. Often when there doesn't seem to be any clear answer to our difficulties, opening the door to the unconscious allows us to tap into new insights. Both play and art enable us to manifest unconscious material. Painting and working (playing) in sand are excellent ways to contact the unconscious.

Directive and Nondirective

Depending on the therapist's judgment, directive or nondirective techniques can be utilized. In both play and art therapy this decision takes into account the presenting issue, length of time available for therapy and client's needs. The flexibility of the two therapies enables these needs to be met on an individual and unique basis.

Variety

In any therapy, the therapeutic techniques must respond to the client's ever-changing and individual needs. There is a great variety of media choices when using art materials, ranging from watercolours to clay. Similarly, the playroom offers any number of play activities. The expansive variety of each therapy creates the flexibility needed to ensure that each client has what she requires.

Active Participation

Therapy is not about finding a therapist who will cure the client. It requires that the client take an active role in the resolution of his situation. Play and art therapy involve the client directly and actively. This involvement sparks the entire process and clients are empowered by their participation.

Giving Life To Fantasy

When we give voice to our fantasies, they become a valuable part of the therapeutic process. When a child is "being" a knight on a white horse or an adult is painting a picture of the perfect solution to her dilemma, their acts are creating ideas, hope and energy.

Use of Symbols

Symbols have the power to evoke genuine emotions. The symbolic enactment of an event can be a deeply moving experience. In art, the symbols can take a two- or three-dimensional form. In the playroom, the element of movement and life can be added to enhance the development of the symbolic event.

Physical and Emotional Discharge

The process of therapy can create the need to release tension and physical energy, accompanied by related emotions. Play therapy is ideally suited to this purpose. Many play therapists have specific areas and toys in their offices that elicit this response. In art therapy, clay is an excellent medium for both adults and children. Large canvases can also offer a more physical experience of the art process.

Reliving the Experience

The act of drawing or playing out a past event begins to conjure the emotional tone of the original event. Both hidden and overt emotions can surface. This feeling of "it's as if it were happening right now" is of prime therapeutic importance when managed by an experienced play or art therapist.

Relaxation

At times the most important thing a client can do is to relax and become totally absorbed in the task at hand. Art is an excellent vehicle for losing oneself in the process. Likewise, play is a natural relaxant for both children and adults.

Visual Data

There are two sets of visual data available to both the play and art therapist. As the client engages in therapy, his body posture, facial expression and level of tension can be noted. In addition, we are able to study the actual product of the activity. The drawing and the play event offer important information such as emotional tone, confusion, need for control, and so on.

Liberation from Perfection

Both art and play have the innate capacity to free the client from the need to judge the end result. Play is naturally free of such restrictions simply because it is play. Art created in therapy need not adhere to any of the usual artistic criteria because its most important purpose is to provide a foundation for the therapeutic dialogue.

Ritual

Ritual is a powerful tool used by various cultures for thousands of years and has the ability to affect us at a conscious and unconscious level. The ritual act serves as a catharsis or invocation. Drawing an event and then creating a ritual to destroy or honour that picture can be a very powerful event. Likewise a ritual re-enactment in the playroom can serve to heal at a very deep level.

Respect for the Client

Both play and art therapy are based on the premise that the client has the necessary resources to address her difficulties. The therapist offers ego support and aids in the client's introspection. This basic tenet is rooted in a deep respect for the client, regardless of age or experience.

Themes

The recurring themes that emerge in a client's drawings or play give us an important insight into his perceptions. Often these perceptions lie just beyond consciousness and are an invaluable addition to the emotional understanding of the client.

As I continue to explore the use of play and art therapy, the list of similarities becomes more important. Each therapy is valid and effective on its own, yet the therapist who can move from one to the other is able to respond to the client in an immediate, personalized manner. This response is a vital component of the therapeutic process.

CHAPTER FIVE

THERAPLAY

Dr. Evangeline Munns

THERAPLAY

History

Theraplay is a comparatively new play therapy method in Canada, although it has been used in the United States since the late 1960s. It was initiated by Dr. Ann Jernberg (1979), arising out of a Headstart project in which increased bonding between mothers and their children was a primary goal.

Nature of Theraplay

So what is Theraplay? It is a short-term, structured method of therapy that involves the direct participation of the parents with their child. There is an emphasis on physical, joyful interactions in which the child sees himself as someone who is important, worthy, and lovable. As Phyllis Booth, training director of the Theraplay Institute in Chicago states, "He must come to see, reflected in the therapist's eyes, the image of himself both as lovable and as fun to be with" (Jernberg, 1973, p. 3). Invariably, the self-esteem of the child rises. Spontaneous comments from children such as "This is the best place in the whole world to be" (from a five-year-old elective mute); or, "I could come here forever!" (from an acting-out adolescent) indicate the depth of well-being the children often feel in the theraplay sessions. Theraplay is not a talking therapy. No interpretations are made to the child nor are questions asked. No toys are used. The emphasis is on interactions between child, parents and therapists. Bizarre behaviour is ignored. Healthy and positive elements of the child are focused on.

Appropriate Subjects

Theraplay has proved to be a versatile treatment method. It is applicable to a wide age range: from infants, toddlers, pre-schoolers, latency-aged, adolescents, adults to the elderly. As well, it has been helpful for a diversity of emotional, social and behavioural difficulties: from the aggressive, impulsive child, to the withdrawn, fearful, inhibited child. Obsessive-compulsive children with their orderly, perfectionistic trends learn to lower some of their defenses in response to the delightful, engaging behaviour of the therapist. This is true for the PDD and autistic population as well. Theraplay has been a useful method in making significant changes with autistic children in gaining their interest and responsiveness to human contact. Learning disabled and handicapped children have benefited from theraplay mainly by the emphasis on building their self-esteem.

This has been true for depressed and suicidal children as well. Theraplay is especially suited for adopted and foster children or any child where bonding is an issue.

Theraplay has been used effectively with parents who were suicidal, homicidal, sexually and physically abused, deprived, and neurotic. Just as it is important to strengthen the self-confidence of children, it is imperative that parents learn to feel good about themselves, in order for generalization of therapeutic effects to occur and last. Often the therapists have to concentrate as much on the parents as they do on the child.

After a thorough social and developmental history, the child and parents are assessed using the Marshak Interaction Method (Jernberg, 1991), from which the therapists gain insight into the needs of child and parents. After an initial feedback to the parents, the sessions are preplanned and led by the therapist. In the first sessions the parents observe the therapist and child through a one-way mirror as an interpreting therapist explains what is going on in the therapy room. The therapist models for the parents positive playful interactions with their child. This is followed by direct parental participation with their child under the guidance of the therapist in the last half of the treatment period. (Usually there is a minimum of eight theraplay sessions for the whole treatment period.) The child and his parents are seen once or several times a week for a half hour of theraplay over a three-month period, although treatment can last longer depending on the needs of the child and family. The latter is particularly true of autistic children. (Note that in our agency at Blue Hills we include a half-hour counselling session for the parents following each theraplay session.) After the last session (which includes a goodbye party) the family is seen for four quarterly follow-up sessions during the year.

Theory

The theory underlying theraplay stresses the importance of the early parent-infant attachment. It postulates that the first relationship that an infant experiences is a crucial one, as it serves as a prototype for all other relationships. If that relationship is not a positive or strong one, then the child will likely have problems in relating to others in the future. Theraplay tries to go back to that first relationship in an attempt to replicate and strengthen the healthy aspects of normal parent-child bonding.

Research

Although there is a scarcity of research directly using theraplay, there is certainly a body of scientific evidence supporting the theory behind it—i.e. the importance of primary parent-child attachments. Starting with the early work of Bowlby (1940, 1973, 1979, 1988), Spitz (1946), Ainsworth (1969), Ainsworth & Bell (1970), Main & Weston (1981) and Main, Kaplan, & Cassidy (1985) to current research projects around the world such as Sroufe, Cooper & Dehart (1992), Rutler (1994) and Van Emmichoven & Ruiter (1994), there is a great deal of significant research that indicates the importance of early attachment and its effects on later personality adjustment.

Techniques

In order to get a clearer picture of what goes on in theraplay one needs to review the basics of healthy, normal parent-infant interactions. The time a mother spends with her baby involves a kaleidoscope of behaviours and emotions that form an interplay of giving, receiving and sharing. In this process, normally a strong feeling of love, caring, empathy, and affinity for each other occurs. Dr. Jernberg from her observations of normal interactions in the nursery describes some of the delightful facets of this process:

> Daily, the mother in the nursery with her baby nuzzles his neck, blows on his tummy, sings in his ear, hides his eyes (or hides her face) when playing "peek-a-boo" and nibbles his toes. She picks him up, twirls him, spins him, rocks him, bounces him, flips him, and jiggles him. She holds him close and nurses him. She powders him, lotions him, combs him, washes him, pats him dry, and rubs him. She whispers, coos, giggles, hums, chatters and makes nonsense sounds. . . . In addition she holds him . . . restrains him . . . protects him, defines his life space, his property . . . his use of time, his degree of deviation from safety (and soon, what is morally appropriate and not appropriate for him to do and be). And finally, by gently teasing, chasing and eluding (and returning), she remains one step ahead of him, thus encouraging him both to learn the art of mastery and to enjoy the challenge (Jernberg, 1979, p. 4).

The interactions that form the basis of attachment between parent and child have been categorized into five areas: structuring, challenging, intrusion/stimulating, nurturing, and playfulness. The areas emphasized in theraplay vary with the needs of the child.

Structuring

In the normal home the parent is in control and makes rules for the child so she is aware of time and space around her: "Yes, you can throw your ball, but not the cup of milk/ yes, you can touch the table, but not the hot stove or electrical outlet/ yes you can play and make noise during the day, but at night you need to be quiet and try to sleep." There are rules and conditions to which the child has to adapt. The parent structures the child's world to some extent and makes it organized and predictable, and in this process makes her feel safe and secure. Likewise, the theraplay therapist chooses and leads the activities, gives clear directions for the child to follow, and helps the child to obey them. This is done in a firm but playful way, with humour and the use of "paradox" if necessary. Structuring is emphasized with children who are impulsive, aggressive, and frequently out of control, or with children who come from chaotic homes.

Challenge

In the normal home, the parent encourages the child to take risks, but always within the child's capacity to succeed. She encourages the child to reach a little for that toy or to sit up without the pillows to support him, or to let go of the mother's finger and to waddle those first steps alone. She does this by enticing the child playfully and praising efforts or rewarding with an approving smile.

In theraplay, the therapist challenges the child in games such as jumping a little higher in a jumping game, or remembering a longer sequence of claps in a clapping game, or pushing a little harder in a thumb, arm or leg wrestling game, etc. The therapist praises the child for whatever effort the child makes. The therapist gives the message, "I believe in you. You can grow bigger, stronger, and healthier. You can take risks." An example of this occurred in work with a five-year-old autistic child who was afraid of heights. First, the therapist had her jump up and down on the spot; then jump from a kindergarten chair into the therapist's arms; then jump from an adult-sized chair, and finally from the top of an office desk. It was in effect a de-conditioning process and it worked.

Challenging is stressed with children who have been overprotected, who are timid, fearful, or who have no confidence in themselves. It is also used when children need an outlet for a lot of tension or aggression. It gives the therapist a terrific opportunity to praise the child and to make her feel what a capable, strong person she is turning out to be.

Intrusion or Stimulation

A mother usually intrudes on her baby; she does not just let her baby lie in the crib for hours. She plays peek-a-boo, lifts the baby up and down, touches noses, playfully tickles him, rubs his tummy, kisses his forehead, fingertips or toes, coos and makes funny sounds, gazes deeply into his eyes and he into hers. Out of hundreds of intimate encounters like these, the baby gains an awareness of who he is and who his mother is, and the boundaries of each. In the process he gains the self image that he is delightful and capable of giving much pleasure and joy to his parents.

Likewise the therapist intrudes and stimulates the child in often surprising and fun ways. He may also play peek-a-boo, or patty-cake, or pease porridge hot, or other clapping games if it is an older child. He may play a "hello-goodbye" game, where he lifts the child and touches noses with him while he says "hello," and pulls the child away for the "goodbye" phase. He may play "popcorn toes," where he guesses what is in the child's sock—will it be popcorn or jelly beans or lollipops?—and then he tugs the child's sock off and pretends to discover "popcorn" toes (younger children especially delight in this game). A therapist and child may throw cotton balls at each other or pretend that snow is coming down on them.

Nurture

Every normal mother nurtures her baby; she cuddles and caresses her baby, rocks her, hums and sings to her, feeds and bathes her, powders and lotions her, and changes her diapers. In numerous ways she lets the child know that she is well loved and very precious to her.

In every case, nurturing is given to all children in theraplay. No matter what problem the child has, he also has a need to feel cared for. In every session a feeding activity is included. This may be simply feeding the child potato chips (therapist takes a chip and offers it to the child), or a favourite cereal (such as Honey Cheerios) or fruit (grapes, apple slices, etc.). If it is felt the child needs to be regressed to an earlier level, then the therapist may feed him a lollypop, freezie, or bottle of juice or milk while cradling the child in his arms and singing a lullaby. Surprisingly, the latter is often effective with aggressive, "tough" boys who have a strong underlying need to be loved just as a baby. Hiding "Smarties" on a child's body and then having a parent find and feed it to the child is always a favourite activity. The therapist nurtures the child in other ways as well, e.g., making handprints or footprints using baby powder or fingerpaints, and then gently washing, drying, and lotioning the child's hands. Finding "hurts" and softly rubbing cream on them or putting a Band-Aid on them fosters a feeling of being cared for. "Beauty Salon," where the therapist combs the child's hair, paints her face, adds a crown, frequently noting the child's beautiful features as she touches her face, leaves the child feeling very special.

Playfulness

Parents ideally take time to play with their child. When there is a "letting go," a sharing of the child's imaginative world, a willingness to lose oneself in the creativity of the moment, when there is humorous teasing, gaiety, and laughter, the child reaches moments of joy with his parents that makes life rich and rewarding for all. Laughter and exhilaration are profound healers for everyone involved, and the theraplay atmosphere promotes this.

The theraplay therapist strives to make his activities as engaging and delightful as possible. From the cheerful greeting he gives the child, to the checkup at the beginning of each session, to the main body of the session (challenging, nurturing, structuring, and /or intruding), to the clear ending, the therapist tries to convey a feeling of warmth and acceptance to the child. Quiet, calm, gentle moments of intimacy are interspersed with more boisterous ones.

As mentioned previously, which of the five areas are to be concentrated on is dependent on the needs of the child and the parents. For example, aggressive, impulsive children need structuring and nurturing. On the other hand, an obsessive-compulsive child or an overachiever would already have too much structure in her life, so playful intrusion/stimulation and nurturing would be emphasized instead. A fearful, timid child or hysterical, immature child would need appropriate challenging activities. An autistic or PDD child would benefit from intrusion/stimulation to help break down his barriers to intimacy.

Whatever the activities chosen, the atmosphere in the theraplay room is generally a happy one. If a child resists, then the therapist tries to turn the negative behaviour into something positive and regains control; e.g., if a child spits, the therapist may say, "Hey, what a good spitter you are. Let's see if you can spit right on that spot" (it might be the therapist's big toe). Or if the child kicks, "What a strong kicker you are. Let's see if you can kick higher. We're going to measure how high you can kick!"

Inappropriate Subjects

Not every child is suitable for Theraplay. The following are examples of such children:

1) Children who have been recently ill or had surgery. These children need a quiet, calm period in their lives to recuperate.
2) Children who have been physically or sexually traumatized recently. They are often in urgent need of the gentle, nurturing aspect of theraplay, but because there is a lot of physical contact in the theraplay activities, it is felt that a period where more traditional methods of play therapy are used first would be recommended. Theraplay has been used with sexually and physically abused children, but care must be taken not to be too intrusive and a child's refusal to participate in an activity must be respected. Abused children should neither be forced nor hurried, and a slow, gentle approach by a trusted adult is advocated.
3) Children who have recently lost a close family member. These children need a quiet period in which to grieve.
4) The fragile child that is completely overwhelmed or panics at the approach of adults. This kind of child needs space and gentle desensitization. Traditional nondirective play therapy would be recommended where the child makes his own decisions.
5) Sociopathic children who are very egocentric and spend their lives fulfilling their needs at the expense of others (Jernberg, 1983). A behaviouristic approach is sometimes helpful with these children.

Innovative Forms of Theraplay

Theraplay has been used in different formats: individually when parents are not accessible, family theraplay when parents can be present, and group theraplay. At our centre in Blue Hills Child and Family Services in Aurora, Ontario, we have used theraplay in innovative ways. First, we have always had a parent-counselling half-hour session following theraplay to discuss events at home and to guide and support the parents in their endeavours. If there were troubled siblings then we have sometimes included them, and this has been planned for at the beginning. As an example, we worked with a deeply disturbed family where all members needed help. The husband and wife emotionally and physically abused each other and this treatment was extended to their three children. Each of the children had his own therapist working on an individual basis in the same room at the same time, but coming together for group theraplay towards the end of the session so that sibling issues could be addressed. When the parents came in they interacted with all three children. Needless to say, marital issues had to be worked out with these parents.

Because of our long waiting list for clients, we have started doing multiple family theraplay, where up to four children have been seen at the same time. As well, we have done marital theraplay, group theraplay with troubled preschoolers (including autistic children), group theraplay with pre-adolescent and adolescent residential children, and last year with a mother and teenage son group where healthy bonding was an issue.

Training Program

Our training program in theraplay and nondirective play therapy, which lasts approximately three years, includes a practicum where our twenty interns and externs are directly involved in the treatment of our clients under the supervision of two certified trainers. For more information please contact:

Dr. Evangeline Munns
34 Burton Grove
King City, ON, Canada
L7B 1C6
Phone: (905) 773-4323 ext. 363

or

Dr. Linda Wark
Executive Director,
Theraplay Institute
1137 Central Ave.
Wilmette, Illinois, USA
00091
Phone: (847) 256-7334

A SAMPLE OF THERAPLAY ACTIVITIES

Entrance

Giant steps in
Horseback ride
On tip-toe while whispering
Walk in backwards
Dance in
Greetings by shaking hand and foot at the same time

Checkup

Counting body parts of child, e.g., teeth, toes, fingers, freckles
Warm and cool body parts
Measure height with stacked pillows
Measure body parts, e.g., smile, dimple, arm muscle, little finger
Wiggly and quiet body parts

Nurturing

Rock child in blanket held by two or more people while singing a lullaby using child's name
Powder prints (hand or foot)
Finger paint handprints; then carefully washing, drying and lotioning hands
Pass lotion on noses
Lotion on hurts
Band-Aids on hurts
Feeding: feed each other—eat potato chip off of a body part
Find shape of a letter or number on palm of hand that was first powdered
Cotton ball touch: child closes eyes—can he feel touch of cotton ball and where on his body it is touching?
Cotton ball soothe: move cotton ball gently all over child's face, hands, arms, feet
Feet touch under blanket
Beauty parlour
Make one nice observation about person sitting next to you
One potato, two potato (the person ending with the potato gets hugs from everyone)
With finger draw shapes, letters or numbers on back of child and he guesses what you are drawing
Back massage
Give freezie, lollipop, or baby bottle to child in blanket in adult's arms

Intrusion/Stimulation

Popcorn toes (guess if child's toes are popcorn or jellybeans before taking sock off)
Hide under blanket with child while parent tries to find you
Silly bones (touch matching body parts together)
Smartie hunt (hide Smarties on child and parent tries to find them and then feeds them to child)
Toss child from arms to arms of adults
Peek-a-boo with pillow or hands
Jell-O toes
Blindfold person; bring another person to him and he guesses who that person is by touching him
This little piggy . . .
Itzy-bitzy spider
Round and round the garden like a teddy bear
Row your boat while sitting on each other rocking
Slip and grip: lotion hands liberally; adult grips child's hand while she tries to slip out
Three-legged race
Blow bubbles together
Pop cheeks as air goes out
Jiggle child on lap and ask "Why aren't you sitting still?"
Fanning child with pillow, cloth or blowing
Roll up child in blanket and parent finds him

Structuring

Mother May I
Green Light, Red Light
Pattycake
Pease Porridge Hot
Imitating clapping sequences
Raise arm or leg as slowly as you can
Body or hand outline
Simon Says
Follow the Leader
Stacking Hands
Pass a Message
Duck, duck, goose (On "goose," people running in opposite directions meet and hug)
Floppy doll: make each body part loose and relaxed

Challenge

Cotton ball fight

Donut dare (in circle everyone takes a bite while avoiding breaking the donut apart)

Races (forward, backwards, sideways, crawl, hop, slow, fast)

Balancing object on head

Water fight with squirt containers

Thumb, arm, and leg wrestle

Blanket tug-of-war

Dancing on toes of therapist

Seed-spitting contest

Licorice-eating contest

Balloon toss

REFERENCES

Ainsworth, M.D.S. (1969). Object relations, dependency and attachment: A theoretical review of the infant-mother relationship. *Child Development, 40*, 969-1027.

Ainsworth, M.D.S., & Bell, S.M. (1970). Attachment, exploration and separation: Illustrated by the behaviour of one year olds in a strange situation. *Child Development, 41*, 49-67.

Ainsworth, M.D.S., Blehar, M.C., Waters, E., & Wall, S. (1978). *Patterns of attachment: A psychological study of the strange situation.* Hillsdale, NJ: Erlbaum.

Bowlby, J. (1940). The influence of early environment in the development of neurosis and neurotic character. *International Journal of Psychoanalysis, 21*, 154-178.

Bowlby, J. (1973). *Attachment and loss: Vol. 2. Separation: anxiety and anger.* New York: Basic Books.

Bowlby, J. (1979). *The making and breaking of affectional bonds.* London: Tavistock Publications Ltd.

Bowlby, J. (1988). *A secure base. Parent-child attachment and healthy human development.* New York: Basic Books.

Jernberg, A. (1979). *Theraplay. A new treatment using structural play for problem children and their families.* San Francisco: Jossey-Bass Inc. Publishers.

Jernberg, A. (1983). Therapeutic use of sensory-motor play. In Dr. C. Schaefer & Karen O'Connor (Eds.), *Handbook of play therapy*. Toronto: Wiley.

Jernberg, A. (1991). Assessing parent-child interactions with Marshak Interaction Method (MIM). In Dr. C. Schaefer, Karen Gitlin, & Alice Sandgrun (Eds.), *Play diagnosis and assessment*. New York: Wiley.

Main, M. Kaplan, N., & Cassidy, J. (1985). Security in infancy, childhood and adulthood: A move to the level of representation. In Dr. Bretherton & E. Waters (Eds.), *Grooming parents in attachment. Theory and research: Monographs of Society for Research in Child Development, 50*, 66-104.

Main, M., & Weston, D. (1981). The quality of the toddler's relationship to mother and to father as related to conflict behavior and readiness to establish new relationships. *Child development, 52*, 932-940.

O'Connor, K. (1991). *The play therapy primer*. Toronto: Wiley.

Rutler, M. (1994). *Clinical implications of attachment concepts: Retrospect and prospect*. Paper presented at the International Conference on Attachment and Psychopathology, Toronto, Canada.

Spitz, R.A. (1946). Analytic depression. *Psychoanalytic study of the child, 2*, 313-342.

Sroufe, L., Cooper, R.G., & DeHart, G.B. (1992). *Child development: its nature and course*. Toronto: McGraw-Hill.

Van Emmichoven, Z., & Ruiter, C. (1994). *The relationship between quality of attachment representation and cognitive processes in a normal population sample*. Poster presented at the International Conference on Attachment and Psychopathology, Toronto, Canada.

CHAPTER SIX

ART AND PLAYROOM EQUIPMENT AND OBSERVATIONS

Betty Bedard Bidwell

ART AND PLAYROOM EQUIPMENT AND OBSERVATIONS

This chapter gives an overview of the most commonly used equipment in the playroom. The therapeutic approach employed is for the most part non-directive, with some directive techniques, particularly connected to art therapy. The information in this chapter is based on my own observations, and is intended to assist you towards developing an understanding of your client's work, of the value of the equipment, and of your role as the therapist in the therapeutic process.

Over several years, I have had the opportunity to do consulting work with a number of different agencies and students (interns). At one particular agency where I was supervising, several staff expressed a concern about the continuous cycle of aggression that never appeared to change, despite the length of time in therapy. After a number of suggested unsuccessful interventions, I asked to see their therapy rooms. Once I saw the rooms, I began to realize why the aggression in the playroom was reoccurring.

These rooms were full of broken and damaged toys and equipment. There was no tactile equipment, such as sand, water, or clay for the clients to have the opportunity to self-nurture. Unfortunately, this room that was meant to help children move through their issues in a natural, non-intrusive manner in fact encouraged them to be stuck with their anger and frustration.

The therapy room does not need to be full of expensive toys; in fact, therapy can take place in a number of places: the travelling therapist with equipment is testimony to this fact. What is needed, regardless of where the therapy takes place, is equipment that allows the client the opportunity to process issues in her own particular way. Children and youth are extremely adaptable as well as flexible, and will very creatively make the equipment work for them; however, they still need the basics to support their work.

Often during the therapeutic process clients that have issues of anger, aggression and frustration will use the therapy equipment to express these feelings through their play. Initially, you will find that three-quarters or more of the client's play will consist of aggressive forms, with little or no self-nurturing. As the process continues, the self-nurturing play increases, and the aggressive play decreases, until the client's play is almost completely self-nurturing and creative with little or no aggressive forms.

This is also the case when clients use games during therapy. Frequently, the client that feels powerless and hopeless, has low self-esteem and struggles socially, feels the need to cheat while playing games or while role-playing. This client must be the winner or heroine in order to feel powerful. As the client begins to feel stronger within (a condition that often coincides with the development of the therapeutic relationship), a shift takes place. The client begins to play fairly with the therapist. As power and conflict issues become less important themes for the client, the need to control by being the winner or the hero ceases to be the prime concern. Instead, the therapeutic relationship becomes the main focus. In fact, often the client will cheat or change the rules so that the therapist will start to win. As time progresses, the rules become fair and consistent so that the game is played on an equal basis with lots of fun, playfulness and teasing. A comfortable balance occurs, not only within the therapeutic relationship, but frequently within the client's home, school and community life. These parallel changes in the client outside of therapy are amazing and exciting to track. This tracking is done respectfully (with the necessary confidentiality forms signed), through teachers, doctors, recreational counsellors, and parents.

Keeping caregivers, as well as other professionals, involved is essential for the total growth and progress of the client. Of course, confidentiality is an important issue, for the client needs to know that he is respected. Although one hour a week of therapy is important for the client, it is by no means the only support the client needs to help make changes. Just as no person is an island, so no therapist with her input, or type of therapy, can stand alone. There are and always will be several components to an individual's life that need to be considered and appropriately addressed.

To understand the value of the equipment, and to understand how and why a client may process a certain way, we need to review a few other factors. In art and play therapy, in fact in most forms of therapy, there are themes, or what we may call "issues," on which a client works. These themes are exhibited and processed in many ways, using different techniques, equipment and written processing. The client processes by working through his particular theme(s) with the support of the therapist. The therapeutic relationship provides the safety, security and structure that allows this very important work to be accomplished.

The most common themes or issues that occur in therapy are the following:

Abuse (family, physical, sexual)
Chaos
Power/control
Anger/sadness
Trust/relationships
Fear/rejection/failure/abandonment
Nurturing/deprivation
Boundaries/intrusion/security
Violation/protection
Self-esteem/self-worth/empowerment
Anxiety/stress/frustration
Confusion
Identity (social and/or sexual)
Loyalty/betrayal
Illness/loss/death/separation/loneliness
Adjustment/change
Divorce/acceptance
Hopelessness/helplessness/loss

While this list is probably not conclusive, it has been invaluable in assisting me with understanding the client's process. The original list was presented by Dr. Bryan Norton, a psychologist/play therapist in the United States, but I have added several themes to it as I have encountered them. You will probably add more as your work evolves and as you develop your own style. Never lose sight of the fact that your clients are your best teachers; each one will take you through several journeys of her life, which is an invaluable experience and gift.

Along with the themes to track your client's processing, there are **four types of play** through which he uses the equipment to process his themes (issues):

Sensorimotor: tactile play that is self-nurturing and can be regressive.

Symbolic: social, dramatic role playing.

Construction: developing and creating through art materials, etc.

Games With Rules: relationship-building, self-esteem, developing social skills.

The client uses the equipment in different types of play to help process her particular themes. The client's age or stage in the therapeutic process has no bearing on when or why she will choose particular pieces of equipment or how she will decide to work through the issues.

Besides themes and types of play, Dr. Bryan Norton has defined **five stages of play**. These are:

1) The early exploratory stage, wherein the client enters therapy exploring the playroom, the equipment, the therapist and the limits.

2) The later exploratory stage, in which the focus is on the therapist and the role he plays.

3) The limit-setting stage, where the client needs to test the rules and limits of the playroom as well as those of the therapist. This occurs because of the client's need to feel safe and secure in the situation before being able to move on to the next two stages.

4) The early therapeutic stage, in which the relationship with the therapist is the prime focus, and where the client truly starts to do his most intense work. True therapy occurs here.

5) The later therapeutic stage, wherein the client finishes up her work to the point at which she is most comfortable, and is also the stage where termination occurs.

The following outline of equipment in the playroom and the therapeutic journey is meant to assist you to better understand some of your clients' processing. This is based on my observations of over twenty years of working with children and youth. It is my hope that you will take this outline and develop it from your own experience and add to it what you learn from your own clients and teachers.

SANDBOX

Types of play: Sensorimotor
Symbolic
Construction
Games with rules

Themes most common:

Power/control
Anger/sadness
Fear/rejection/failure/abandonment
Nurturing/deprivation
Boundaries/intrusion/security
Violation/protection
Self-esteem/self-worth/empowerment
Anxiety/stress/frustration
Confusion
Loyalty/betrayal
Illness/loss/death/separation/loneliness
Adjustment/change
Chaos

Sandplay is tactile and healing, allowing the client to self-nurture while working through difficult issues.

The sandbox in the playroom is truly the most used piece of equipment, and viewed by clients as by far the most valuable. Frequently, clients may choose to process entirely with the sandbox to the exclusion of the other pieces of equipment. All four types of play can occur in the sandbox; in addition, any of the client's specific themes may be processed there.

Clients may choose to engage in either directive or non-directive play in the sandbox. The play may be symbolic in nature. The client is able to nurture herself while working through difficult issues. In addition, the client is able to be in total control of the sand, with no right or wrong way to work with it, thus avoiding frustration during processing.

WATER PLAY

Type of play: Sensorimotor

Themes most common:

Power/control
Anger/sadness
Fear/rejection/failure/abandonment
Nurturing/deprivation
Boundaries/protection
Self-esteem/self-worth/empowerment
Anxiety/stress/frustration
Confusion
Loyalty/betrayal
Illness/loss/death/separation/loneliness
Adjustment/change
Chaos

Water play allows the client to regress, to learn to self-nurture, and thus to do a great deal of healing.

The client may or may not need the therapist to be involved in the water play. Clients may feel the need to be rocked or to be fed by the baby bottle; or may simply need the therapist to play with them.

Water play can be used by the client to self-nurture; or the doll may be used to wash or to nurture. In either case, the effect is the same—the promotion of healing.

Please note that it is essential that the client use the washroom prior to water play, as experience tells me that accidents do happen!

PUPPETS

Types of play: Symbolic
Construction

Themes most common:

Power/control
Anger/sadness
Fear/rejection/failure/abandonment
Nurturing/deprivation
Boundaries/intrusion/security
Violation/protection
Self-esteem/self-worth/empowerment
Anxiety/stress/frustration

Confusion
Loyalty/betrayal
Illness/loss/death/separation/loneliness
Adjustment/change
Chaos

The entire list can be and often is role-played with the puppets. Clients develop elaborate and entire scripts about their issues.

The value of puppets is extensive. The use of puppets allows the clients to do creative problem solving. They are able to process issues that are painful, but in a non-intrusive manner. Most important of all, the clients are in complete control of their life stories and outcomes.

Puppets are the second most used and popular type of equipment in play therapy. Puppets can be used anywhere, and in a number of different ways by the client. Clients can make their own or choose their puppets to represent many characters in their dramatic play. Often the client will request the therapist's involvement in his puppet shows. There appears to be no "perfect" puppet to have in your playroom, but what appears to be more essential is the variety and flexibility of the puppets. You will start to collect the type of puppets according to your client's needs. Once again, follow your best teacher, your client, to find what will work best in your playroom. You may also decide to use different puppets in the playroom other than the puppets with which you choose to travel. I have three puppets that accompany me to schools, hospitals or presentations, which are not the puppets that are frequently used in the playroom.

The chapter on Puppetry by Marg McBride will help you to understand the value of puppets and how you may choose to work with them.

CREATIVE CENTRE

Types of play: Sensorimotor
Symbolic
Construction

Themes most common:

Directive art

All of the themes listed above are often dealt with through the therapeutic technique of art therapy. Play and art therapy are closely linked together in the creative centre.

Non-directive work in the creative centre allows the healing process of creativity to focus on self-esteem, self-worth, and empowerment.

This area is equipped with paper, clay, markers, paints, sparkles, braiding lace, beads, glue, wood, material of all sorts, tissue paper, straws, Popsicle sticks, and so on. As time goes on, your clients will make other suggestions for your supply list. Art therapy can take both approaches: directive and non-directive.

(Please note: Directive art should not be used with children under the age of nine. Too often children are pushed beyond their abilities to deal with certain issues. I have found that young children are eager to please and will draw what they are asked to draw and become overwhelmed by the results.)

Art therapy is a very powerful technique and needs to be used carefully and respectfully in awareness of the client's capabilities as well as her readiness. If a child is allowed to use the creative art area in a non-directive, creative manner, she often develops better self-esteem and self-worth, and also feels more empowered.

Clay is truly marvellous for clients of all ages to work with. Issues of anger, encopresis, enuresis, and tactile self-nurturing are frequently worked through while clients use clay. The other benefits to using clay are that it is fun, playful and a tension release.

The creative centre/arts area is where the younger clients tend to go after they have dealt with some of the more intense issues with the other equipment. The clients aged nine and up tend to go to this area first, then to the other equipment later in the therapy.

DRESS-UP CLOTHES AND MAKEUP CENTRE

Types of play:	Symbolic Construction
Themes most common:	the same as the sandplay themes listed previously.

The value of the dress-up clothes and the makeup centre lies in the fact that it is here that the client will do role-playing around identity and sexual issues. Role-play often occurs around family violence, physical and sexual abuse, and situations of chaos that cause stress.

DOLLHOUSE WITH FAMILY FIGURES

Type of play: Symbolic

Themes most common:

Power/control
Family sexual and physical abuse
Divorce/separation
Chaos/stress
Trust/relationships
Fear/rejection/failure/abandonment
Boundaries/intrusion/security
Violation/protection
Anxiety/stress/frustration
Confusion
Role identity issues
Loyalty/betrayal
Illness/loss/death/separation/loneliness
Adjustment/change
Hopelessness/helplessness/loss

The dollhouse particularly allows play around family issues, which tend to be a major area of concern for most of our clients. I have three dollhouses so that the client has the opportunity to deal with issues of divorce and separation: Mom's house, Dad's house and, in some cases, a residential setting or foster home.

KITCHEN SET

Type of play: Symbolic

Themes most common:

Abandonment
Trust/relationships
Divorce/separation
Chaos/stress
Nurturing/deprivation

Mother/child issues
Boundaries/intrusion/security

The kitchen set is most valuable with clients who have eating disorders, mother/child issues, or power/control issues around eating.

BABY DOLLS

Type of play: Symbolic

Themes most common:

Loyalty/betrayal
Anxiety/stress/frustration
Violation/protection
Boundaries/intrusion/security
Mother/child issues
Trust/relationship
Fear/rejection/failure/abandonment
Abuse (physical/sexual)
Hopelessness/helplessness/loss
Nurturing/deprivation

In playing with the dolls, the client may be very nurturing or very abusive. I have found it useful to set aside a particular doll for the child who displays a pattern of abusive play. This doll is stored for the client's use, and he is allowed to process the abuse through playing with this doll. I also have a very special doll, called Michelle, which I use to break the cycle of abusive play. Michelle is very well dressed and cared for. If the client begins to get rough with Michelle, I point out how fragile she is and model how she needs to be cared for. Gradually, the client tends to be less aggressive with the particular doll set aside for his own use, while at the same time exhibiting more nurturing behaviour toward Michelle, and thus letting go of aggression and past anger. Many mothering and abuse issues begin to be resolved when the client starts to nurture Michelle.

MUSICAL INSTRUMENTS

Type of play: Construction

Themes most common:

Self-esteem/self-worth/empowerment

Use of musical instruments is a form of constructive play, as clients put together tunes and enjoy them. It is a playful part of being creative.

Musical expression most often takes place in the later therapeutic stages, when the client is quite close to termination and to finishing therapy.

GUNS

Type of play: Symbolic

Themes most common:

Aggression
Chaos
Abuse
Power/control
Anger
Fear
Protection

Although the use of guns in play is controversial, I have toy guns as part of my play therapy equipment because children do tend to want to act out gunplay and will frequently make guns out of seemingly innocuous objects if none are provided. In families with a history of violence, wife assault, or alcoholism, guns are often a part of the client's background, and the feelings around them need to be dealt with.

In using guns in play therapy, I have found it useful to have certain rules. There must be no pointing of the gun at the therapist, especially at the face. Usually clients want the therapist involved in this play, but even though I may be involved, I choose not to shoot back at them or towards them. Although the clients may want me to role-play the perpetrator, I make it clear that I will not accept that role, and that I am not comfortable with shooting them, hitting them, tying them up, force-feeding them, locking them away, or using abusive language towards them. I choose not to repeat that abuse for them; I will support them in their need to process the abuse, but will not be a part of it.

PUNCHING BAG AND MINI-TRAMPOLINE

Types of play: Sensorimotor
Constructive

Themes most common:

Anger/aggression
Frustration
Hopelessness/helplessness
Empowerment
Nurturing/deprivation
Boundaries/intrusion
Security

This equipment is available to younger children to help them let go of their negative energy, and in doing so a great deal of their frustration and anger is released.

Initially, the children are interested in the punching bag and will use the trampoline later. The use of the trampoline allows more energy flow, opens up the client for a discussion, and creates a desire to talk and to share. In fact, you may find that some clients will do all of their talking while on the trampoline!

It is also helpful to redirect some children who have difficulty focusing or are very hyperactive to spend some time first with this equipment. They then seem to be able to calm down and to seek another type of equipment that allows them to self-nurture.

MASKS AND PLAY CLOTHES

Types of play: Symbolic
Constructive

Themes most common:

Power/control
Trust/relationship
Boundaries/intrusion/security
Violation/protection
Self-esteem/self-worth/empowerment
Identity (social and/or sexual)
Adjustment/change.

Masks and play clothes allow the client to work out multiple themes.

The client may use the masks and clothes available or may make them out of paper, plaster, clay, cloth, and so on.

Streetproofing

Streetproofing is directive in nature, and is used in the later therapeutic stages and in termination.

It is essential that both children and adults be given guidelines so that they are not revictimized. They are still vulnerable, even though they have been dealing with their abuse through therapy.

Streetproofing can be accomplished through the use of videos, cue cards, journal processing, art techniques and storybook reading that addresses these issues.

Each piece of equipment that I have described has its own value, but the emphasis in play therapy is still upon the therapist and upon the whole therapeutic relationship. In describing and examining each piece of the playroom equipment, we must not lose sight of the relationship between the therapist and the client. The greatest piece of equipment is you—the therapist—and the relationship that you and the client develop together as you both work toward the client's healing.

CHAPTER SEVEN

PUPPETS AS ALLIES IN THERAPY

Marg McBride

PUPPETS AS ALLIES IN THERAPY

> Pup-pet (pup'it) n. 3. One slavishly subject to the will of another; a tool. 4. A toy in the form of a person; a doll.
>
> *Funk and Wagnall's Standard College Dictionary*

Personal choice is absent from this definition. A puppet has no options.

Children entering therapy frequently arrive there because they are "stuck"—stuck because they have lost their sense of personal power, the power to choose. They may be responding to stress with negative assumptions about their role in their families. Puppet-like, they repeat patterns of unproductive or unpopular behaviour.

Puppets are concrete objects that speak to the child's imagination. They invite a child to take physical control of them while providing a safe distance from her real-life experience. Thus puppets allow children to act out delicate problems without expressing them verbally. Perhaps this is why puppets are such effective tools in a child's search for self.

Nancy Renfro, in her book *A Puppet Corner in Every Library* (1978), explains this concept well:

> For a child, a puppet becomes an ambassador between his inner and outer world. . . . A puppet serves as an alter ego for a child's thoughts and desires and he feels no inhibitions about expressing them. . . . When a puppet is placed on his hand, the child can easily hide behind this transparent facade and feel secure in the knowledge that he is not being seen. Whatever the child projects through the puppet, he feels no responsibility: the action and words are by someone else. When a puppet is placed on the hand of an adult, the child forgets that the adult is there, making it possible for a communication barrier to be completely broken down; for a moment a shy child becomes expressive, a normal child is more fluent, and a hyperkinetic child is calmed.

To these observations I would add that the very act of wearing and manipulating a puppet is empowering. The child feels a sense of control by making the puppet talk, by making it move, by teaching it and telling it.

It is critical that we who work with children are sensitive to and respectful of the tremendous risk a child takes when she loses herself in fantasy with a puppet.

It is also valuable for us to experience for ourselves this special relationship between the puppet and self. This can be done in a variety of ways. Much of my experience has involved working with children in libraries: making puppets, teaching children how to make them and performing puppet shows. Most importantly, observing and listening to children as they play with puppets has taught me that observing children in play is a privilege. This is a time when, as Renfro suggests, all barriers are down. Barriers dissolve between a puppet and puppeteer. They also dissolve between puppets and audience.

As teachers, therapists and concerned parents, we can attend performances for children by professional puppeteers or children. We can observe children's classes in puppetry in public libraries. We can observe the magic that occurs between the puppets and the child audience. We experience the chemistry that occurs between the child within us and the puppets. By attending workshops in storytelling, puppetry, mime, mask making and clowning, we may open ourselves up to identifying with that vulnerability the child experiences when he picks up a puppet before us in therapy. The more we grow ourselves in the art of creating and fantasizing, the more we can "be there" for our client during therapy.

Renfro tells us that children feel safer in expressing their feelings through a puppet because of the distance it creates between the child's association of those feelings with that of his physical reality. At the same time the child is very vulnerable because his defences are down.

Using Ready-made Puppets

Many of us use ready-made puppets and dolls as part of our play therapy collection. I like to use anatomically complete puppets with movable mouths and removable ears. The movable mouths enable the child to speak through the puppet, to vent her rage or sadness or confusion verbally as well as physically. It allows her to practice saying "No!" for example, while acting out scenes of sexual or other abuse.

Here is an example of how it can work:

Ben was using a boy puppet. I had a Dad puppet on my hand. Both puppets have movable mouths. Ben ripped the ears off my Dad puppet and said to me, "You be the Dad."

"You've taken off his ears," I commented.

"He never listens to me," Ben explained.

Ben then talked through his puppet about how he would throw Dad in the river and he ended by demanding to know what Dad thought of that suggestion.

As the therapist, without speaking through my Dad puppet, I commented that Dad probably couldn't hear without his ears.

Ben put the ears back on Dad.

As Dad, I then said, "Thank you, Ben. I knew that you were angry but I couldn't hear what you were saying. Will you tell me again?"

"You never listen to me," said Ben, with less vehemence this time.

Again I spoke for Dad: "I'm sorry, Ben, sometimes I get so busy I forget to listen."

With this, Ben's puppet gave the Dad puppet a kiss and then Ben, without his puppet, said to me: "I'm tired of this game. Let's play something else."

This typifies productive play with ready-made puppets. We must be alert to prevent a child from becoming stuck in a destructive play pattern with puppets or dolls. In Ben's case, he invited me to join him in a way that enabled me to acknowledge his anger. If I had allowed Ben to throw the Dad puppet in the river, that action would have caused the abuse to accelerate, and I would need to intervene further. Allowing the child to get stuck in a negative space blocks the flow toward self-healing. Without disclosing the details of Ben's play to his real father, I could convey to him Ben's feelings of rejection and anger and suggest that Ben needed more one-on-one time with his dad. It has been my experience that most aggressive play with puppets is an indicator of unease within the child as a response to his stressful environment.

In addition to boy, girl, mom, dad, grandma and grump puppets, I have a moveable-mouth villain and assorted animals.

Reversible storytelling dolls are wonderful additions to a puppet collection. These fairy tale characters contain the Jungian "shadow" in some way in their reversed form, e.g., Red Riding Hood and the Wolf, Miss Muffet and the Spider, King George and the Dragon, Snow White and the Hag. Children sense the dichotomy inherent in these characters. An awareness of dichotomy helps to open the door for self-acceptance: acceptance of both their positive and negative natures and of the blend of these qualities in other people.

Let us take the example of the reversible doll, Miss Muffet and the Spider. Children and adults respond to Miss Muffet in surprisingly different ways. A class of six "trainable retarded" children were learning nursery rhymes. I decided to use the reversible doll to illustrate the rhyme. Children took turns in telling the rhyme while using the doll, and their speech became more discernable. They were less conscious of their audience of peers and moved eagerly from this step to acting out the rhyme as part of a group.

In a training session for therapists, a woman who chose to play with Miss Muffet was surprised by the "hair" she felt when she reached under the puppet's skirt. Peggy later disclosed that the fur-like spider concealed under the doll's skirt startled her because she thought of pubic hair. From her reaction it appeared to me that this might have prompted a new awareness in Peggy of her sexuality.

Let us now examine the three significant experiences a child has when she makes a puppet and brings it to life.

First of all, the mere act of making a puppet is empowering. Then by telling a story with the puppet she gives voice to her own feelings. Finally, she must risk a development of trust in order to perform the story she has invented with the puppet she has made.

One Boy's Experience of Making a Puppet

Kevin is sewing. He is nine years old, but as he works, his face takes on the look of an innocent five-year-old. As he coaxes the needle laboriously in and out of the buttonholes, his mouth twists with the effort. Meanwhile, Michelle, Kevin's younger sister, takes a different approach to making her shirtsleeve puppet. She is bubbly and talkative. She breezes through the construction and then looks for something else to do.

Even after several sessions in a Saturday morning puppet club at the public library, Kevin still barely communicates with his peers or me. I wonder what has prompted his mother to enrol him in the public puppetry class for children nine to thirteen. Each week Kevin comes, listens, works and then goes home again without interacting with any other person.

After eight weeks, the children and puppets are ready to perform for a public audience. Groups of two to four children cluster behind the puppet stage to perform the fairy tales of their choice.

Kevin's puppet appears on cue and suddenly, to everyone's surprise, its big voice thunders incomprehensible sounds to the audience of sixty or so children and adults. When Kevin emerges from behind the stage to take a bow, his eyes are as bright and wide as those of his button-eyed companion.

After fourteen years, the memory of this child's performance remains vivid to me. Following the puppet show, his mother, full of delight, said that this was the first time Kevin had completed anything. She was surprised that he had even made the puppet, much less made such a striking public appearance.

Because my job in this case was simply to teach puppet making and not to provide therapy I did not press the mother for details about Kevin's verbal, social and co-ordination difficulties. In hindsight, I see that Kevin was a child with low self-esteem, who perhaps was learning disabled or suffering from some form of speech impediment, possibly even autism.

Kevin's story typifies the sense of personal empowerment that children may gain from creating objects and then bringing them to life. Puppets allow a child to complete this experience. "It's just like being God," as another child in my puppet club once aptly put it.

Kevin's benefits were threefold. He created, he gave life, and he gave life before an audience. All of these steps demanded courage. Every step became easier with successful completion of the previous one.

Practical Puppet Construction

Here are some examples of simple puppet construction as well as suggestions for providing support. These may be used with an individual in therapy or with any group of children. I prefer to use materials that are readily available in most households, because this gives the child an experience he may repeat with little or no expense.

Madeline L'Engle (1980, p. 51) reminds us that, "What looks like a hat to a grownup may, to a child artist, be an elephant inside a boa constrictor."

For all adults working with children, respecting this is the challenging part: our perceptions are ours, the child's are hers, and we have no right to influence a child's creative interpretation. The exception occurs if the child asks for support or indicates in some way that the cathartic experience will be lost for her if the adult does not give some guidance.

For example, a child might say "I can't do this," or "This puppet is dumb," or "I can't make this right." Support offered to the child in dealing with an overwhelming challenge in construction is necessary at this time. You may discuss ways to make things work and offer to help. Again the challenge to the adult is to avoid taking over, "doing it for" him and thereby disempowering the child.

Acknowledge the child's feelings: "You're feeling angry/sad because things aren't going the way you want them to." Then you may suggest, "I wonder what would happen if we used ______ to attach the eyes," or, "I wonder what else could be used to hold eyes on?" A child will usually respond to this type of suggestion.

In general, I try not to interfere beyond making certain that the puppet is structurally sound. I leave the child to lose herself in communing with the materials and with herself.

Sample 1: Shirtsleeve Puppet

(For children of any age.)

This is the kind of puppet Kevin made.

Sever an old shirtsleeve at the shoulder. Then turn the sleeve inside out and bind the end that used to be attached to the shoulder tightly with string or a rubber band.

Now turn the sleeve right side out again and stuff the bound end with wadded newspaper or cloth scraps. Your puppet now has a head. Bind below the stuffed area to create a "neck" loosely enough so that the child can insert an index finger and middle finger to support the puppet's head. Cut holes in the sleeve so the puppeteer's thumb and remaining two fingers may protrude to form hands. Buttons, yarn scraps and other bits of fabric may be sewn or glued on to create features and clothes.

Sample 2: Paper Bag Puppet
(For children of any age.)

The mouth on this puppet is moveable. Its facial features may be coloured on or made from fabric scraps, buttons, bits of yarn and paper.

To begin, open a bag to expose the fold line that forms the bottom. Construct or draw the upper portion of the puppet's face (including the top lip) onto the bag bottom. The lower lip and jaw of the puppet's face must appear below the fold line on the bag front in order for the mouth to move (see illustration).

Now slide your hand inside the bag and hook your fingers into the groove formed by the bag bottom and fold. By flexing your fingers when you speak, the puppet will appear to talk.

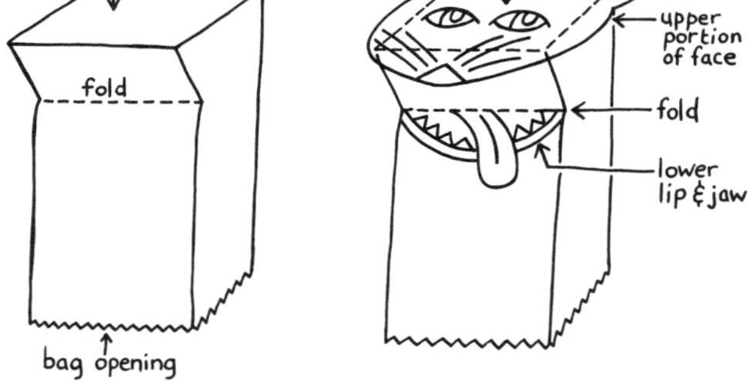

Sample 3: Papier Mâché over Plasticine
(Best with children age nine and older.)

Sculpt a head from Plasticine (play dough or clay will not work) over the neck of a pop bottle or a foil-covered heavy pressed paper cone available at craft stores. Make exaggerated features in the Plasticine. These will lose definition as paper is layered over top, so make eyes, ears, nose and mouth big to begin with. Draw Plasticine down the bottleneck by about three cm. to form the puppet's neck. Apply a liberal layer of petroleum jelly to the entire head.

Tear regular old used newspaper into small strips (approximately 2 cm. x 5 cm.) Tear, but keep in a separate pile, pieces of unprinted newsprint paper or other plain lightweight paper. Mix a liberal amount of thin non-toxic wallpaper paste. Dip individual pieces of old newspaper into the paste. Remove excess paste with fingers and apply pieces to the puppet head, overlapping them as you go. Apply a second layer in the same way using the unprinted paper. (This helps you distinguish the number of layers.) Allow these layers to dry completely, beyond the reach of small children, at least a day or two, in a well-ventilated area. Apply two more layers, alternating printed and unprinted paper. The puppet head should have a total of four layers of paper.

When the head is perfectly dry, separate the papier-mâché mould from the Plasticine base by running a sharp blade from the neck edge on one side of the head, up the neck, over the head and down to the other side. The papier-mâché head will split in two, leaving the sculptured Plasticine behind. Using two layers of papier-mâché, reconnect the front and back portions of the head. You now have a lightweight original puppet head. It may now be painted using any kind of paint, however, acrylic paint provides long-lasting colour and doubles as a protective coating. When the paint is fully dry, decorate with buttons, sequins, yarn and fabric scraps. Clear-drying, all-purpose glue works well.

Tracing a hand on a piece of paper may make a pattern for the puppet body, and then drawing a dress-like shape around it. Make sure the neck end is big enough to fit generously halfway around the neck edge of the puppet head. Pin the paper pattern on a double layer of fabric and cut.

Using a machine or a short running stitch by hand, sew the puppet's body sides together from top neck edge to bottom, but leave the top and bottom open. Turn the body right side out.

Apply glue liberally to the neck edge of the puppet head. Insert the head into the body and hold firmly in place until the glue begins to set, about ten minutes. Allow the glue to dry thoroughly for twenty-four hours, and then it's "Show Time!"

Sample 4: Magazine Stick Puppets
(For any age, including adults.)

These puppets may provide quick clues to how a client is feeling.

Have on hand any heavy paper of bristol board weight, clear Mac-Tac (colourless adhesive plastic), wooden Popsicle sticks or tongue depressors, magazines, glue and scissors.

Cut a picture from a magazine. Glue it onto the heavy paper. Cover it with Mac-Tac and re-cut the shape. Paste a stick on the bottom edge, on the wrong side of the shape, to form a handle.

Feelings that Puppet-making Can Generate
Simply making any puppet may be enough for some clients and too much for others. The image that the child chooses to make the focus of his puppet and what he creates may evoke such intense negative feelings that he may wish to destroy his puppet. This usually indicates that the child is on the threshold of some significant realization.

I may say to him by way of acknowledging his feelings, "You feel so angry/sad/scared you want to throw your puppet away." Then I would have them speak strongly in defence of saving the puppet.

"But it's ugly, I hate it," the child may argue.

"I saw how hard you worked," I reply. "Will you give it to me? I will keep it in a safe place."

At this time I would offer a shoebox that the child can decorate (as a coffin, if he wishes) and I put the date and his name on the box with the rejected, but saved, puppet inside.

When the child is ready to deal with the issue, he knows that I accepted the feelings he poured into the making of his puppet. He knows where the puppet can be found. I safeguard any work given to me in trust—it may be months before it is looked at again.

A child may experience deep feelings during the making of any kind of puppet. However, the sense of personal empowerment will increase if he chooses to bring the puppet to life rather than lay it to rest. The choice of what to do next remains with the child. The risk involved in this part of the process is his.

Bringing the Puppet To Life

The newly made puppet, like Frankenstein's creature, is now ready to be "given life." "Giving life" can mean miming—doing actions without words—or it may mean giving voice as well. Try to leave the choice up to the child. Regardless of how a client chooses to bring life to his character, he is telling a story. We must watch with our third eye and listen with our third ear, letting our intuition guide us in our response.

Unless invited by the child, I rarely intervene in this process. If I am unclear about what theme he is working through, I may reflect back to him what I see or hear the puppet doing.

For example, if I see the puppet in a despondent posture or if the child is pretending to cry, I may say, "Something has made the puppet sad." Often this will trigger an explanation from the child of what is making the puppet sad. I am careful at this time to leave the child's communication of feelings to the puppet. If the child connects with feelings that erupt outside of the puppet character I may say, "Playing with the puppet is reminding you of something sad/something which made you angry."

Interventions should begin before a child becomes excited by a negative theme and loses touch with reality. Early intervention keeps the child connected with the present through communication with the therapist.

A child will benefit from the independent play with his puppet and from interacting with the therapist. However, performing before an audience in a group setting may be more empowering still. Again the child leads the way in this decision.

Performing before an Audience

Kevin's experience with performing as part of a group before an audience was a strengthening experience for him. His risks were more public than those taken by children in therapy. However, small groups of four to six children with the support of two therapists may achieve similar benefits.

Group work in puppetry provides the opportunity for participants to take risks on many levels: making a puppet in the presence of others, sharing and creating stories, speaking and being listened to, having all the attention and being attentive to others.

Professional puppeteers often use a stage to create distance between themselves and the audience. Many client puppeteers prefer to have their puppet appear from behind a stage. The stage can be anything that provides concealment: a solid-backed chair or couch, a large cardboard appliance box with a cut-out window through which puppets may appear, a cloth stretched across a doorway, or a table turned on its side. Any object large enough for the child to hide behind can set the scene for a story the child wants to tell.

A group of children working together for the first time appreciates the anonymity of ad-libbing a familiar folk or fairy tale while manipulating puppets from behind a stage. Most of these stories include a victim, villain, hero or heroine and often an omnipotent figure. Cinderella, for instance, is a victim; the stepmother and sisters are villainous. She is saved from poverty and suffering by the prince, with the help of a fairy godmother.

We can identify with Cinderella's plight and celebrate her liberation from it. Similarly, for children in therapy, Cinderella provides a character that can speak for their personal suffering and abuse. They may yearn for liberation from anger and oppression. A ready-made tale such as this can allow a child to voice, from a distance, her own suffering.

I believe, as Rudolph Ekstein (1983, p. 417) suggests, that perhaps therapists who work with all children and adolescents

> . . . not only should know the technical and theoretical literature but also should be concerned with fairy tales and children's stories, with mythology and religious myths of all

> countries, of all persuasions. Behind the language of faith, the language of magic, the language of hope and the language of despair is psychological truth. We must learn this language and thus identify with the suffering of the child, with the meaning of his private mythology. In turn, at times he will internalize that part of us that wishes to understand him, that speaks his language. Then he may ask how to translate into our language, a language that he knows exists, a language that will help him venture out of his island of despair and secret, often forbidden, longings, to the mainland where the rest of us usually reside.

I draw your attention to the word "usually" in that last sentence: "where the rest of us usually reside." We must remember that we have all dwelt in fantasy worlds for varying lengths of time. In a practical sense, knowledge of the mythology of various cultures will help us to build bridges with the client whose culture and literary heritage differs from our own.

In conclusion, let me emphasize that I feel we should learn to connect with "the puppet" within ourselves as well as in others. Let us use all of the tools at our disposal in order to become sensitized to how children choose and relate to puppets. These tools may include: our memories of our own childhood experience, the ancient fairytales of our culture, our client's own favourite toys, and our ability to listen and observe.

The observation of children at play with puppets is a privilege. Their vulnerability is amplified because barriers dissolve and we must respect this.

Puppet making is an empowering act involving three distinct steps: creating the puppet, giving it mobility and/or voice, and giving it life before an audience. Each step involves courage and risk.

As therapists we must support the child in the creative process by giving assistance when asked, or when a technical weakness in the construction of the puppet may threaten a child's success. Our perception is not the child's and we should withhold artistic judgment of her work.

We must respect the child's decision to stop at any step in the creative process and be willing to keep for her, in trust, the work that may help her to recall her feelings when she is ready.

In my practice, I tend to make a lot of use of puppets, especially those with moveable mouths. They are a valuable asset in the play therapy setting, but we may need to intervene if a child becomes "stuck" in destructive play with puppets or any other toy. Reversible storytelling dolls illustrate the dichotomy of potential "good and evil" within us. They can lead clients in a symbolic way to greater self-acceptance and thus to an expanded acceptance of others.

Every person has a story to tell and puppets are a powerful storytelling medium. By broadening our knowledge of fairy tales, religions and mythology, we will become better able to identify with the mythology of our clients or students.

If we pay attention, we will find that our clients are offering us an opportunity to learn a new way of listening. If we listen carefully through the filters of fantasy, we may hear the whispers of psychological truth.

REFERENCES

General

L'Engle, M. (1980). *Walking on water*. New York: Bantam.

Puppetry Bibliography

Angler, L. (1997). *Making puppets come alive: A method of learning and teaching hand puppetry.* U.K.: Dover Publications..

Ekstein, R. (1983). Play therapy for borderline children. In Schaefer, C. & O'Connor, K. (Eds.), *Handbook of Play Therapy*. New York: Wiley.

Gates, F. (1978). *Glove, mitten and sock puppets*. New York: Walker and Co.

Hunt, T., & Renfro, N. (1982). *Puppetry in early childhood education*. Austin, Texas: N. Renfro Studios.

Jenkins, P. (1980). *The magic of puppetry: A guide for those working with young children*. USA: Prentice Hall.

Philpott, A. (n.d.). *Puppets and therapy plays*. Boston: out of print.

Renfro, N. (1978). *A puppet corner in every library.* Austin, Texas: N. Renfro Studios.

Renfro, N. (1979). *Puppetry and the art of story creation*. Austin, Texas: N. Renfro Studios.

Ross, L. (1969). *Hand puppets: How to make and use them*. New York: Lothrop, Lee and Shepard.

Ross, L. (1978). *Scrap puppets: How to make and move them*. New York: Holt, Rinehart and Winston.

Williams, D. (1966). *Paper bag puppets*. Belmont, California: Fearon.

Wilt, J. (1977). *Puppets with pizazz*. Waco, Texas: Creative Resources.

Bibliography of Picture Books for Use in Art and Play Therapy

Dreams, Nightmares, Fear of the Dark

Condy, R., & Hazby, N. (1990). *How to get rid of bad dreams*. New York: Scholastic Publishers.

Drawson, B. (1977). *Flying Dimitri*. Canada: Orchard Books.

DePaola, T. (1976). *When everyone was fast asleep*. New York: Holiday House.

Ivens, P., & Cook, L. (1974). *If I were all these*. Toronto: Burns & MacEachern Ltd.

Mayer, M. (1968). *There's a nightmare in my closet*. New York: E. Dutton.

Sendak, M. (1988). *Where the wild things are*. New York: Collins Children's Book Group.

Waber, B. (1972). *Ira sleeps over*. Boston: Houghton, Mifflin.

Monsters

Asbjornsen, P. (1992). *The three billy goats gruff.* New York: Harcourt.
McKee, D. (1980). *Not now, Bernard.* London: Red Fox.
Munsch, R. (1983). *David's father*. Toronto: Annick Press.
San Souci, R. (1994). *The Hobyahs*. New York: Delacorte Press.
Sendak, M. (1981). *Outside over there*. New York: Harper, Row.
Steptoe, J. (1980). *Daddy is a monster . . . sometimes*. New York: Lippincott.

Miscellaneous

Pappas, M. (1982). *Sweet dreams for little ones*. San Francisco: Harper.
Wise Brown, M. (1997). *Goodnight moon*. New York: Harper Collins.
Zolotow, C. (1972). *William's doll*. New York: Harper and Row.

CHAPTER EIGHT

A SYSTEMIC ART THERAPY ASSESSMENT FOR USE WITH CHILDREN

Barbara Dorrington

A SYSTEMIC ART THERAPY ASSESSMENT FOR USE WITH CHILDREN

Abstract
This chapter describes a six-session art therapy assessment package using concepts based on systems theory, now generally known as systemic therapy. Two concepts are introduced (circular questioning and externalizing the problem) as useful ways of obtaining detailed information in children's art assessments. Emphasis is placed on how the therapist asks questions in each succeeding session. Suggested topics are included. Examples of art pictures complete the description of each session.

To date, most art therapists have developed their own unique ways of assessing children. Such diversity of approach has enabled art therapists to develop a rich and creative style that can be applied to many therapeutic situations. In fact, it was only in the 1940s that two American artists and educators, Florence Cane and Margaret Naumberg, combined psychoanalytic theory with art activities to develop what is now known as art therapy (Cane, 1951; Naumberg, 1947). Consequently, art therapy is just past its infancy as a valued therapeutic approach. There is a growing need for ongoing evaluation and research to validate the art therapy method. This particular chapter will focus on a six-session art therapy assessment to be used with children as young as five and as old as sixteen. Some agreement appears to have developed in the art therapy literature that the following ideas should be included in the assessment of a child in an art therapy session:

Free Picture
A free picture is one that is done in both the first and the last assessment sessions. This allows the child to spontaneously suggest themes that occur over time. Along with producing the picture, children are encouraged to tell a story about their free picture.

Some art therapists prefer to include the immediate family members in the first and last assessment sessions and may even encourage family members to participate in a drawing activity as a way of understanding their issues and concerns. Drawings may be completed by each individual in the family; or they may be directed as a group to complete an exercise with only one picture emerging as a family group project (Kwiatkowska, 1978).

Kinetic Family Drawing

A kinetic family drawing activity has family members doing something together with the client (Burns & Kaufman, 1970). This particular drawing is completed by the individual child. Kinetic family drawings suggest action and movement. The family members usually include only the immediate family, but the child may draw more distant relatives, friends or neighbours as "his family." The reasons why the child chooses to include these people should be explored with him. However, drawings of unusual members should not be discouraged. Although instructions to the child are left vague, e.g., "Draw yourself doing something with your family," the idea is to draw all family members in an activity. Children regularly choose such activities as going for a walk, watching television, or eating dinner with family members. Sometimes each of the family members is involved in separate activities in the same picture. In spite of the direction, some children may choose to draw the family as if they were posing stiffly for a photograph because he finds it hard to think of an activity that the whole family does together.

Kinetic School Drawing

A kinetic school drawing includes a teacher and classmates doing something together with the client (Prout and Phillips, 1974). The child is told, "Draw yourself at school doing something with your teacher and classmates." Much of the time, children will include only the teacher or only a classmate or two in the drawing. Therapists should always ask the client to explain why certain important people like other children in the class have been left out. This assignment can be an especially difficult one for learning-disabled children, who work laboriously at designing desks and tables as part of the background for the picture.

Kinetic Drawing With Friends

A kinetic drawing "with friends doing something together" allows the client to choose a friendship situation in the immediate neighbourhood or in a school or a community group situation. This assignment sheds light on the social situation of the client (less structured than the school milieu) by providing a medium for her to describe how friends are made and how she has been able to fit into her peer group. Occasionally, children will draw an adult friend or an imaginary friend if they feel they have no age-mate peers. This allows the therapist an opportunity to assess the potential social skills of the child by asking questions about these types of relationships as well.

Squiggle Game

In the Squiggle Game (Winnicott, 1971), the therapist makes a squiggle on paper and then asks the child to "turn it into something." The child's creation may be something quite realistic or it may be imaginary: he may turn the squiggle into arrows, guns, princesses, animals, ghosts, cartoon characters, pretty designs, suns, moons or flowers.

Projective Picture

Projective pictures are intended to project feelings and philosophies and may include such themes as: Draw how you feel today; draw yourself and your family as animals; draw your ideal place; draw your safe place; draw a road map of your life; visualize your world in colours and symbols (Oaklander, 1978).

What Is the Systemic Art Therapy Assessment Package?

It is helpful for the art therapist (or any therapist or counsellor) to adopt a theory base as a map or a guide as to how he will work with a client. Just as a chess player needs to strategize his next move, the art therapist needs to strategize how he can help his clients find solutions to their problems. An art therapy assessment will give children who are verbally silent, anxious or verbally non-compliant a "voice on paper" with which to express the problems in their lives.

Systemic art therapy always looks at the child in context—how the child is with her family as a whole, how the child behaves when she is just with her parents, or how she interacts when she is just with her siblings. But there is more. How does this child react with her teachers? Does she react differently with her teacher if her classmates are present? How does she interact with her friends? Does she interact differently if both her parents and her friends are with her?

I believe that the word "systemic" is a key word for the art therapist because the therapist examines the client's behaviour when he is in the "system" of his family, and in the "system" of the community (his friends, the clubs he belongs to), and in the "system" of school (his teachers, his classmates, his guidance counsellor).

If a photographer were told to follow a child around for an entire day and take at least one hundred snapshots of her, a more systemic picture of the child should emerge. In the morning, she may be groggy and quick to spar with her siblings. On her way to school, she may be chipper, engaging in excited conversation with her best friend. At school and in the classroom, she may appear confused and disoriented, and be unable to complete the academic lesson. In the evening, she may respond warmly to her mother reading her a story. Only minutes later, she might argue plaintively with her father not to put her to bed yet.

In an individual art therapy session with a child, the art therapist naturally focuses on that individual. At this moment, the child is in a therapeutic system (therapist and child). As the child and therapist relate to each other, it becomes the "systemic" art therapist's task to bring alive the other systems in which the child lives, works and plays. At times it may even almost feel as if the family, friends or teacher were in the therapy room.

The systemic art therapy assessment package is designed to include pictures and specific questions that will highlight the many and varied relationships a child has in his life.

Preparing for the Initial Systemic Art Therapy Session

A meeting with the entire family or at least the child's parents should be planned for at the beginning and also at the end of the therapeutic contract (contracts tend to average about six weekly sessions and can be renewed by agreement of both parent[s] and therapist). Some systemic therapists prefer to alternate an individual art session with the child by having meetings with the entire family in order to stay current with any progress or difficulties faced by all family members. This may also alleviate the inappropriate expectations of a parent who feels the therapist should see the child and cure him of his ills independently of the family.

The goal of the first interview is to gather basic information about who is in the family and to identify other people involved with the child's problem. Changes in the family system should be explored, such as deaths, illnesses, births, older children leaving home, marriages, residential moves and changes in the parents' careers or jobs. The therapist's expectations about how future art therapy sessions will be handled should be shared.

I usually advise the child that stick figures are discouraged and ask her simply to draw as well as she can. Emphasis is placed on having fun drawing and not on how artistic the child is. Also, the child is informed that many of the drawings will include using lead pencil on blank white paper when given a specific task, but there will be opportunities to use crayons, coloured pencils, markers and magazine cutouts for free choice productions. Over forty years ago, Irene Dewdney, a Canadian art therapist, initially introduced the concept of a "structured pencil technique" using only pencil on paper for structured tasks. Children who tend to come from chaotic environments or children who are often described as hyperactive tend to flourish in art productions when they use art materials that provide more control, such a pencil or paintbrush, rather than the freedom of using their fingers.

This initial family assessment should also allow family members to give their (possibly different) views of the problem. Family members are encouraged to be specific and to give concrete examples. There should be discussion of solutions to the problem that were tried in the past, with attention to including involvement with other counselling agencies or private therapists. The therapist asks the parents and other family members to define their own goals for change.

It may be appropriate with some families to ask each member to draw a picture, using blank paper and pencil only, of what the problem is. This will help highlight what each member feels has gone wrong and it may possibly even generate some ideas about how to solve the problem in a new way.

By the end of this initial family session, the therapist will hopefully have developed enough of an understanding to identify how each family member relates with the others and what descriptive opinions the family members hold about the child's problem. Also, the art therapist will have made some judgments based on her observations of the family group's behaviour during the session. These judgments become what is therapeutically known as a hypothesis (Fleuridas, Nelson & Rosenthal, 1986).

Getting Started: Preparing the Questions for the Art Assessment

Systemic art therapy assessment may be a bit of a misnomer in that many therapists agree it is hard to divorce the therapeutic process from the assessment process. However, the goal of this assessment is to complete an evaluation of how the child views his world and how he sees his problems. The questions that the therapist devises in the systemic art assessment package are designed to highlight differences and changes in the various relationships in the child's life.

If you ask a child the question, "Do your parents fight?" you will probably get a one-word response; or perhaps the child will feel compelled to lie, if he thinks saying "yes" will reveal too much information. However, a carefully phrased question such as "Do your parents fight more before or after your father starts to drink in the evening?" will evoke a much more helpful and detailed answer. The fighting is taken for granted. In fact, if the child feels his parents really do not argue much, he is likely to tell the therapist that the question does not make much sense to him.

Questions that examine relationships—that look at problems as existing between two people rather than as a single problem within one person—are called circular questions (Selvini, Boscolo, Cecchin, & Prata, 1980). These types of questions can be framed in the past, present or future.

Some examples of "past" questions would be: How did your father use to discipline you before he started to drink? Who was most attached to your mother before she died? How was your sister's problem with stealing different before your father moved out of the house?

Some examples of "present" questions would be: How does your sister act silly? How does your family have fun, compared to other families you know? When your father tries to get your mother to stop crying, what does your sister do? Who agrees with you that you don't have a problem with drugs?

Some examples of "future" questions would be: What do you think your mother would do if your father were to stop drinking? What would your father do if your oldest sister left home? If I waved a magic wand and you stopped having these problems, how would your parents react?

Such questions, which focus on the child's relationships, on the child's view of his problems and on attempts at solutions, are the anchor of the systemic art therapy package. Consequently, a comprehensive list of suggested questions is included in each session of this assessment series.

The Systemic Perception of Problems and Solutions

Many families engage in counselling because they view their child as being the problem—that the rest of the family is fine and life would be much easier if only she would cooperate. It is the systemic art therapist's task to develop a new description of the problem so that the child and all family members will feel that the problem can truly be solved. Systemic art therapists see the problem as separate from the child's existence and therefore external to her, which implies that she is not necessarily to blame. This process is known as externalizing the problem (White, 1984).

By asking a lot of questions about the problem and how it has developed, how the child has occasionally not succumbed to the problem, or has escaped from it, the therapist will convince him that he does have some control over the problem. He can make it bigger or smaller, have it happen more or less often, and he can observe how his family reacts when the problem is worse or better. Sometimes, just by personifying the actual problem as if it had a life of its own—such as THE TEMPER MONSTER, rather than Johnny's temper—the therapist will encourage all family members that the problem can be minimized or tamed. It is very hard to totally eliminate a problem altogether and parents should be advised that relapses are very common before true success has occurred (White, 1984; Munro, 1987).

Session 1 of the art therapy assessment focuses on a number of questions a therapist can ask to assist with externalizing the problem. Working on one or two problems at a time may make some positive changes in the other problem areas that have been identified.

THE SYSTEMIC ART THERAPY PACKAGE

Session One: Approaching the Child in a New Way about the Problem

The interaction is all-important. Parents may respond to the child's problem with anxiety and anger. Teachers may respond with indifference or avoidance. Friends may respond with mockery and snobbishness. Therapists should respond with interest, even excitement and enthusiasm. What appears to be a problem for others is a creative solution in the eyes of the therapist. For others, the child steals because he is bad. To the therapist, the child steals to bring his divorced parents together for a common cause. For others, the child wets his bed because he wants attention he doesn't deserve. To the therapist he wets his bed as a novel way of showing his tears, since he knows that boys aren't supposed to cry.

Instruction: Setting the Tone
Ask the child to verbally define the problem. Ask questions about problem definition before actually having the child draw her picture of the problem. Suggested questions are:

> What do you think the problem is in your family?
> What does your mother think the problem is? Your father?
> Who is the person that thinks the problem is really big?
> Who doesn't think there is a problem?
> Who would help you with the problem?
> Who wouldn't help you with the problem?
> Whom would you ask to help you with the problem?
> Whom is the problem a secret from? (Especially helpful for abuse case.)
> If it is a secret that has to be kept from someone special, how old will you be when you tell your secret to that person?
> How long will the problem take to go away? (Does the child see an end solution to the problem?)
> What will have to happen for the problem to be really solved?

The Drawing: Draw a Picture of What You Think the Problem Is
The instruction to the child should state "You can draw yourself or anything you want, but your task is to show me the problem on this paper so that I can see it."

The introduction of the visual aspect—being able to *see* the problem—aids the child in viewing the problem as external. Once externalized, she may see the problem as being more readily solved. If the problem remains internalized, she may view the problem simply as part of her being. It is helpful to have the child develop the problem on paper as if that problem had its own life.

Questions to Ask after the Drawing
Art therapists are encouraged to develop their own questions that they would routinely ask about any picture. The following questions are examples of the usual style when asking about problem definition:

What happens when the problem appears? (Ask for details.)
How many times in a day does the problem happen? In a week?
At what time of day does the problem usually happen?
Who is usually around when the problem happens?
Is the problem worse now or was it worse before?
Do you always know when the problem is about to happen or does it just happen? (Clarifies how much control the child believes he has over the problem.)
Who is usually the first person to find out that the problem has happened again?
Who could help you from having the problem happen as much as it does?
What is good about having the problem?
Who would be happiest if the problem happened less? (Usually indicates who finds the problem the most disturbing.)
What have you tried before to keep the problem from happening? (Gives information about past solutions that have been tried.)
What do you think you will try next to have the problem happen less? (Examines future solutions to be tried.)
Do you think the problem will ever go away completely? (Gives realistic information about elimination of the problem versus minimization of the problem.)

Development of Graphic Size of Problem
It is helpful to determine the size of the problem in the child's eyes. This can easily be accomplished with the use of a simple graph. A visual graph is more concrete for the child than a verbal 1-10 scale where the child is asked to grade the size of the problem in his head.

After determining the number of sessions that will occur in the art therapy assessment (usually four to six sessions), design the graph according to the number of sessions as follows:

WEEK	1	2	3	4	5	6

At the end of the first session, ask the child to draw a circle on the week 1 mark that depicts the size of the problem. This chart will then be used again by the child at the start of each subsequent assessment session; this will graphically demonstrate the size of the problem over time, just as the best assessment information comes from a study of a sequence of art pictures over time. The graph is also in keeping with the therapist's attempts to externalize the problem for the child. Indeed, the problem is developing a life of its own.

Sometimes the child does not feel he has a problem at all. He may view the problem as being that his mother does not think he has enough friends. He may believe that one close friend is enough. The picture of the problem and the problem graph can be adapted to show that the problem is his mother's belief that he is friendless. The therapist and the child may then work together to formulate a plan for the child to demonstrate to his mother that he is playing with more than one friend.

Examples

The first picture (picture 1) is one child's version of The Problem. This eight-year-old boy has been brought to therapy because he has been stealing. The boy describes the problem as the urge to steal taking control of his arms. The arms are drawn large, suggesting he has not yet obtained control over the stealing. However, he is smiling and he verbalizes to his therapist that he himself is very upset at the trouble the stealing has caused him in his life. In this very first session, the child seems committed to working on the problem of stealing.

Picture 1

Note:* *The dark areas on the head and arms are brown and the lighter areas are orange

In picture 2, a ten-year-old girl describes her problem as being slow to do what her mother wants. "Slow listening" has caused her mother to yell at her frequently and she resents her mother's demands to act her age. In this picture, the girl (with the 27 on her shirt) has just been yelled at by her mother because she has walked through the garden and gotten her shoes muddy. Her mother (the figure in the bathing suit to the girl's right) has just told her off for not listening. (The therapist reframed the problem as being "slow to listen.") Unlike the first picture, the girl does not believe she has a problem. The girl has drawn herself as being the same size as her mother and, in fact, she feels more like her mother's confidante than her daughter. In the session, the girl delights at the fact that the water is about to hit her mother. Unlike the first picture, the girl is not committed to work on the problem but she may be convinced to accept trying to change this behaviour so that her mother will yell at her less, hopefully creating a more positive mother-daughter relationship.

Picture 2

Picture 3 is an example of one twelve-year-old girl's problem chart about sleeping arrangements. This girl has been frightened to sleep alone because of a break-in that occurred about six months previously (when both she and her divorced mother were out of the house). Over a four-week period, the girl is highly successful and finds that she has only needed to sleep with her mother on two occasions in the first week. The idea of the problem chart caught on so well with this girl that she voluntarily chose to start working on a second problem—getting her homework done.

Session Two: Balancing the Emotions

Just as it is important for the therapist to remain neutral about the information being discussed, it is impossible for the child to become neutral about what he is reporting. The child is likely feeling very negative about a number of experiences and people in his family. It is helpful for the therapist to assist in highlighting both the positive and negative experiences for him. It is likely that other people in his family have contributed to the problem and these same people will be needed to find the solution.

Instruction

Ask the child to add this week's notation to the graphic "size-of-the-problem" chart, once again using a circle. It is helpful for the child to see the size of the problem increase or decrease over time. In some cases, the therapist may wish to have the child draw the problem circle on a separate piece of paper each week and then compare it to the problem circles of the previous weeks.

Picture 3

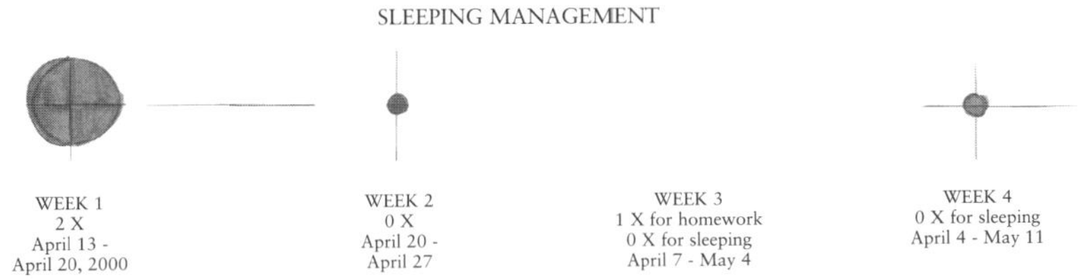

The child should be asked questions about the graph each week until the graph has been completed. Examples of such questions may include:

> What is different about the problem since last week?
> What is the same about the problem?
> How did the problem get to be bigger/smaller than last week?
> Whom did you talk to about the problem?
> Who helped you with the problem?
> What did you do to help make the problem bigger/smaller?
> If you didn't do anything, what can you do to keep the problem smaller?
> What do you think you will try to do over the next week to keep the problem smaller? (Getting the child to think about controlling the problem.)

Who can help you keep the problem smaller?
What good things have happened because you still have the problem?
What good things have happened because the problem is smaller?
How will you approach them to help you? (This may result in the child requesting the therapist to intervene in a family session. Such a move is very appropriate, as ultimately the parents must become involved if the solution is to last over time.)
Who do you think will want you to fail?
How might they try to make the problem worse?
What will you do then? (Helping the child to gain strength over the problem.)

The Drawing
Your instructions might be, "Draw a picture of your family doing something together. Draw in every person that you feel should be included in your family and please do not use stick figures." Once again, it is important for the therapist to ask, in his normal questioning style and before proceeding with the addition of the systemic questions, straightforward, informational questions about omissions, unusual additions, size and placement of figures on the page, etc. Once again, remember that the systemic questions are the ones that focus on the relationships, feelings and expectations between two people in the drawing.

Do not hesitate to ask the child more questions when it is not clear what has been drawn in the picture. Understanding of all aspects of the picture is most important at the assessment level even if it results in the child feeling hurt that the therapist has not understood the picture. The therapist, by her actions as the therapeutic relationship develops, can reassure the child in many other ways that their time together is valued and positive. Some systemic questions to ask about the drawing might be:

What two people get along the best in this family?
What two people get along least well in this family?
Who is the happiest? The angriest? The most sad?
What do you like the most about your mother? (Your father, aunt, brother etc.)
What do you like the least about your mother? (Your father, aunt, brother etc.)

Whom are you closest to in the family?
Whom do you share your secrets with?
What two people fight the most in the family?
Do they fight with words or with actions?
Whom can you go to for help in the family?
Who would you say has the most problems in your family?
Whom do they go to for help?
What do they do to solve their problems?
Does anyone ever drink alcohol to solve problems? (Promotes disclosure of positive and negative solutions used in the family.)
How does your family have fun together?
Do you ever think the problems in your family could go away altogether? (Questions the reality of the child's goals.)
If it were a year from now, do you think the problem you are working on will still be a problem then? (Promotes future thinking for minimization of the problem.)
Who in the family will still think it is a problem a year from now?
Who will continue to help you so the problem won't get so big again?

The questions are purposely arranged to promote a balancing of both positive and negative information. In this way, the child will not be overcome by the size of the problem but will provide the necessary information to develop the assessment information to the fullest.

Example: Draw a Picture of the Family Doing Something Together

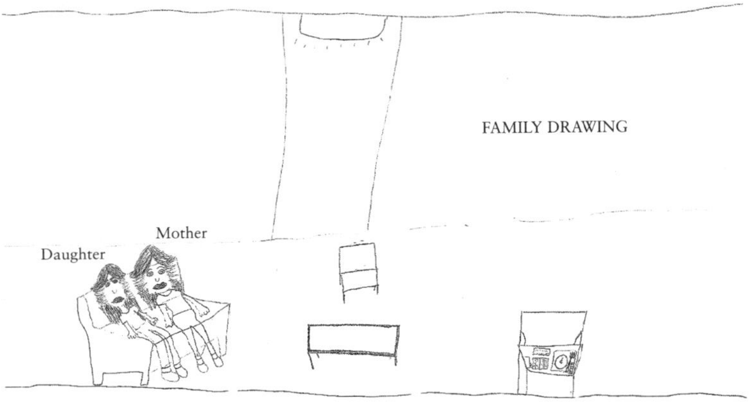

In this family, there is only a recently divorced mother and her daughter. This twelve-year-old girl drew herself and her mother sitting together, unsmiling, on a couch, watching television. I have noticed that a number of children who chose the activity of watching TV with their family do so because they spend little time in a more action-oriented activity. Television watching is a passive activity requiring no direct need to communicate with each other. This particular child was concerned that her mother was depressed from her recent divorce and was fearful to leave her alone. The girl tended to shadow her mother at the expense of playing with her own friends. In spite of the girl's unhappy look, she was insistent that she had a close as well as pleasurable relationship with her mother (which is likely true as evidenced of the close proximity of the two figures). On the other hand, when the mother was shown the picture, she was able to identify the unhappiness of both figures in the drawing.

Session Three: Maintaining Neutrality

With each successive session, there is danger in developing a strong alignment with the child. The use of repetitive questions such as, "What would your mother say . . ." and "What would your father say . . ." assist in maintaining neutrality. The child should be told that the therapist will share the main content of the session with the parents.

Instruction

Ask the child to add another notation on the graphic size-of-the-problem chart. At this point, new questions about the graph may include:

> Are you now stronger with this problem than in our first session together?
> What have you been doing to gain control over the problem?
> What have you asked your parents to do to help you gain control over the problem?

It may be necessary at this point for the therapist to assist in the development of a plan of action to correct the problem. This may include requesting a family session to design the plan with the parents involved. No matter what course of action the therapist decides upon, the art therapy assessment should continue as described to obtain the most complete and useful information.

The Drawing
"Draw a picture of you in your classroom. Include the teacher and some of the students if you like."

We specify drawing a classroom picture rather than a drawing at school because, without specific directions, a number of children will draw themselves out in the schoolyard. A schoolyard drawing may come later and will yield different information to a "draw yourself with friends" picture.

Questions to Ask after the Drawing

Tell me the story about your drawing.

How does the teacher act differently than your parents?

Who has the most fun in the classroom?

Who is the most unhappy in the class?

Who gets along best with the teacher? (Supports the view that the child knows there are ways to get along with the teacher.)

What do you think your parents would do if you got along better in the classroom?

What does the teacher do when "Billy" gets along with the other children? What would the teacher do if you got along better?

Who would agree with you in the classroom that you do get along?

How is your behaviour different than it was a month ago in the classroom? A year ago?

If your parents did divorce, how do you think your behaviour would be in the classroom? (Introduces how the child's family concerns would affect the classroom performance.)

In your family, who would be the most pleased if your behaviour improved at school? Who wouldn't care?

At school do you fight more, about the same, or less than the other children do? (Assists the child in comparing himself to the other students.)

What do you like to do after school after you have had a good day? (Promotes the idea of a positive outcome after a good day.)

Example: Draw a picture of you in your classroom

Occasionally a child will spontaneously draw his feelings very clearly. This twelve-year-old boy demonstrates his anger well by shoving the lid of the desk in the face of his teacher, who is drawn as a fierce dragon. The boy easily discussed his effort to match his anger with the anger of his teacher. Verbally, he does not seem bothered by authority figures, yet what he has drawn tells a different story.

Session Four: Looking for Similar Situations

As the therapist investigates the "world" of the client, the child will reveal similar ways of responding to particular persons, especially to his parents and siblings. However, he may find himself responding differently to similar situations when it involves different people. The same situation may not seem so critical or devastating if it involves a more distant relative or friend. The therapist can use this source of strength in the client to help him to respond more successfully to his own family.

Instruction

Once again, ask the child to add to her graphic size-of-the-problem chart. Ask problem questions similar to those noted in the session entitled, "Balancing the Emotions." New questions about the graph may include:

How has your teacher helped you with the problem?
What other people in your life have you told about the problem and how have they helped you?
If an aunt or uncle knew about the problem, what advice would she or he give you?

The Drawing
"Draw a picture of you doing something with friends. It is up to you as to how many friends you would like to include."

If the child suggests that he does not have any friends, the instruction should be changed to, "Draw a picture of you doing something with someone that you would like to be your friend."

Questions to Ask after the Drawing

Tell a story about your picture.
What two people get along the best in the drawing?
What two people get along the worst in the drawing?
What would your best friend say is the nicest thing about you?
What would he say is the worst thing that you have done?
How would you let your friend know that he is a good friend?
What would he do if he knew that you were fighting a problem?
What would you do if you knew that your friend was fighting a problem?
Have you felt more like a friend or an enemy to your friends in the last month?
Do you get along better or worse with your friends when you are not getting along with your family at home?
What do you think your best friend would do if you did not get along with one of his friends?
What would your friend do if you asked him to do something he thought was wrong? Then, what would you do?
What would your mother or father say if you got along better with your friends?
Who agrees with your mother that your friends are always getting you into trouble?
How do you get along with your friends differently than you did a year ago?
What kind of things do you do to have fun with your friends?
How is your friend's family different than yours?

What would your mother say if you wanted to bring this friend home with you today? What would your father say? How do you let your friend know when you are upset/angry/happy/sad with him? How is this different than when you tell your parents how you are feeling?

Example: Draw a Picture of You Doing Something with Your Friends.

THE SNOW FORT

DOING SOMETHING WITH FRIENDS

The picture suggests an overall happy impression with eight-year-old Erin (the largest figure, with eyeglasses, on the left) playing in a snow fort with some of her friends. Her parents describe her as depressed, and, projectively, Erin draws herself as transparent and somewhat separated from her friends. In actual life, she does not know how to talk to her friends and children avoid her because she acts so serious.

Session Five: Relationships Are Central To the Approach

The main object at this point in the assessment is to get sufficient information to promote successful change in the client system. While the therapist develops a unique relationship with the child, the child comes to understand the therapist's desire to know about how she views her family, academic, and peer relationships. The therapist must continue to ask questions that are consistent with his therapeutic approach and style. The therapist should also continue to add relationship questions—past, present or future.

Instruction

The child is instructed by the therapist to add to the graphic size-of-the-problem chart. In this session, the child will be encouraged to look at the problem and his relationships from a future vantage point. These additional problem questions would be helpful:

> Six months from now, will the problem be better, worse or the same?
> Who will think the problem is better?
> Who will have forgotten that there is a problem?
> How long do you think it will take before people will forget that there was a problem?
> Who will think that the problem will never go away?

The Drawing
"Draw a picture of yourself in the future. You should be doing something in the picture that you can tell a story about. Feel free to draw anyone you choose in the picture with you. The picture can be drawn as if it were a month from now, six months, or even longer."

Should the child draw a picture years away from now, she should be encouraged to discuss the picture in detail. It may be that the client prefers to draw such a future picture because she feels quite hopeless with the present situation and this exercise provides the necessary distance from the problem.

Questions To Ask After the Drawing

> How is this time in your life different than what is happening in your life now? What would the problem be like if it were still happening at this time? (A collapsing time question.)
> Who would be the closest to you in your family? Whom would you get along the best with? The worst?
> Who will be the closest to your mother (or your father) when all of you children have grown up and left home?
> Who will likely stay at home the longest with your parents?
> How do you think your mother (or father) would treat you now?
> Who would be the child that causes your parents the most worry?
> If you could look back on this present time, what advice would you give about how to solve the problem?
> Who would agree with you?
> Who would think that it wasn't a problem at all?
> Who will be the most successful and happy in the family?

Who will be causing the most trouble in the family? (Clarifies client's belief as to whether he can successfully change the problem.)
If your teacher (aunt, friend, neighbour) could see you now at this future time, what would she say about you?
Who would be the most surprised?
Tell a story about what your life is like in this picture.
(Attempt to gauge how productive the client feels his life has become.)

Example: Draw a Picture of Yourself in the Future

This nine-year-old boy seemed to feel safe in the therapy session drawing himself at age twenty-five. The boy saw himself as an unmarried airline pilot. In between flights, he saw himself as regularly checking up on his mother and younger brother, who he expected would still live at home with his mother. This boy was in trouble because he felt closer to his separated father, who had recently moved to another city. Also, he believed that his mother favoured his younger brother. His desire for a job in travel may reflect his desire to recapture a closer relationship with his absent father.

Session Six: Nothing Is Predictable

As the therapist approaches the sixth and final session, the hypothesis has likely been well established, the information seems more understandable and complete, and a plan of action is being devised as to how to handle the problem. However, at times during the assessment, a piece of information may be revealed that doesn't seem to fit the description about relationships described by the child, and the therapist should be aware that other pieces of information may follow that don't seem to fit the established pattern. It may be important to begin to unravel the new information in cases where the child wants to hide a more serious problem such as abuse. The therapist will have to judge whether the art assessment will continue beyond this last session in an effort to clarify the piece of the puzzle that does not fit.

The Drawing

"Draw a picture of your favourite kind of day." No art therapy assessment seems complete without some kind of projective drawing. The first documented research on projective pictures had to do with drawing a person in the rain (Oster and Gould, 1987). This type of projective drawing examined how the person responds to stressful circumstances. Is the person able to protect herself in the rain or does she just stand there helplessly? Inclement weather such as rain, snow and hail are often reflective of abusive home environments (Manning, 1987). Manning's study revealed that physically abused children "project their abusive home environment on to exaggerated size and movement of inclement weather in the elicited favourite kind of day drawing." The same study further noted that physically abused children from violent homes rarely included people in the drawing. Warm, sunny pictures with a lack of inclement weather were often seen to be produced by children from less chaotically structured homes and such pictures are more typical of an emotionally stable child. Figures were also usually included. Certainly by asking questions of the child, the therapist can ascertain how in charge of his life the child feels.

Questions To Ask after the Drawing

Tell me a story about the picture.
Where exactly are you in the picture?
Where would you be in the picture and what would you be wearing? (If client is not included in the picture.)
In the picture, who would help you to get to a safer place? (If the picture shows inclement weather.)
Who in your family would want to be in this picture with you?
If this is your favourite kind of day, how would you describe your least favourite kind of day?
What would you be wearing?
What would your mother say about your being outside on this kind of day? Your father?

Who else would you like to include in this picture?
What would they be doing?
How would you describe this picture? Happy? Sad? Angry?
If I had asked you to draw this picture last week, how would it look different? (Does such a picture generally reflect the child's mood or just today's mood?)
What would your mother say to you if I showed her this picture? Your father?

Such a picture may indicate the level of stress that the client is feeling. Due to the projective nature of this exercise, it is desirable to consider all sources of information about the child and compare it with the rest of the assessment information that has been verbally reported by him. These sources of information would include: looking at any patterns that emerge from all of his drawings; any discussions with parents and other family members; any verbal or written reports from other agencies, doctors, teachers, police and other professionals; any observations noted by the waiting room receptionist or other employees at the centre where the child is coming for counselling; any "gut" reactions or hypotheses developed by involved therapists that may need further exploration.

Example: Draw a Picture of Your Favourite Kind of Day

This eleven-year-old boy draws himself enjoying a day of fishing where he has already been successful at catching two fish. The boy has lived in a violent home. The chaos is clearly depicted in the excessive amount of inclement weather and the swirls in the water. In spite of the chaotic environment in which he is fishing, he seems relatively content even if he is alone.

Feedback Session

At the end of any art therapy assessment, it is helpful to the client and the therapist alike to re-examine all the created art products. The child may be able to identify some common themes or changes in the pictures as they are placed side by side. It is also helpful for the art therapist to encourage the child to draw a final free picture that will be some measure of his present state of mind about the problem situation that he is facing.

Some art therapists prefer to have this termination session prior to the family's feedback session, if it is likely that no more work with the client will occur. However, if the therapeutic plan is to engage the family in ongoing family therapy, one last individual session with the child after the feedback session will allow the therapist and client one further hour to discuss the reactions of the family members. The art therapist may take this final opportunity to strategize with the client as to how he can seek the help of the family members who feel the most positive about him.

The word *termination* implies the "end of something" and it becomes the therapist's task to celebrate with the child the end of this phase of individual therapy. The child may be "graduating" to sessions with the entire family or there may be no present need to continue any form of therapy. Completion of the art therapy assessment is an accomplishment and needs to be recognized. Appropriate ceremonial activities may include working on a joint picture together to share with the family, a snack at the local coffee shop or even a walk down to the park. In this way, the child easily recognizes his successful participation and completion of the art therapy assessment. The art therapist and client, having formed a unique relationship over a short period of time, can also feel positive about saying a proper goodbye.

Summary

An art therapy assessment can adopt systemic principles and bring the family alive for the child on paper. Many families will bring a child to a counselling centre in the first place because she is seen as having a problem; so the fact that a therapist willingly spends some assessment time with her supports the parents' perception that the child is in need of help.

The systemic art therapist, in supporting the notion of the problem, also supports the notion of a problem as something that is external to the child and therefore as something that can be productively changed. There are solutions to problems. By asking "circular" questions that focus on relationships in the family, the individual art assessment may provide some new answers for the child and ultimately for the family. The child begins to feel that he is a positive part of the battle to gain control over the problem that has been plaguing the family.

The addition of systemic concepts in the traditional art therapist's repertoire will enhance not only the understanding of the problem but may also provide some new information about how to change the negative interactions in the entire family system. Art therapists have known for a long time how to encourage their clients to draw and to talk about their experiences. The difficulty is in asking the right questions.

REFERENCES

Buck, J.N. (1948). The H-T-P technique: A qualitative and quantitative scoring manual. *Journal of Clinical Psychology, 4*, 317-396.

Burns, R.C., & Kaufman, S.H. (1970). *Kinetic family drawings (K-F-D): An introduction to understanding children through kinetic drawing.* New York: Brunner/Mazel.

Cane, F. (1951). *The artist in each of us.* New York: Pantheon.

Efron, D. (1985). *The tiger-shark model of systemic therapy.*

Fleuridas, C., Nelson, T., & Rosenthal, D. (1986). The evolution of circular questions: Training family therapists. *Journal of Marital and Family Therapy, 12*, 113-127.

Keith, D., & Whitaker, K. (1981). Play therapy: A paradigm for work with families. *Journal of Marital and Family Therapy,* **Vol. No.,** 243-254.

Klepsch, M., & Logie, L. (1982). *Children draw and tell: An introduction to the projective uses of children's human figure drawings.* New York: Brunner/Mazel.

Kramer, E. (1971). *Art as therapy with children.* New York: Schocken Books.

Kwiatkowska, H.Y. (1978). *Family therapy and evaluation through art.* Springfield, IL: Charles C. Thomas.

Machover, K. (1949). *Personality projection in the drawings of a human figure.* Springfield, IL: Charles C. Thomas.

Manning, T. (1987). Aggression depicted in abused children's drawings. *The Arts in Psychotherapy, 1987, 14*, 15-24.

Montalvo, B., & Haley, J. (1973). In defence of child therapy. *Family Process, 12*, 227-244.

Munro, C. (1987). White and the cybernetic therapies: News of a difference. *A.N.Z. Journal of Family Therapy, 8*, 183-192.

Naumberg, M. (1947). *Studies of the "free" art expression of behavior problem children and adolescents as a means of diagnosis and therapy.* New York: Coolidge Foundation.

Oaklander, V. (1978). *Windows to our children.* Moab, Utah: Real People Press.

Oster, G., & Gould, P. (1987). *Using drawings in assessment and therapy: A guide for mental health professionals.* New York: Brunner/Mazel.

Prout, H.T., & Phillips, P.D. (1974). In defence of child therapy. *Psychology in the Schools, 11*, 303-306.

Selvini, M.P., Boscolo, L., Cecchin, G., & Prata, G. (1980). Hypothesizing - circularity - neutrality: Three guidelines for the conductor of the session. *Family Process, 19*, 3-12.

Weber, T., McKeever, J., & McDaniel, S. (1985). A beginner's guide to the problem-oriented first family interview. *Family Process, 24,* 357-364.

White, M. (1984). Pseudo-encopresis: From avalanche to victory, from vicious to virtuous cycles. *Family Systems Medicine,* 2, 150-160.

Winnicott, D.W. (1971). *Therapeutic consultations in child psychiatry*. London: Hogarth Press.

CHAPTER NINE

BECOMING A THERAPEUTIC STORY TELLER

Greg Lubimiv

BECOMING A THERAPEUTIC STORYTELLER

Once upon a time . . . these simple words are the introduction to millions of stories and when they are spoken, something almost magical happens. Bodies squirm to find a comfortable position, eyes become fixated, breathing becomes controlled and there is a sudden quiet in the space around the storyteller.

Once upon a time . . . when we hear these words we ready ourselves to be taken on an adventure, to be transported to a world of wonder and imagination, where everything and anything is possible.

For centuries storytellers have taken all of us on countless journeys and adventures, through past, present and future, to new worlds and into our own minds and souls.

Although we often think of stories as just for children, the power of stories is no less for adults. Stories have been used to entertain, to teach, and to provide a link for us to our past, present and future. Since man first began to communicate, stories have been used to create understanding. In fact, stories precede the development of formal language, as our early ancestors utilized drawings to depict a successful hunt, the death of a tribal leader or the coming of the winter. Once language did develop, stories were mostly utilized to create meaning out of chaos. Stories therefore provided grounding, stability and predictability. Fears about the sun not rising were quelled by the story of the sun god who would rise each morning from the same mountain to provide the people with light and warmth.

We are all storytellers, whether we realize it or not (and most of us don't). Take a moment now and pick up a pen and a piece of paper. Try to go back to your childhood and pick one of your earliest memories. Write down that memory in as much, or as little detail as you wish. When you finish, read your memory out loud to yourself. Take a few minutes to do this now.

If you have completed this task you have just told a story to yourself. It is one of many you will likely tell today—why you were late, the new movie you just saw, a funny story about something your youngest child said—these are all stories we tell to others to define our world and share it with them.

However, stories can be more than just history and fantasy; they are also capable of having significant impact on the listener, in terms of altering values, beliefs, behaviours and feelings. If we could just understand how to weave the "healing" stories and release the "storyteller" inside of ourselves, then what an impact we can have on those children, youth and adults with whom we work!

Milton Erikson provided inspiring leadership in the study and use of stories and metaphors to assist people to enhance their own growth and development. Over the past 20 years in particular there has been an incredible growth in the utilization of therapeutic stories and in the understanding of why stories have such impact.

This chapter will not dwell on the scientific/existential part of storytelling. You may refer to one of the readings in the bibliography to better understand this. Rather, I am interested in providing stimulus for you to reach into yourself to become a storyteller and to use stories in a therapeutic way.

As well, I would like to provide you with some of the key building blocks to creating therapeutic stories for children (but also for any age and any system).

This chapter is designed to provide you with practical, concrete skills and tools to build and use stories. The key will be for you to complete the exercises that appear in the following pages. The more diligent you are in doing the task the more you will learn and the more effective you will be as a storyteller. Practice will make the difference between just playing baseball and being the M.V.P.

The following is adapted from a story by Robin Moore (1991).

THE STORY STONE

Once upon a time, near the beginning of man's time on earth, there was a young boy named Sawqua who lived with his family in a small village. The village depended on fishing and hunting to survive and everyone helped out whether they were young or old.

Each day was always the same. The people awoke. Those who hunted would hunt. Those who caught fish went fishing. Those who prepared food waited for the day's catch to be brought to them.

One day Sawqua, who helped with the fishing, asked his father, "Why is it that the yellow light in the sky falls down each day?"

His father looked at him and shook his head. "No one knows, but we all fear it will never come back when it is gone."

Sawqua went to his mother and asked, "Why is it that we do not have wings like the raven?"

His mother looked at him and shook her head. "No one knows."

Sawqua kept wondering, but stopped asking questions because it just seemed to bother everyone. One day, though, as he was returning from his fishing trip he stopped to rest by a large stone that lay on the side of the path. He lay back against the stone and enjoyed the warmth coming from the smooth surface. Just then he heard a voice.

"Would you like to hear a story?"

Sawqua looked around but saw no one.

"Would you like to hear a story?" the voice asked again.

Sawqua jumped up and looked around for who it was that could be talking to him. He suddenly realized it was the stone he had been lying against.

"Are you talking to me, old stone?" asked the boy.

"Yes, I am. Would you like to hear a story?" the stone repeated.

"What is a story?" asked Sawqua.

"A story is a when someone tells you about something that has happened and why it happens. It is when your imagination dances and your mind travels to places it has never been," answered the old stone. "My journey is to be able to look out at all the valley and all the animals and trees and people, and my stories will take me there," added the stone.

"Please, tell me a story then," pleaded Sawqua.

As Sawqua sat down the old stone began to tell the child a story about why the raven was black. Then he told him about the fiery ball in the sky and why it rises and falls each day. Then he told him story after story after story. Sawqua was spellbound. He listened to every word, and in fact found himself seeing each story as it was told.

Sawqua noticed it was almost dark and jumped up. "I must go home, but can I come tomorrow to hear more stories?"

"Yes, and each day after that, you may come and I will tell you stories," replied the stone.

Sawqua did come back the next day, and the next day and the next. And each day the stone told him more stories . . . until . . . until it was nearing the winter. The stone had finished a story just before dark when he said to the boy, "That is the last story I will tell. My time has come to an end."

Sawqua looked at the stone with tears in his eyes. "You can't leave yet. You have not finished your journey."

"It is through you that I will be able to complete my journey," replied the stone.

"But stone, I don't want you to go!" cried Sawqua. "I want to hear more stories."

"I have no more stories . . . but you must now share the stories I have told to the others in your village. With each story told I will grow bigger and bigger. I will always be with you and soon will watch over all that is around me and that I love." With that the stone became silent and cold.

Sawqua cried and cried, and for the next few days, would sit at home and refuse to eat or talk.

Sawqua's mother was becoming very worried and she came up to her son. "Sawqua, what is wrong?"

Sawqua shook his head and looked down at the ground. "The stone is gone and I will not hear any more stories."

His mother looked puzzled. "What is a story?"

Sawqua explained in the same way the stone had explained to him. Then he told his mother a story. She sat back in amazement and listened to every word. When Sawqua finished she ran out of the tent and brought back all the villagers she could find. "Listen to the story my son will tell you."

Sawqua was very nervous and he feared he would lose his voice, but he began to speak and told all the stories he had heard from the stone. As he did this, the old stone began to grow and grow and by the time the last story was told it was a majestic mountain overlooking the whole valley.

When Sawqua told the last story the stone had told him, he became very sad. The other villagers were also sad and asked for more. But Sawqua had no more to tell. His father, though, stood up and said out loud: "I have a story. I would like to tell you about when my father was alive and we went to hunt for the great white bear."

When Sawqua's father had finished another villager told a story and then another and another. As time went on Sawqua's people would go to other villages and soon stories were being told everywhere.

It was the first day of spring when Sawqua sat at the village fire with all the villagers gathered around to hear the evening's story. It was his turn to tell the evening story and Sawqua wondered what story he

would tell, but as he looked up at the great mountain, whose snow-covered peak glistened in the sunset, he knew.
Sawqua stood up and announced in a firm voice, "Tonight, I will tell you a story about the stone that became a mountain."

RELEASING THE STORYTELLER WITHIN

One of the first barriers to overcome in order to be an effective storyteller is the belief that you are not or cannot be a storyteller. As previously mentioned, you already are a storyteller. We all are. Avoid comparing or competing if you want to move forward. You do not have be "as good as" or "better than" anyone else.

One of your first tasks, if you are not convinced that you are already a storyteller, is to listen to others and to yourself in the course of a day. Pay attention to the personal stories you hear and to the personal stories you are telling—about why you are late, how you first met your partner, getting stuck in the storm, how you got the stain on your pants.

These are all stories, personal stories, not necessarily therapeutic (although they can be), but certainly they are stories that create definition, understanding, or linkage.

In your work with children, become more aware of their stories and ask questions to elicit their own personal stories, e.g., "Tell me about your friends/Tell me about what you like to do/Tell me about what went well for you this week."

In particular I would like to encourage you to begin to write down some of your stories. These will be useful later, when you begin to develop more expertise in utilizing metaphors and re-framing.

Exercise 1
On a piece of paper write down how you got your name. You may select your first name, last name or all of your names. If you don't know, call someone you think may know. This may be a parent, aunt, uncle or older sibling. If you are unable to do this and still do not have any "story," then I would ask you to create a story about your name. Make one up and write it down. Over the next few days ask some people you know about where their names came from. Pay attention to their body language as they tell you.

Exercise 2
Think back to when you were a child and pick a family tradition/ceremony/ritual that you remember. Write down what this tradition was. Over the next few days ask people you know about their childhood traditions and share yours with them. Pay attention to body language as you listen to their stories.

Feedback
One of the things you should notice from these exercises is that when a person "moves" into a "story," a transformation usually takes place. There is a shift, sometimes subtle, sometimes exaggerated, in posture, voice tone, energy or affect. Often all of these shifts occur as the teller engages in his story. The one area I would like you to pay particular attention to is the affect or feeling tone. Stories tend to reconnect that person to the feeling he had at the time of the story or will reflect the linkage he has currently.

For example, a widow tells of meeting her husband for the first time. As she tells her personal story she giggles and blushes, or begins to cry as she revisits her grief/loss. Another example: as the young girl tells about her encounter with a barking dog her face takes on a look of fear and she begins to lose her breath as she talks faster and faster.

I have found that the more meaningful the personal story is, the greater is the feeling she had at the time of the story—and vice versa.

This will be very important to remember and to utilize as you move into therapeutic storytelling. In fact, one of the most essential ingredients to powerful healing stories is the affect within the story and the accuracy of connection of the feelings to the listeners and their own inner stories.

Exercise 3
One of the best sources of stories is in literature, which is all around us. Read children's books, especially those labelled as "self-help" books. Books designed to help children with death, making friends, going to the dentist, going to school for the first time, and so on, are good sources to begin your transition from personal story to metaphoric story.

Summary
We are all storytellers and need only allow our voice to touch the ears and minds of others. As you develop your comfort level to tell stories

and as you practice listening to the stories of others you will find yourself more ready to use storytelling as a therapeutic tool in working with individuals, families, groups and systems.

You may want to consider checking out your area to see if there are any storytelling groups that you can join. These organizations are quite prolific and hold regular sessions and conferences at the local, national and international level. These are not geared towards therapy; rather, they focus on the oral traditions of storytelling and the sharing of various historic and personal stories. As well, you will have an opportunity to be exposed to a huge variety of storytelling techniques.

BUILDING BLOCKS OF EFFECTIVE THERAPEUTIC STORIES

The art of storytelling is composed of many wonderful skills, tools, and techniques, many of which are unique to each storyteller. Consider Edward Munsch, the children's storybook writer. Although not a therapeutic storyteller in the formal sense, one can very much appreciate how well Mr. Munsch connects to his large audiences of children (and their parents) through his very special brand of storytelling. You may also consider someone such as Bill Cosby, who tells stories with a comical twist, making the listener chuckle or laugh out loud because we can relate so well to his tales.

In this chapter I cannot explore all the nooks and crannies of storytelling; however, I would like to concentrate on a few that I believe are essential to therapeutic storytelling. These include:

- Metaphors
- Reframing
- Using a storytelling framework
- Using effective storytelling processes

Metaphors

A metaphor is simply a figure of speech in which a word or phrase denoting one kind of object or action is used in place of another to suggest likeness or an association between them. They are often helpful in creating understanding, awareness and new learning. For example, I remember speaking with a young girl, aged eight, who was telling me that when her mother shouted it made her feel angry. Anger is a hard thing to measure; however, if we can use a metaphor then I can get a better idea of what the child means in terms that are familiar to me. I ask her, “If your anger were a volcano, could you describe it to me?” The young girls then answers, “It is a huge volcano, the biggest in the whole world, and it is full of lava which just sits and sits, then when it’s mad the lava bursts out the top and burns everything. It doesn’t care about anyone and can’t stop once it starts.”

This use of a metaphor gives me a much clearer picture of the anger this girl has. It also gives me a wonderful way of speaking with the child as we continue to work together: “How hot is the lava now?” “Are there ways of cooling the lava?” “Are there times the volcano does not explode?”

I have found metaphors very powerful in helping people to find a way to talk about something in a way they can measure, picture, touch, smell, etc. I have also found that metaphors create a much easier way for many to talk about their pains, issues, ideas, etc. Early in my career I thought that this was especially true for children, but I don’t think that it is any less helpful for adolescents and adults.

When you are using metaphors, similes, and analogies one of the important aspects you must remember is that all symbolism is not universal. When I use a particular metaphor to describe something, it may be interpreted in a different way than I meant, especially at the unconscious level. The following exercise will help to illustrate this fact.

Metaphor Exercise 1: Finding Meaning in Metaphor
Imagine that you are in search of a hidden strength within you. You decide to take a journey to the Himalayan mountains to seek the advice of a Tibetan lama. You arrive at the doors of the monastery and knock. In a few moments the great wooden doors slowly open and you are greeted by an old man in orange robes. You say to him, “I am in search of a hidden strength so I may know myself better.”

“I know, my child,” he replies. The lama takes your hands in his and looks deep into your eyes and says, “*Your Hidden Strength Is Like the Wind that Blows in the Fall.*”

Then he leaves and the door closes. Look back at his words to you and write down what hidden strength he is referring to. There may be more than one, and you are invited to write as many as you wish. Write them down now.

Metaphor Exercise 2: the Uniqueness of Metaphor
I would like you to take Metaphor Exercise 1 and give it to at least six people. These may be friends, your team at work, etc. You may do it individually or with a group. Have the people you use it with tell you what they wrote down; however, always allow anyone the choice of not sharing it if they so wish. When you have completed at least six responses then reflect back on this section. You may wish to review it, as you have some additional experience to relate to now.

Discussion

What should be emphasized by this experience is:

> The unique way in which individuals apply the metaphor to their own lives (you will have several "teachings/interpretations" for the same "story").
>
> The influence that someone's interpretation for themselves will have on others. (As others are sharing their personal meaning, especially if this is a group exercise, the listener[s] will apply some of what the storyteller has learned to their own lives.)

In order to use metaphors we need to develop our capacity to identify and find them as quickly as possible. Often we use or listen to metaphors but as they are woven into our language they remain veiled in the communications we give and receive. (I'm hungry as an elephant, your goose is cooked, your eyes are like diamonds.) In creating stories and metaphors for therapy, we need to be much more aware of our use of metaphors and have a conscious process for selecting particular ones to fit specific situations.

The following exercises will provide some right-brain calisthenics in relation to identifying and creating effective metaphors.

Metaphor Exercise 3: The Same but not the Same.
In this exercise you can select a word from the list below or choose one of your own: for example, "dig." Write down the first phrase that comes to you to express the meaning of this word. The first phrase that comes to me is to "dig a hole with a shovel."

The next step is to write the word again and to see if you can find a different meaning for the same word.

> "dig": to understand, as in "do you dig it, man?"
> "dig": a home, a place to live, as in "nice digs you live in."
> "dig": an insult, as in "did you get the dig she made at him?"

Fill in a meaning for the next word:

"chair": ______________________________________

Now try to find new ways to use the same word, but with slightly different meanings.

"chair": ______________________________________

"chair": ______________________________________

"chair": ______________________________________

Proceed with some or all of the following list:

light	right	play	run
soft	well	sick	ball
paper	line		

Now try some of your own words. You will find that this will not work for every word in our language; however, it does for an extraordinary number. As you practice this more you will find new meanings more easily and faster. This is another exercise that works very well in a group, with adults or children.

Metaphor Exercise 4: Stretching the Image
Go back to the last exercise and take your original or root word and begin to write down common phrases or sayings in relation to the word or different forms of it.

For example we started with the word "dig."

> "He's digging his own grave."
> "What great digs!"
> "Dig in (banquet)!"
> "If you dig any deeper you're going to reach China."

Another word we can try is "light."

"You are the light of my life."
"I can see the light at the end of the tunnel."
"I feel lighter than air."

Practice doing this with the other words you worked on earlier and see how many you can come up with. Take your list and consult with others to see if they can add any more.

Metaphor Exercise 5: More Stretching
Take a piece of paper and write down several headings. For example:

Feelings	Images	Sounds	Animals	Songs

Fill in one of the headings with a word. In this case we can choose a feeling—"**mad.**"

Feelings
mad

Now fill in the other areas in relation to the word "mad." Try to find at least two for each heading, but you can add more if you wish. The end result should look something like the following:

Feelings	Images	Sounds	Animals	Songs
mad	volcano erupting	explosion	T-Rex	*These Boots are Made for Walking*
	Wrestling match	shouting	alligator	*Don't Come Home Tonight*

You may add all kinds of other headings such as actors, songs, smells, etc. You may start your root word in any of the headings. For example, start with an object such as a camera. Then fill in the other areas as much as you can.

Discussion
What you are trying to do in the above exercises is expand your right-brain thinking and in particular to be able to create metaphors much more easily and with greater creativity. Your development of creating and utilizing metaphors will also be a tremendous aid in the next building block— reframing.

Reframing

As human beings we can often become locked in a particular view of the world (internal or external) in which there is no solution to an outstanding problem or issue. Subsequently, a sense of helplessness, powerlessness and hopelessness can result. Reframing helps a person take a new perspective on her problem that allows new solutions to emerge and be explored.

Reframing:

provides a new perspective on an old problem makes the situation/issue manageable/solvable empowers the person and provides hope

Several years ago I was working with a 13-year-old boy who had a learning disability and was several years behind his classmates in academic achievement. Larry considered himself "stupid," and with this label ended up not even trying new ventures, as he would only fail again. The fact that many of his peers also called him names such as "stupid," "dopey" and "moron" didn't help. To Larry, his whole problem in life was related to the issue of being stupid, something he had been convinced he was born with and could do nothing about. This left him feeling helpless, powerless and bitter.

After initially joining with Larry and getting a better sense of him and his world, I utilized reframing as a main intervention tool. Through stories and discussion, the issue of being different but equal was key. More importantly, the issue of being stupid was reframed as *not knowing how to use something*. By the third session, in Larry's stories and in his play he was utilizing the reframe; and then, in the fourth session, he made a major transition in his thinking when he said:

"You know, Greg, I don't think I'm stupid . . . I just don't know how to use my brain yet."

This opened up a whole new world for Larry—a world that gave him a choice and some sense of control over his own life. He now had the option to learn how to use his brain so that he could meet some goals—not necessarily the same goals as everyone else, but goals that he could find fulfilling. Now our therapy moved away from helping Larry with his barrier to change. Now we could work on change, and on helping him to find ways to use his mind that would work for him.

Reframing, like metaphors, also calls for right brain activity and there is a linkage between creating/using metaphors and reframing, as you will see in the following exercises. What you must remember about reframes is that they should:

Fit in the client's context of understanding (e.g., reframing by using references to chemical reactions with a five-year-old will not work).

Accentuate the positive, and place some sense of control or power back with the client (except in some cases where you may want to reframe voluntary behaviour as involuntary).

Utilize reframes in various ways (e.g., in your conversations with your clients, or by embedding them in metaphors and stories).

Reframing Exercise 1: Some Practice in Reframing
The basic premise of reframing is to convert a negative to a positive (for example, "the glass of water is half empty" = "the glass of water is half full," or "the meeting has been cancelled" = "I have some extra time for paperwork," or "my daughter has temper tantrums" = "she has a strong will and won't be walked on").

Review the following problems and try to reframe in order to give a sense of optimism.

My shoes don't fit any more =
My boss always overloads me =
My partner is always jealous =
My partner is never home on time =
Another foot of snow fell last night =
I am so depressed =
I have tried everything =

Don't worry if you struggle with some of these. More practice will help and you will find it easier to find reframes. If you know someone who is the "eternal optimist" in your circle of friends or acquaintances pay more attention to her language and ability to convert gloom and doom to cheer and opportunity. That person is a master reframer (usually without even knowing it).

Mastering the Language in Reframing Therapeutically

In my work with children, couples, families and groups I utilize stories, parables, analogies and metaphors frequently. I have found that where I have used a metaphor or reframe, the impact is magnified if I can utilize a client's root words or metaphors. For example, I worked with a young mother who complained of being "tired" all the time. She had tried resting, holidays, medication, getting help with chores, etc., but nothing seemed to make a difference. Her physical health was good and not a major concern to her. She found that the children took all of her energy and she just had none to spare for anything else.

The reframe I used was "tired" = "bored." One of the stories I used was about a car with bald tires that had a hard time getting anywhere. In the story the car gets some new tires (the car was retired), and it began to travel through some new roads and began to see new things and feel refreshed. I tried to use the client's word "tired" in my reframe and in my story, but with a whole new meaning.

There are many creative ways to utilize client root words or beliefs and to reframe these or create empowering metaphors around them. You will discover them as you use this more and gain more experience and mastery in reframing and metaphors. The following are some exercises you can use to help you on your journey.

Reframing Exercise 2: Linking Metaphors and Reframes to the Client's Language/concepts

Take a problem or issue and in your reframe try to use the root word in the problem statement. Refer back to your metaphor exercises for aid in doing this.

Examples:

Reframe "The boy would run away when he had a problem"
to
"The boy would no longer be run-of-the-mill when he had a problem."

Reframe "The boss fired the employee when he found him sleeping" to
"The boss fired up the employee when he found him sleeping."

Try the following yourself:

I don't see any light at the end of the tunnel.
He's going to have to face the music some day.
Just give him the boot.
No one listens to me when I talk.

One of the things you may have had some struggle with is which "root" word to select. In the first sentence above, you might have selected "light" or "end" or "tunnel"; or you may have chosen the phrase "light at the end of the tunnel." All of these are correct, depending on the emphasis the client used and how they repeat the word or theme or phrase. Also, you may add a verb or change tenses or add a connecting word. There are no formal rules, although the closer you are to the original version and the greater the difference you create in your new wording, the greater the impact.

You may wish to refer to the bibliography to review some of the current literature that focuses on reframing. Like everything else we wish to do well, it will come down to practice in the end.

Storytelling Framework

When you are travelling to a new destination by car it is helpful to have a road map to guide you on your way. As you are driving, you are able to stop where you want, to take a detour or do some sightseeing. When you are building a house it is essential to have a set of plans to provide guidance as to widths, heights, etc. You can add a room, or change the size of the kitchen, or delete the extra shower; however, you still have a plan to which to refer that will keep you on track.

In storytelling, especially as you are developing your storytelling skills, having a "road map" is also useful. Based on my work with stories I have designed a framework that has been helpful, and I would like to share it with you. Again, feel free to add, subtract, expand or set aside any of this to fit your particular style, interests or needs.

Listening Framework

When you are listening to a story your client is telling you there are some key areas to pay attention to:

1. Who are the characters in the story?
In any child's story, for example, he will have animals, objects or people who are a part of the story. These are the story characters and are quite easy to identify (e.g., mouse and cheese, the baby and the alligator).

However, we also know that stories are symbolic and are metaphors for our real lives. Our first task is to try to determine who the characters in the story represent in real life. Some general findings may be helpful. One of the characters is almost always the person telling the story, whether a child or an adult. Other characters usually represent a significant person in the life of the teller (e.g., a parent, foster mother, grandmother, sibling). As storytelling develops, and especially if you use mutual storytelling, you, the therapist, will frequently appear. For children and adults who have been traumatized the main character often represents an abuser or someone integrally connected to the trauma (e.g., bus driver where there was a bus collision).

If you are ever unsure then your safest "guess" is to understand the representation as the child and parent. In determining which character is the child and which the parent, or abuser, or caretaker, it is necessary to take note of the relationships that are portrayed and to compare these to the child's real life. Which of the two characters is best demonstrating how the child may deal with that problem or relationship? For example, the acting-out, aggressive child will usually be controlling, powerful and victorious; the abused child may seek shelter, try to escape or be destroyed in the story.

2. What are the feelings?
During the course of the child's story what is the predominant feeling? Often it will be either anger, fear or sadness, but there are many other possible affectual states which may be demonstrated. Also, you are looking at whether there is any change in feelings from the beginning to the end of the story. Usually, especially when children begin using stories, you will find that the story is quite short, the plot very thin and the affect limited to one or two feelings at the most.

The feelings in the story are the cornerstone of your therapeutic story and the better you can parallel the child's feelings, the more impact your stories will have.

The tricky part of understanding the feeling content in the client's story is in trying to differentiate between the overt and the covert, or hidden, feelings. For example John, aged seven, is quite aggressive with other children and his stories centre around a powerful figure who destroys everything. But under the anger is extreme fear of being hurt and rejected by others. He protects himself by hurting and rejecting others first.

When the client first begins telling stories, the two levels of feelings are not often depicted, or if they are they may be very vague. If this is the case you have an option to just concentrate on the overt feelings for now, or you can make your best guess as to what the covert feeling is when it comes time to tell your story.

One of the options you have to help you decipher stories is to spend a little time after a client tells a story to ask a few clarifying questions. These do not relate to making the material conscious or to analyzing the story with the child. Rather it is a means to help with your understanding of her story.

The following is an excerpt from a storytelling segment with a six-year-old child.

Billy: "Once upon a time there was a gorilla and a lion. The gorilla said that he was the king and the lion had to listen. The gorilla killed the lion and the lion ate all the other animals so that the gorilla would die. The end."

(Note: don't worry about stories making a lot of sense. To the child who sees or feels the story more than they may have words for, it does. This is especially true for young children.)

Greg: That was a great story, Billy. But I don't understand something. You know when the gorilla killed the lion, how did the gorilla feel?

Billy: He was mad.

Greg: And how did the lion feel when the gorilla was mad?

Billy: He was mad too.

Greg: Did he feel anything else?

Billy: He was scared. He didn't like to be killed.

Greg: So the lion was scared and mad, and after the gorilla killed him what did the lion do?

Billy: He killed all the other animals.

Greg: How did the other animals feel?

Billy: They were scared.

Greg: How did the gorilla feel when all the other animals were killed?

Billy: He was scared too.

Greg: How did that make the lion feel?

Billy: He was happy. He hates the gorilla for what he did.

Using open-ended questions and utilizing the child's language as much as possible in order not to influence the story (e.g., I continued to use the word "killed" rather than "hurt" or "fight"), I try to find out a little more about the story, and in particular about the feelings. I now have a better sense that two feelings are in play here: one is anger, but under the anger is fear. I would also hypothesize that the lion is the child and the gorilla his father (who was currently being investigated for physical abuse).

3. What is the problem/issue?
While listening to the child's story I am trying to find the central problem/theme/issue. When I tell my story I want to focus the story around this same issue, which will be embedded metaphorically.

In the majority of your cases you will find that nine times out of ten one of a finite set of common themes will emerge in the child's story. Although you may have more than one theme at play there is usually a central one that will stand out.

The common themes are:

Power/Control	Poor Self-esteem
Belonging	Loss
Safety	Loyalty
Change	Over/Under Responsibility
Identity/Role	Boundaries
Social Skills	Being Different

When a child is not clear on his theme you will usually have enough other information to determine which of the above themes are involved and can use this as the core of your storytelling.

Suggested Storytelling Framework

In creating your therapeutic story the following is a framework you can utilize to assist you.

1. What is your hypothesis/theme/issue?

This was already discussed in the previous section. To start your story you must focus on an issue you wish to illustrate. This is usually an issue in which the client is stuck. It may be having poor problem-solving skills, or not feeling safe, or not having a role in the family. Whatever it is, you need to have it clear in your mind. One of the things to remember is that if you did not get it right, then you will have just told a great story, and whatever the issue is will eventually emerge. There will be other opportunities to "hit the nail on the head."

2. Who are the characters in your story?

In reverse to the child's story, you are starting with reality and then moving to the story characters. Generally, if you are using mutual storytelling you are trying to duplicate the child's characters. If you are just using one-way storytelling then you will almost always use the child as one character and then the primary character connected to the issue you have selected. Usually, somewhere in the story, I add a third party, who most of the time symbolically represents the therapist.

If I am going to depict, for example, the child, her mother and myself, then I need to select characters or objects to represent them in the story. In some of the literature on therapeutic storytelling it is advisable to select characters that have some metaphoric representation to the real-life person. The withdrawn child is the mouse or rabbit. The abuser is the snake or dragon. The child who steals is a magpie or fox. However, my experience has been that it is more powerful and universal to find characters, objects, or animals that have dissonance. Therefore my stories will have an unlikely troupe such as a penguin, a worm and a coconut as the main players. Or I may tell a story about the clam, the teapot and the wishing well.

Although I have not done any research on this, I believe that dissonance, or unusual use of characters, evokes greater right-brain activity and magnifies the effect on the unconscious. As well, there is less opportunity for the listener to race ahead and begin to anticipate the story. This combines to create a more difficult forum to analyze, compare or figure out what is being talked about (which would put the listener into more left-brain activity).

So don't worry about being "off the wall" in your character choices. If you utilize techniques such as Richard Gardner's Mutual Storytelling, characters are determined by those you choose out of the box. Have a wide assortment of animals, objects, and people to select from.

You may also wish to make a condition that the listener will choose the characters and that you try to make them "difficult." I do this for storytelling with my children at night. We call these "imagination stories." My two older children would select two things/people/animals and then I would have to tell a story that included each of them.

3. What is the setting of the story?

Much like characters, I have found that the greater the dissonance of the character the more interesting and right-brain-oriented the story becomes. The clam and worm may be on the moon, or at the zoo, or on a riverboat. The whale and monkey may be mountain climbing or visiting Mars. What is interesting is that as you engage in very creative use of characters and settings you will find that the child's imagination will become richer.

When working with children who have neurological disorders, problems with boundaries, or separating reality from fantasy you may wish to be more limiting in your ideas. In these cases you can choose more connectedness between characters and settings and build in a little more realism.

4. What is the main problem feeling?

This relates to the feelings component we spoke about earlier. Determine the overt and the covert feeling you will have in your story.

5. What is the crisis/challenge?

This relates directly to the first point. The crisis or challenge is connected to the hypothesis/problem/theme/issue; but it is not possible for the character to maintain her old behaviour in order to achieve resolution. Something different is forced to happen.

For example: The issue is that the child is unable to co-operate with others. He is a loner and likes to control others. In the story I would centre the theme around co-operation. The characters would represent the child, a friend, and me as a third party. The process used in relationships, control, fear and anger would be built into the story. The overt feeling would be *anger*, and the covert feeling would be *loneliness*. As the main character engages in each dysfunctional relationship he and the other animal are suddenly caught up in a situation where if they don't co-operate they will face terrible consequences (e.g., pumping out water from a sinking boat—one can't do it alone, both are needed). The characters find themselves co-operating and they are successful. From this there is new learning, new feeling and adjustment made in thinking/behaviour.

6. What is the desired outcome?
The desired outcome is the antithesis of the problem. Loneliness is replaced by belonging, fear to safety, difficulty in expressing feelings to expressing feelings with ease.

7. New learning is achieved.
In the story the protagonist achieves some new learning. This means that there must be a clear depiction of what the new learning is. Although a metaphor or reframe or other form of symbol may be used, the narrator must also detail what has happened. This is why I often use the third party.

For example: Based on the desired outcome, the worm learns that it is okay to be different in size or shape or have a "different" sort of name. What is important is to feel okay about yourself and try your best. With this built into the story, I would narrate something like this . . .

. . . and so the worm crawled back home feeling very good about himself. He crawled tall and proud. Just before he arrived at his hole the marble rolled by and noticed the worm. "Hi, Squiggles," said the marble. "You look really happy today. What's up?"

"Me, I'm up," said Squiggles as he stopped to wiggle. "It was just like you were talking about yesterday. If I stopped worrying about who I wasn't and thought more about just being me then everything would work out."

"Wow!" exclaimed the marble. "I'm so glad your life is perfect now."

"Hey," said Squiggles, "nobody's perfect. I still might feel sad or mad or sorry for myself sometimes. But not most the time, because I have a secret weapon."

"A secret weapon? What is it?" asked Rolly.

"I'll show you," said Squiggles. With that he pulled out something from his pocket and stated, "Whenever I feel a little glum and it doesn't leave me, I look into a mirror," Squiggles held a little mirror in front of him, "and I tell myself, 'Just do your best.'"

"Great," said Rolly. "I think I'll do that when I feel down." (And so the two friends went on their way. The main character uses the new learning.)

8. The main character achieves the desired outcome

9. The new feeling is evident

10. Ending

Make sure in your ending you don't build in a message that everyone lives happily ever after. I try to build in that life is not perfect. We are not perfect. There still are times we may become angry, have a hard time talking about feelings, or resist trying something new. However, even though not perfect we can apply the new learning to make things better than they are.

If you follow the framework to create your stories you will find storytelling becomes more automatic and easier as you go along. You will also find that with practice you become faster at telling stories and more accurate. Currently, I create most of my stories within the session; however, this is not crucial. Write the story between sessions and then deliver at the next session. Ask for help from a colleague or look up some of the stories that are already written to see if they can be used or adapted.

Here is a suggested worksheet to help you at first:

Storytelling Framework

1) What is your hypothesis/theme/issue?

____

2) Who are the characters you want to use?

Real	Story
____________________	____________________
____________________	____________________

3) What is the setting of the story?

____

4) What will be the problem feeling?

Overt ____________________________________

Covert ___________________________________

5) What is the crisis/challenge? (Refer to #1)

____

____

6) What is the desired outcome?

____

7) Character becomes open to new learning.

8) Character uses new learning.

9) Character achieves desired outcome. (#6)

10) New feeling is achieved.

11) Ending with realism.

Putting It All Together
With the above ingredients and framework you are now ready to create a story. First let me provide an example. Then you can go through the framework and write your story.

Susan is a nine-year-old with mild learning disabilities. She is distracting in class, often doing silly things that the other children laugh at. She has no close friends and is often teased due to her plump appearance and slow nature. She responds by shrugging her shoulders and saying, "I don't care," or "sticks and stones . . ." When asked about friends she states she doesn't need friends and is happier without them. She relates well to adults. She is the daughter of a single mother who is on welfare and works part time. Her mother is weak on rules and feels sorry for her daughter.

Susan is quite compliant in the room but is cautious with her play. She will not try new things and does not like to lead. I would like to tell her a story using the framework.

First let us fill in the blanks in the framework.

1) What is the hypothesis/theme/issue?
   Susan acts silly to hide from the fact she feels incompetent. She has very poor self-esteem.
2) Who are the characters?

Real:	Susan	Story:	Tiger
	Peer		Cricket
	me		Seashell

3) What is the setting?
   Golf course
4) What are the feelings?
   Overt: Aloof, distant
   Covert: Lonely, sad
5) What is the crisis/challenge?
   Something happens that forces the main character to be competent and to reach out to someone else and risk being hurt.
6) What is the desired outcome?
   The main character develops self-esteem and realizes she does care.
7) The main character becomes open to new learning.
   The main character learns that what you think about yourself is

the most important thing and that everyone gets hurt some of the time in relationships.

8) The main character uses the new learning
 She does what it says in #7.
9) The main character achieves the outcome.
 As in #6.
10) What is the new feeling?
 Confidence and feeling happy.
11) Ending
 Make sure there is realization that some relationships still hurt.

And Now the Story . . .

THE TIGER WHO DIDN'T CARE

Once upon a time, a long, long time ago there lived a tiger named Jesse who loved to play golf. The only thing was that the tiger just never played. He would often arrive early in the morning to watch all the other animals play golf. Sometimes he would run out and grab the ball in his mouth then hide it in the tall grass. Sometimes he would move the flagpole that showed the hole you had to aim for and everyone would hit the ball in the wrong places.

The other animals would often laugh at what Jesse would do, except when he did it to them. When that happened they would be mad at Jesse, or they would call him names, like "Clawless," "Mr. Spaztick," and the one that was the worst, "Elephant." (Tigers just hated being called Elephant.)

When this happened Jesse would just look over his shoulder and exclaim, "I don't care." Jesse would try to look like it didn't matter—that it was okay not having friends. But it wasn't. Deep down inside he felt . . . he felt . . .

Just then Jesse noticed Betty Cricket coming down the golf course. He had an idea and he ran off to hide behind some bushes. He watched and he waited as Betty Cricket came closer and closer. He giggled as he thought about how much he could scare her when he hopped out and roared.

He crouched down very low behind the bushes and waited. But, just then he heard a voice. It was very faint: "Hey, I don't think that's a great idea."

The Tiger looked around but saw no one. The voice spoke again. "I'm over here, by the stump."

Jesse looked over at the tree stump and saw a large seashell. "Is that you talking, seashell?" Jesse asked.

"Yes, but my voice is very tiny so you have to hold me up to your ear so I can talk to you."

Tiger picked up the seashell and held it to his ear. "My name is Ocean and I have been watching you for some time."

"You have been watching me?" Tiger said with surprise, then he remembered not to be interested. "So what, I don't care if you were or weren't."

"Listen, Jesse," said Ocean, "telling me you don't care is like telling me you are not a tiger. It just isn't true."

Jesse found himself getting angry and a little bit scared. He didn't want anyone finding out what he really felt. And what he really dreamed. If that happened he would just be teased and hurt even more.

"You know, Jesse," continued Ocean, "I was a lot like you when I was just a tiny seashell living on an island in the Pacific Ocean. The other animals and shells around would often walk on me and laugh at my little round spot on my head. They would tease me and call me names. I didn't like it. Then I found an answer. At least I thought I did."

Tiger was quite interested. "What was the answer?"

"It was to stop caring. To turn myself off and not have any feelings. When I had a problem with this I would just act silly, and then when everyone laughed it was because I wanted them to and it didn't hurt me."

Tiger was very interested now. This sounded just like him. He thought he was the only one in the whole wide world that thought that way.

"But I was only fooling myself. Because I did care. It hurt me to be lonely and I was so sad. Then I had to be more foolish and pretend harder to stop my secret feelings."

Tiger stared at Ocean. It was incredible. It was like she was talking about him in every way. He had never told anyone how lonely he felt. How much he wanted to have friends and play golf with them, but he was so afraid of being hurt more it just seemed easier to be silly and pretend he didn't care.

Ocean continued. "But, you know what, Tiger? I learned something really different when I met a strange new friend. She was a cricket—a very wise cricket with one antenna that was crooked. She somehow knew that I wasn't telling the truth about not caring. With the cricket's help I stopped worrying about what everyone else thought and instead thought more about me. But not feeling *bad* for me—feeling *good* for me. I wasn't perfect, but I was as good as any of the others around. I also learned that everyone gets hurt sometimes. Even the cricket had been called names or had someone try to step on her. But most were okay . . . and no matter what happened she said to herself, 'I'm okay. I will try to do my best and that's the best I can do.'"

Ocean took at deep breath. "I started to say the same thing to myself. And instead of being silly I would try to help other animals, or share with them, or try to learn something they could do, or teach them something I could do."

Tiger took a deep breath. "And it works . . . now you do everything well and no one teases you anymore."

Ocean shook her head. "No. It doesn't work all the time. But most of the time it does and when it doesn't I tell myself, 'I'm okay. I tried my best and that's the best I can do.'"

Ocean looked at her watch and noticed it was two o'clock. "Oh, my goodness, I have to get home. Can I come back tomorrow to visit."

Tiger nodded. "Sure, Ocean." Then he turned around and saw that the cricket was almost at the bush. He crouched down behind that bush and was ready to jump. When the moment was just about there, Jesse's eyes opened wide and his mouth dropped. One of Betty Cricket's antennae was crooked. Why, Betty Cricket was the same cricket that had helped Ocean. If that was true then Jesse could not fool her.

Jesse began to think over what Ocean had said. Maybe it wasn't so crazy. If it worked for her maybe it would work for him. Jesse stood up and walked over to Betty.

"Hi, you're Jesse Tiger, aren't you?" she said.

"Yes, and whatever you've heard I really don't care," Jesse quickly blurted out.

Betty looked into Tiger's lonely eyes. Tiger felt her staring into him and he said something he didn't expect. "That's not true, you know. I do care. I just don't want to be hurt."

Jesse was shocked. Now he'd done it. Now he would be mush for everyone. He turned to run away when Betty held out her leg to shake his paw.

"I am pleased to meet you, Jesse. You know, everyone is worried about being hurt, but all you can do is do your best."

Jesse smiled. For the first time in many years he didn't feel lonely. And even though he realized that he may be hurt sometimes, like the seashell and the cricket had said, he really wasn't any different from anyone else.

Now it is your turn. Think of a child you could tell a story to. The child may be a client you had, or one with whom you are currently working, or maybe your own son or daughter, or niece or nephew. Think about the age of the child. One of the factors to keep in mind is that the younger the child, the shorter the story. The sample story above, for example, would not be appropriate for a four-year-old.

Now that you've thought of the child, think of the problem/issue/hypothesis. It may be self-esteem, fear of the dark, being too friendly with strangers, being a bully, or whatever comes to mind.

With the storytelling framework in front of you fill in all the blanks. When you have done this, fill in the rest by adding colour, sounds and movement. Try to picture, hear and feel the story as you are writing it.

Take as much time as you need to complete the story, but do try to finish it.

When you are finished read it out aloud and make any changes that you think are necessary.

If you have completed all of these steps then give yourself a pat on the back. Congratulations on your story! (If you didn't complete it then maybe think of a story about someone who wanted to be a master violinist but never practiced.)

Processing Ingredients

The majority of fun in creating therapeutic stories is having the opportunity to tell the tales to those who are listening. Like magic, it is vital to know how to do the trick, but if you can't perform it well, then it just fizzles. This does not mean that everyone must tell a story like I do, or like Edward Munsch or Bill Cosby. It does mean that you need to find your own style and develop techniques that will assist in capturing attention, stimulating curiosity and creativity. The following are some of the areas you can explore; have fun with it and practice. Make your own list and find what works, but be prepared to make adjustments, as listeners are never all the same.

1) Sounds
   a) Voice
      Use different voices for different characters. You don't have to be gifted or a ventriloquist. Find three voices that you

can do comfortably and use these for the different characters and stories.

b) Sound effects
As you tell the story try to make sound effects to match the content of the story. For example, the trees were whistling . . . make the whistling noise. The door creaked open . . . simulate the creaking noise. The dog barked . . . go ahead and bark.

c) Music/singing
This is especially effective for younger children and for groups of children.

d) Accompaniment from the listener(s)
Again, this is particularly good for young children and for large groups. As you stomp through the woods have the child(ren) stomp with you. Use a key word that will come up several times. Whenever you say it they make a noise, or say a word, or do something in unison.

2) Nonverbal communication

a) Facial expressions
Make facial expressions appropriate to the content. When the character is crying, take on a crying posture.

b) Eye contact
Give eye contact to the listener(s), except where this is culturally to be avoided (such as with first nations).

c) Gestures
Use arm and body movement. Exaggerate movement to make the point. These will fit in very well and provide more energy to the story and to the listener as well.

3) Movement
You need to consider three separate arenas for movement.

a) Your movement in telling the story. Are you going to sit down or move around.

b) The movement of the characters in the story. Are they changing positions, scenes, walking, running, driving, etc.

c) The movement of the listener(s). How much do you want. When it is not planned for and the listener(s) are beginning to shift and move about you are probably losing them and need to come to an end to create a point of attention or interest.

4) Silence
Silence carries a lot of power when used correctly, perhaps once or twice during a story, especially at a time where you want the listener to do some thinking or to raise curiosity/interest. Watch that you don't over-use this or leave silence for too long. Again, the younger the audience, the shorter the period of silence and less you would use this.

5) Paralleling/miming the story
During the story you can play out the parts, in terms of movement. For example "The monkey swung from tree to tree" could be acted out by pretending to swing from vine to vine like Tarzan.

Conclusion
Storytelling is a powerful tool to use in assisting people who are in need. This not only includes children, but also adolescents and adults. This chapter was designed to give you a concrete and practical start to effective storytelling. The rest is up to you. If you allow the storyteller in you to come out, believe in the power of stories, and practice you will become a therapeutic Aesop.

"Good Luck and Good Endings"

REFERENCES

Bandler, R. & Grinder, J. (1975). *Frogs into princes.* Moab, UT: Real People Press.

Barker, P. (1985). *Using metaphors in psychotherapy.* New York: Brunner/Mazel.

Bassin, D., Wolfe, K., & Thier, A. (1983). Children's reactions to psychiatric hospitalization: Drawings and storytelling as a database. *Arts in Psychotherapy, 10*, 33-44.

Bettelheim, B. (1976). *The uses of enchantment: The meaning and importance of fairy tales.* New York: Grove Press.

Brink, N. (1982). Metaphor creation for use within family therapy. *The American Journal of Clinical Hypnosis, 24*, 258-265.

Cameron-Bandler, L. (1978). *They lived happily ever after.* Cupertino, CA: Meta Publications.

Davis, N. (1990). *Once upon a time . . . Therapeutic stories to heal abused children.* Oxon Hill, MD: Psychological Associates of Oxon Hill.

Edwards, B. (1979). *Drawing on the right side of the brain.* Los Angeles: Tarcher.

Gardner, R. (1974). Mutual storytelling: A technique in child psychotherapy. *Acta Paedopsychiatrica, 38*, 253-262.

Gindhart, L. (1981). The use of metaphoric story in therapy: A case report. *American Journal of Clinical Hypnosis, 23*, 202-206.

Gordon, D. (1978). *Therapeutic metaphors.* Cupertino, CA: Meta Publications.

Hoffman, L. (1983). Imagery and metaphor in couples therapy. *Family Therapy, 10*, 141-156.

Jung, C. (1964). *Man and his symbols.* New York: Holt, Rinehart and Winston.

Kagan, R. (1982). Storytelling and game therapy for children in placement. *Child Care Quarterly, 11*, 280-290.

Kopp, S. (1971). *Guru: Metaphors from a psychotherapist.* Palo Alto, CA: Science and Behavior Books.

Lankton, S. & Lankton, C. (1983). *The answer within: A clinical framework of Eriksonian hypnotherapy.* New York: Brunner/Mazel.

MacDonald, M.R. (1982). *The storyteller's sourcebook.* Detroit: Gale Research Co.

Maguire, J. (1985). *Creative storytelling.* New York: McGraw-Hill.

Mills, J. & Crowley, R. (1986). *Therapeutic metaphors for children.* New York: Brunner/Mazel.

Moore, R. (1991). *Awakening the hidden storyteller.* Boston: Shambhala.

Oaklander, V. (1978). *Windows to our children.* Moab, UT: Real People Press.

Plaget, J. (1951). *Play, dreams and imitation in childhood.* New York: Norton.

Rosen, E. (Ed.) (1982). My voice will go with you. New York: W.W. Norton & Co.

Wallas, L. (1985). *Stories for the third ear.* New York: Brunner/Mazel.

Wildgen, J. (1975). Once upon a time . . . or how to teach retarded children to tell stories. *Dissertation Abstracts International, 36,* 899, B.

Xianyi, Y. & Yang, G. (Trans.) (1981). *The zen master Hakuin: Selected writings.* New York: Foreign Language Press.

OTHER RESOURCES

National Storytelling Association
P.O. Box 309
Jonesborough, TN
37659
Phone: 1-800-525-4514

T.A.L.E.S. (The Alberta League Encouraging Storytelling)
10523-100 Ave.
Edmonton, Alberta
T5J 0A8
Phone: (403) 424-7764

The Storyteller School of Toronto
412A College St.
Toronto, Ontario
M5T 1T3
Phone: (416) 924-8625

Stone Soup Stories of Winnipeg
35 Cordova St.
Winnipeg, Manitoba
R3N 0W7
Phone: (204) 489-6994

CHAPTER TEN

IMPLEMENTATION OF PLAY AND ART THERAPY PROGRAMS IN THE SCHOOLS

Donna Cuthbertson

I would like to dedicate this chapter to the memory of my father, Hilliard Stiner. His sense of humour, acceptance and loving guidance made "being a kid" easy for me.

IMPLEMENTATION OF PLAY AND ART THERAPY PROGRAMS IN THE SCHOOLS

Over the past twenty years while working in various agencies I have always counselled through play, and I have seen positive growth in many children. Throughout this chapter I will share my experiences of introducing play therapy in our schools, and how this has had positive effects on many children's self-confidence and self-control. Among those referenced in this chapter are ideas taken from Dr. Garry Landreth (1991), as well as Virginia Axline (1964, 1969), a pioneer in the field of play therapy. By the time you have read this chapter, you will be able to identify practical and key factors, as well as the necessary steps to consider in order to implement an effective play therapy program in a school system.

The play therapy program has been shown to assist students in maximizing their opportunities to learn and to better cope within their classrooms. As a counsellor working within a school system, I find that most of the children referred to me are not able to gain maximum benefit from their learning environment. My role as a counsellor is to provide opportunities for children to feel important and capable, thus enhancing their beliefs in their own abilities and strengthening their self-esteem.

Play therapy and art therapy provide empowerment for students when mastery is experienced, and when the students develop the skills necessary to function successfully in a regular classroom, at recess, and within their community. This program is extremely positive, powerful, and instrumental in assisting successful integration of our students with exceptionalities.

Implementation: Our Beginnings

A play therapy program became a reality in the Durham Region Roman Catholic Separate School Board after I attended a full-day conference with Larry Corrigan, Principal of St. James Catholic School, in Ajax, Ontario. The speaker at the conference was Dr. Garry Landreth, the director of the Center for Play Therapy at the University of North Texas. The following two comments made by Dr. Garry Landreth most strongly influenced Larry and me. Dr. Landreth first stressed the benefit of a child experiencing a positive relationship. He then commented that in Irving, Texas, an elementary school does not open without an equipped, staffed playroom as part of their school program.

It appeared to Larry and me that the school system in Irving, Texas, was acknowledging the need for, and benefits of, a playroom for their students. Based upon our impressions of Dr. Landreth's message, Larry and I felt motivated and confident that the students in the school communities at the Durham Region Roman Catholic Separate School Board could benefit from a similar program. Since our understanding and acceptance of the importance and power of play were further confirmed by the expertise shared at the conference, we felt confident that we could successfully introduce this program to our school personnel and parents. As a result of this initial venture, the Durham Region Roman Catholic Separate School Board now has three schools with a playroom in each. Further, there are other schools that have expressed an interest in beginning the play therapy program in their setting.

Developing Awareness

Careful planning in setting out an acceptable process needs to take place for the successful implementation of a play therapy program in a school. It is essential that you have full support of the administrative personnel of the school, as well as that of the supervisory officers of the board.

In being an effective salesperson for this program, you need to familiarize school staff and parents with the philosophy and value of play. The staff and parents need to recognize your confidence in a program that assists students in achieving their potential. The importance of teamwork in increasing the effectiveness of the program needs to be stressed. Presentations to school personnel and parents should include references to practitioners in the disciplines of play and art therapy, as well as child development. The following information can be used in a presentation to support and develop an awareness of the benefits of such a program in their school.

The concept of the value of play and art is certainly not new. As Axline (1969) says:

> For children play therapy is a unique learning experience under the most favourable growth promoting conditions possible and is viewed from a developmental perspective with objectives consistent with those of the school: to assist children in learning about themselves and their world. Play therapy is based on the fact that play is the child's natural medium of

> expression. Toys are children's words and play is child's language (p. 9).

Piaget (1962) and Landreth (1991) found that "play bridges the gap between concrete experiences and abstract thought and it is the symbolic function of play that is so important" (p. 9). Landreth (1991) indicated that "play involves the child's physical, mental and emotional self in creative expression and can involve social interaction. One can say the total child is present when the child plays" (p. 13). The play therapy program is consistent therefore with school objectives.

The ultimate objective of elementary schools is to assist the intellectual, emotional, spiritual, physical and social development of children by providing adequate learning opportunities. Our responsibility is to help children get ready to profit from the learning experience offered. Children cannot be made to learn. Even the most effective teachers cannot teach children who are not yet ready to learn. (Landreth, 1991, p. 33)

Landreth (1991) has outlined that in play therapy children learn:

> Self-control and responsible freedom of expression
> To respect themselves
> Their feelings are acceptable
> To responsibly control their feelings
> To be creative and resourceful in confronting problems
> Self-control and self-direction
> Self-acceptance
> To make choices and to be responsible for their choices
> (pp. 82-84).

In addition, Axline (1969) shared that:

> The therapeutic value is based upon the child experiencing himself as a capable, responsible person in a relationship that tries to communicate to him two basic truths: that no one ever really knows as much about any human being's inner world as does the individual himself and that responsible freedom grows and develops from inside the person. The child must first learn self-respect and a sense of dignity that grows out of his increasing self-

> understanding before he can learn to respect the personalities and rights and differences of others. (p. 67)

Axline (1969) has incorporated Rogerian principles into eight basic guidelines in developing non-directive child-centred play therapy. These guidelines, revised by Landreth (1991), state:

> The therapist is genuinely interested in the child and develops a warm, caring relationship.
>
> The therapist experiences unqualified acceptance of the child and does not wish that the child were different in some way.
>
> The therapist creates a feeling of safety and permissiveness in the relationship so the child feels free to explore and express self completely.
>
> The therapist is always sensitive to the child's feelings and gently reflects those feelings in such a manner that the child develops self-understanding.
>
> The therapist believes deeply in the child's capacity to act responsibly, unwaveringly respects the child's ability to solve personal problems, and allows the child to do so.
>
> The therapist trusts the child's inner direction, allows the child to lead in all areas of the relationship and resists any urge to direct the child's play or conversation.
>
> The therapist appreciates the gradual nature of the therapeutic process and does not attempt to hurry the process.
>
> The therapist establishes only those therapeutic limits that help the child accept personal and appropriate relationship responsibility. (pp. 77-78)

It is important in the presentation to indicate that it is valid to use the playroom as a place to support a child in developing positive peer relationships. Feeling in control of their environment and experiencing positive peer interaction can only enhance the children's ego strength. In a survey of inner city schools it was found that "the best predictor of academic achievement was the child's sense of control over the environment" (Landreth, 1991).

Oaklander, in a 1994 conference, spoke about an "I/thou" relationship where two people come together with honour and respect. Many therapists stress that the attachment/connecting relationship is the most influential factor in the child's being able to reach his potential. Oaklander further stated that "most kids in therapy have two big problems: one is making contact and the second is that they do not feel good about themselves." The message emphasized to school staff and parents is that it is more important to know how you feel about the child than mundane facts about them.

Play therapy in the schools can help children who have a need to connect better. The child is given an opportunity to work out issues and to remove obstacles that stand in the way of learning. In the playroom the child is the most important person. The child is completely accepted, and, not subjected to judging, can be her true self. In describing play therapy, Axline (1969) shares that "it is a unique experience for a child to suddenly find adult suggestions, mandates, rebukes, restraints, criticisms, disapprovals, support, intrusions gone" (p. 16). What is underlined and stressed to school staff and parents at the conclusion of a presentation is that, without the provisions made in a school system for play and art therapy programs, most children would never have the benefits of such a unique experience.

It is suggested that the presentations be given to three distinct groups: the school staff, the parent association, and the general parent population of the interested school. It is important to build on the receptivity of each constituent group, and to encourage the sharing of ideas and impressions throughout the process.

Parents as well as the school staff need to be aware that the Play and Art Therapy program is considered to be an integral part of the school curriculum, complementing the school philosophy and made available for the child when needed. Often a detailed description is included in the school newsletter, to inform parents who are unable to attend meetings.

An initial reaction from some parents may be: "I don't want my children to waste their time playing, I'm sending them to school to learn." Included in Appendices 10-A and 10-B are the poem *Play Today*, and an information sheet, *Why Play/Art Therapy with Children?* which I share with parents and school staff in addressing such concerns.

It has been noted that once the presentations have been made, and faith is established in the value of the play therapy program, most parents and school staff are receptive to whatever would benefit any student in their school.

To date it has been the parent associations that have generously given their respective schools a donation of money for materials, after the presentations have been made. Donations have ranged from $200.00 to $400.00. Thus far the parent associations have allocated a sum of money annually from their budgets to replenish resources in the playroom. The cooperative effort of parents and school staff working together keeps the commitment to the play and art therapy program alive.

Role of Child and Youth Counsellor

As a child and youth counsellor in the Durham Region Roman Catholic Separate School Board, I am responsible to six schools each week. As a result of referrals from school team meetings, I see students on a regular basis. Where it has not been possible to establish a playroom in a school, with the commitment and support of both school staff and parents play therapy has nonetheless been made available to students, since I choose to use play therapy as my way of counselling. In such cases, I provide my own materials, contained in a portable play therapy bag. I have outlined the list of materials later on in this chapter. In schools where a play therapy program is fully implemented, the playroom is accessible by students under the supervision of school personnel, as well as those students referred to the child and youth counsellor caseload. Continued support is given by providing ongoing in-service sessions for "client-centred, non-directive play therapy" (reflecting responses, limit setting). I am also available as a resource to school personnel as required.

In my position of child and youth counsellor for the Durham Region Roman Catholic Separate School Board, I would not be conducting the formal assessment of a child, as assessments are the responsibility of the board's psychologists and psychometrists. Information obtained from the assessments is made available to me, upon the referral of a child to my caseload. Often during play the child presents me with opportunities to make informal observations. My personal observations, as well as concerns presented at a school team meeting, involving parents and school staff, assist me in determining the goals I hope to help the child achieve, through play experiences. The "counselling intake form" I have developed helps me to keep each child's profile clear. The basic and pertinent information recorded is useful to refer to when completing my end-of-school-year reports. A copy of the counselling intake form is included in Appendix 10-C.

Qualifications of School Personnel

In choosing school personnel who will play a supportive role in supervising in the playroom, the administrators are selective in choosing staff members who are free to let their ""inner child" come through. Recognizing that play therapy allows for "play, humour and fun" (Lubimiv, 1994, p. 13), the staff member needs to be supportive, understanding, caring, and unconditionally accepting, as well as receptive to an adult-child relationship. It is not difficult to find a staff member within a school to fit the aforementioned criteria. School personnel need to believe in the importance and power of play as well as have knowledge of child development. Often this staff member is an educational assistant.

To be at ease with the power of play, I encourage school personnel to read *Play Therapy*, by Virginia Axline (1969); *Dibs in Search of Self*, by Virginia Axline (1964); *Play Therapy: The Art of the Relationship*, by Garry Landreth (1991); and *Wings for Our Children*, by Greg Lubimiv (1994). My own knowledge base was extended when I had two occasions to further my training in play therapy in Texas. In that setting, I was able to experience first hand how "child-centred Play Therapy is an attitude, a philosophy, and a way of being" (Landreth, 1991).

P.A.W. or C.A.L.M. Room

The term "therapy" often creates an emotional reaction in parents and school personnel. To avoid or restrict the program from being available because of the reaction to the word would be unfortunate.

I have worked together with school staffs and encouraged them to be creative in developing a title that best describes what they feel this program offers their students. Two of my schools have named their program the P.A.W., or "Play and Wellness," program. This is the name used throughout our school board when making reference to this play therapy program. The third school has chosen to call their room the C.A.L.M., or "Create and Let Mend," room. I also like this title, as the child is immediately given a sense of what is possible when you say they are going to the C.A.L.M. room. I would also avoid calling the room a "playroom," as the older elementary students may feel embarrassed to use it.

The students have never questioned the titles, and the parents quite like the carefully selected name of this special room. Once the child has spent time in the playroom, no matter what her age, she looks forward to the next time.

Permission and Consents

The preventive role of play therapy is considered part of our school board's proactive intervention measures. Although the administration of the school determines the parameters within which the play therapy program is offered, there are necessary procedures to follow in referring a child for this program. A school team meeting would be scheduled in order to address the concerns about a particular child. School personnel, parents and student services resource staff contribute to the discussion, and the school team decides how best to meet the needs of the child.

If a decision were made to involve the child in a play and art therapy program, the parents would be requested to sign a consent form. Should the occasion arise that a parent is not able to attend a school team meeting, then a consent form is attached to a covering letter explaining the school's play therapy program. These are sent home for parental signature. An example of this consent form appears in Appendix 10-D. In Appendix 10-E, I have included a form that one school chooses to use for teacher referral to the school team.

Obviously, if a crisis situation arises and time is needed in the room to reduce stress or to assist in de-escalating negative behaviour, there would not be time for a signed consent. This opportunity provides the child a chance to regain his composure and eventually return to the regular school environment. Parents are appreciative of this positive management.

When the room is used for social skills development with a few peers, then consent is not obtained, as the social skills program is considered to be an extension of a regular classroom activity. Or if a student seems to be having a "bad day," he may also use the play therapy room. In this circumstance, a parent or legal guardian would be informed.

Confidentiality

At our first session, I let the child know that what she says and does in the playroom is private and confidential. I stress that I will not share any information with anyone unless the child wants me to or unless she is not safe. I let the child know that she is free to talk about her session if she chooses to.

"Children must always be protected from potential physical harm from themselves and others" (Landreth, 1991, p. 147). I let the child know that if I hear or sense that he needs help "to be safe," I will talk to someone who can help him "to be safe." I do not ask for permission from the child if I need to contact another person but I most often will talk to the child about it prior to doing so. Whenever I have needed to consult with another adult or agency, the child has been hesitantly receptive.

"Obviously, the words you choose to explore the concept of confidentiality must fit the age and cognitive abilities of the child you are working with but, in some way, the above messages are conveyed to the child" (Barnes, 1991, p. 8). I feel this honesty, respect and concern that is conveyed to the child right from the initial contact contributes to the therapeutic process.

I do not share specific information from a session with a parent or teacher but I may relay what the child felt good about, or focus on the child's strengths. I feel that sharing this can promote a positive mindset and thus enhance relationships between parent and child and between teachers and children. In addition to advocating for the child I may share with teachers and parents what I feel may be their child's defence mechanisms to protect himself, rather than their perception of "intentional" negative behaviours. This selecting of information to share from a session seems to allow parents and teachers to be more supportive, once they have a better understanding of the child.

Scheduling

Scheduling has been an individual school decision. One school has a select number of staff members who have volunteered to be available either during their program preparation time or during the recess break, on an "emergency, on call" basis if a child is in crisis. In most cases, the educational assistants are regularly scheduled to be present when specific students use the room. These students may be scheduled any time from daily to weekly, depending on room and staffing availability.

A schedule for a student needs to be predictable and consistent, in the same way that the rest of her school program is. The time allotment for each session varies from twenty minutes to fifty minutes, depending on the number of students scheduled per day. Twenty minutes may be better than nothing, but forty to fifty minutes is preferable.

Scheduling for the frequency of visits to the playroom also needs to be considered. Some children use it only once or twice, some children use it regularly for a few weeks or a few months, and others may need this support throughout the entire school year.

Space

The most common initial comment from school personnel is, "We don't have any space." Once school personnel believe in the benefit of having a playroom, it is amazing how resourceful the school is in rearranging or reprioritizing in order to "find" space. In one school, the servery is now the playroom. Once the refrigerator and range were removed, and shelves, sandbox and easel moved in, you would have thought the room was meant to be a playroom. In another school, computers were moved from a separate computer room in the library, and that room is now a playroom. A third school uses a former science preparation room for the playroom. In other schools we are considering gym storage rooms and rooms attached to classrooms or libraries. Each school is unique, with space that could be made available for the play therapy program.

Not all spaces are usable, and there are certain qualities to look for when searching for space (realizing that not all these qualities would be available in each school):

Window	for brightness and for the child to look out of
Sink	for easy cleanup, water play
Shelves	to have toys visible, organized and inviting to play with
Light-coloured walls	for brightness
A private place	with lessened interruptions and minimal noise
Floors	should be easy clean vinyl or indoor/outdoor carpet
Warm décor	posters, stencilling, drawings

Room dimensions	a 12' by 12' square-shaped room is preferable for the adult to be "physically present" from all angles.

Materials

Lubimiv (1994) says "what the therapist uses as their tool is less important than how it is used" (p. 88). With limited funding and resources, we are justly reminded that "as a play therapist you must learn to make use of any material around you and make it into a game" (Lubimiv, 1994, p. 90).

The following is a list of materials I see children freely choosing to use:

large white or black board (attached to wall or portable)
markers or chalk brush
easel (or paper taped to wall)
school desk or table (table top for clay, tracing, etc.)
two or three child-sized chairs
floor pillows
paints and varying sizes of brushes
scissors
Oogly (non-hardening clay)
rescue vehicles
road mat with buildings
Construx or Lego (building material)
sand table
miniature plastic animals (zoo, farm, prehistoric, domestic)
rubber snake
trees, fences, bridges
people, families
doll house
baby bottles
puppets (people and animals)
puppet theatre
hats
purse, costume jewellery, play money
toy soldiers
army equipment
doctor's kit
"Lone Ranger" mask
stress balls

nerf balls
telephones (at least two)
cooperative games
Ungame (self expression game)
My Homes and Places game
tracing books (Wacky Animals, Silly Monsters)
Capture a Feeling card game
Ups and Downs with Feelings bag
paper (all sizes and kinds, e.g., newsprint, construction, tissue, sketching)
origami materials
paper airplanes (child makes own)
embroidery floss (for friendship bracelets)
craft materials (wool, pipe cleaners, glue, thread, masking tape, fabric, felt, cotton balls, buttons, beads, magnetic tape, glue gun, ribbon, varying sizes of bead eyes)

When I send out a notice in the school newsletter asking for donations of specific items, I stress "selected" materials rather than "collected."

Some of the aforementioned items may be in classrooms not being used (like the four big floor pillows I have in one playroom), and teachers would be happy to donate them to your playroom. Most of the art supplies can be gathered from the school supply cupboard. Garage sales and dollar stores often have the small items, such as plastic animals and rescue vehicles, available at a nominal cost. It is not the amount of materials that is as important as the freedom of the materials to present themselves for creativity, mastery, and esteem building.

It is possible to set up a playroom on a "shoestring budget"! Due to financial and budgetary constraints, such an approach is a good selling feature when presenting to parent associations and school boards.

When I go to schools that do not have a specific playroom set up, I carry a portable play therapy bag of selected materials. I also use plastic storage containers for transporting and storing my materials. I set out my materials in an organized, tidy and inviting way in any available corner I can find, before going to the classroom to meet the child.

Portable Play Therapy Bag

The following materials are those I carry from school to school, and are consistently used in a variety of ways:

hand and finger puppets
Oogly non-hardening clay
hats
crayons, markers
paper (all sizes)
masks
rescue vehicles
people
craft materials and books
army vehicles
army people
nerf balls
stress balls
doctor's kit
Construx, Lego, Knex
masking tape
cooperative games
Ungame
tracing books and tracing paper
Capture a Feeling card game
Ups and Downs with Feelings bag
paint blocks and brushes
empty yogurt containers for water
glue
scissors
paper

Even if the school does not have a spare room, there is often a drawer, shelf or a cupboard that you can use for storing art supplies. It is economical as well as task efficient not to transport such materials from school to school.

Each therapist will choose her own "tools" or strategies depending on her own interests, abilities and beliefs. The specific materials are not as important as the opportunity for developing a relationship between the adult and child. The child feels that someone cares. I have included in Appendices 10-F, G, and H a list and brief description of some of the resources I have found to be useful. The resources are equally acceptable in a permanent or portable play therapy program configuration.

Strategies

Role-playing

Role-playing is an opportunity to practise alternative options in responding to conflict and for expression of feelings. I demonstrate for the child the way in which I believe he would naturally interact and allow him to experience being the other person. I then use a more appropriate, less threatening response, using tones of voice, as well as selective words. We then discuss how the child felt about each response. Inevitably, he chooses the second response, often unaware that his response may have sounded like the first. Once the child is aware and has modelled these alternatives, he is better equipped to respond appropriately.

Positive Self-Talk

The child and I discuss how it is possible to be in control of the "tapes" of messages received from others. It is not possible to control what others say and do, but the child and I discuss how we can control the effects of others on us. Depending on the age and receptiveness of the child, we may verbally role-play, or write positive self-talk statements on banners, mobiles or pennants. The child may take his artwork to post it where he can readily see it. I find this effective with children who are being bullied and for those children who are depressed.

Relaxed Breathing or Diaphragmatic Breathing

I show the child how to breathe in through her nose and out through her mouth. To help the child stay focused, I encourage her to put her hand on her tummy. She can feel her tummy go out when she inhales and go in when she exhales. This technique can be used when the child is hurt, angry, sad, frustrated, anxious, getting silly, or scared. Relaxed breathing is a therapeutic tool that we can make accessible to our clients. I encourage them to share this with their peers, teachers and parents. The more automatic this breathing focus becomes, the more likely it will be used when needed.

Bibliotherapy

The reading or the sharing of books that relate to issues with which the child may be dealing helps him to feel "he is not alone." I share children's books related to ADHD, autism, grief, being bullied, or feeling different. Book titles I have used are included in the listing of suggested resources at the end of this chapter.

Cooperative Games
In introducing a cooperative game to a child I state: "We will need to work together and cooperate to be able to . . ." I explain the expectations of the game and how it is necessary to anticipate possible upcoming trouble spots in the game. We can choose to avoid the trouble or be prepared to advance, by using a selected card that enables us to effectively deal with the difficulty. Once the child successfully completes the cooperative game, he has experienced the effectiveness of working together cooperatively. The taking of turns and decision-making are effective strategies of skills the child can use for problem solving and successful interactions outside the playroom.

Crafts
Utilizing crafts in the playroom enables the child to make choices and to be creative. While working with art and craft materials, the child is absorbed in what he is doing, while anticipating with excitement the end product. He may ask for help or he may work independently. Often crafts provide an opportunity for the child to nurture, when he makes something for himself, a parent, or friends. Positive interactions, sharing, and having fun all contribute to the development of a "special" relationship between the child and the adult.

Although these aforementioned strategies and activities may appear to be directive, the child is free to choose what she wants to do. For example, some children never choose crafts, but instead choose toys, sand, or painting. Others may choose only crafts. The range of resources and activities available to the children will depend on the therapist's preference or style. I have included a list of suggested resources at the end of the chapter.

Personal Philosophy and Approach
My focus while in the playroom is to develop a positive relationship that both confirms and affirms that the child is accepted and capable. I believe the child's potential is there. The child only needs an opportunity to express and experience it. Once her self-esteem is heightened, she is better able to approach life more confidently.

I have seen that when a child has achieved emotional relaxation, he is able to experience empowerment to be resourceful in making positive decisions to confront his problem.

I feel that the innovative feature of this play therapy program is that it can be used by any student with any exceptionality. The child is accepted for who he is, as a whole person, who he wants to be, and what his strengths and limitations are, while at the same time drawing on his amazing inner strengths. You let the child lead; you follow. This philosophy presupposes that the child knows himself and is capable of working the conflict out in a safe environment. The following poem (Landreth, 1994) illustrates quite strongly the tenet that underlies this philosophy.

> I tried to teach my child from books,
> He gave me only puzzled looks.
> I tried to teach my child from words,
> They passed him by, oft unheard.
> Despairingly I turned aside,
> How shall I teach this child, I cried?
> Into my hands he placed the key,
> Come, he said,
> "Play with me."

Depending on the specific exceptionality or need of the child, the therapist would draw upon his expertise to support the child creatively. Opportunities to experience feelings of calmness, capability and importance are valuable for everyone. While there are students who may act out very apparent problems, there are also many quiet students who may be in need of play therapy support. These quiet students also need this "safe haven" in which they can talk, or vent their feelings, in their own way. The play therapy program can be an appropriate support for students throughout the elementary school.

There are four key messages that can be felt by every child:

> I hear you
> I care
> I understand
> You are not alone

Since loneliness is a concern for many children, the one-on-one interaction makes the child feel special. It is important to make encouraging statements to the child. "Encouragement recognizes effort, praise recognizes the end result. In an encouraging playroom your worth is just a given" (Landreth, 1991). Many children feel a great sense of accomplishment after being in the playroom. That success enhances a child's belief in her own abilities outside the room.

Building Peer Relationships
I have found that the playroom is also a safe place to develop peer relationships. I often see children who feel they do not have any friends. If the child expresses the wish to invite a peer to our session, then arrangements are made. The child may choose to invite a classmate to his next session, or he may choose to make something to show the class or to share with a peer. At other times the child may choose to arrange an activity in the gym or outdoors involving a few selected peers.

The skills developed through positive play interactions in the playroom between children often continue to be used in the classroom and at recess.

Group play therapy is not as common a practice as individual therapy. To be effective in group play therapy, the therapist requires unique skills and training.

Working with Siblings
I have also found that working with a child and his siblings, especially if they are twins, gives you a lot of information. You can find out who is a leader, who is a follower, and what each sibling expects of himself.

Depending on the issues presented, you may find yourself supporting a different sibling at different times (be careful to give equal attention). I experienced this while working with twin boys. One had ADHD (attention deficit hyperactivity disorder) and was academically delayed. The other was a perfectionist, strong academically, and had assumed responsibility for both himself and his brother. Recognizing immediately that there was too much stress on each of them, I addressed my observations with them. Our sessions involved opportunities to empower the student with ADHD and to lessen the frustration of his brother, who felt that he needed to be perfect. The boys chose cooperative games, card games, painting, building, and sometimes they just talked. I found the activities that required taking turns were most beneficial for a successful outcome.

By the end of the school year there was much less pressure felt by the boys and they appeared happier. Both parents and teachers also made this comment.

The sibling play therapy approach seemed to bring faster results in this case.

Limit Setting

Limit setting is in essence the creation of therapeutic boundaries. Although the child is free to choose to do what she wishes in the playroom, therapeutic boundaries need to be set in order to provide a safe place. At the beginning of the initial session I share the following limits with each child:

> You need to be safe
> I need to be safe
> The materials cannot be broken

Naturally you will have your own personal limits, but it is important to be predictable and consistent so that the child can make decisions and maintain self-control. "The freedom to choose exists within the boundaries of limits" (Barnes, 1991).

I personally do not feel limits are called for until they are necessary. If given too many limits in advance, I feel the child is restricted and unsure of what he is "allowed" to do. This takes away from the child's belief that you trust him. There is no doubt you will have the occasion to reinforce additional limits.

A technique I have found to be effective is to remember A.C.T. (Landreth, 1991, p. 223):

> A Acknowledge the child's feelings, wishes and wants.
> C Communicate the limit.
> T Target the alternative.

For example:

> A Emily, it sounds like you wish you could stay in the playroom longer.
> C Your time is up for today.
> T You will be able to come back next Thursday.

(The child is more willing to leave if she is made aware of when she is returning.)

This is also a great technique to share with parents and teachers. Often by simply acknowledging the feelings of the child, you can sense the lessening of resistance, and the decreased need for a power struggle. The child hears that you "understand" how he is feeling and can trust you.

Termination

I feel there are two terminations to consider in a play therapy program. First, there is the termination of each session. It is important to let the child know when there are five minutes left in a session. This gives the child time to end his "work" and to be prepared to proceed to his next school activity. I chuckle when I recall the response from a four-year-old boy in junior kindergarten when I informed him there were five minutes left. In his four-year-old voice he said:

> Daniel: You said that last time, it is my time to say!
>
> Myself: You feel it is not fair for me to say what time you go back to class this week because I said so last week.
>
> Daniel: Yah.
>
> Myself: (Pointing to the clock) OK, Daniel. You can tell me when this big hand gets all the way down to the six and we will go back to class.
>
> Daniel: (Playing and looking up at the clock periodically) It is almost at the six.
>
> Myself: Thanks for telling me, Daniel. You tell me when it is right at the six, OK?
>
> Daniel: Donna, it is at the six. Time to leave. (He opened the door, reached for my hand and skipped back to class.)

Recognizing immediately that Daniel wanted control, I was able to give it to him. While Daniel was given control, this did not affect anyone else and he got what he needed at that moment. When a child does not want to leave the playroom you have an occasion to set a limit and "ACT."

The second termination I refer to is the ending of the therapeutic relationship. With most children, the ending of the school year dictates the termination (at least for a few months).

If I feel the child no longer needs to be part of this program or if the child indicates she is ready to terminate the relationship then we decide together when the last session may be. The child needs time to work out how she may be feeling about leaving one safe, caring connection in hopes of establishing another. Some children react minimally, and for others it may be unsettling. "The process for actual termination will need to be started two or three sessions prior to the final session" (Landreth, 1991, p. 330).

The availability of the student within a school setting makes it possible to extend the amount of time between sessions when considering termination. Rather than seeing the child on his usual weekly schedule you may see him biweekly or monthly, until termination. This scheduling provides the opportunity for the child to prove to himself that he can manage and seek support if necessary. Once a weekly schedule is no longer needed, most students feel it would be more helpful to be seen less frequently than not at all. Some readers may interpret this as a dependency, but I disagree. I feel that if the child is part of the process in decision-making, we need to respect his decision as well as rely on our understanding of how to best meet his needs.

This "tapering off" of sessions seems to be the most beneficial process and support for empowering most students to best manage in their school community. Entire chapters have been written by therapists dealing with the topic of termination (Lubimiv, 1994, chapter 8; Landreth, 1991, chapter 15).

Barriers and Rewards

In an ideal situation, it is expected that the implementation of a play and art therapy program in a school system would work as smoothly as has just been described. However, things are not always as simple and straightforward as they appear to be. Discussions, negotiations, and barriers are all part of the implementation process.

I would encourage those interested in setting up a similar program in their school setting, to look beyond those barriers. Such barriers may be the extent of receptivity to the concept, lack of trained staff, amount and extent of release time available for training and in-service, and the limitations of space and financial support. This chapter has described how the barriers can be overcome with creativity, and the collaboration of all stakeholders. As a result of my experiences, I promote play and art therapy as an extension of the classroom program. I am convinced that the benefits of the play and art therapy program outweigh the barriers and obstacles that must be overcome when introducing any innovation into a new setting.

The energy that has been put into establishing the play therapy program in the three schools of the Durham Region Roman Catholic Separate School Board has been well worth the effort and determination of all who have been involved. "Sharing our enthusiasm with others causes us to lose nothing at all, and we quickly discover that enthusiasm is contagious" (Kern, 1990, p. 10).

The following are comments and observations that serve to affirm the value of the innovation of having play and art therapy available in a school setting.

"The C.A.L.M. Room is a place of freedom for some of the children I work with! It has become a room of safety and unconditional caring and the children really feel this. They are free to be open, free to be children in the sense of being able to play with no pressure. They enjoy being able to make their own choices, pressure free."
Rita Somers, educational assistant, St. Patrick Catholic School, Ajax, ON

"A very sad, frustrated little girl cannot bring herself to enter the classroom. Whatever may be bothering her, she is not yet prepared to begin her day at school. A much happier girl returns to our classroom after having spent time in the C.A.L.M. Room where what is expected of her seems more bearable. Not only can she can be herself, she also begins to realize that someone is there to listen in a place that offers her choices—choices in how to spend that special time and prepare her for her day."
Emily Delaney, grade one classroom teacher, St. Patrick Catholic School, Ajax, ON

"In the turmoil of the these confusing times, it is often difficult to be a child. Through play, the P.A.W. Room gives our children unconditional acceptance and the tools to deal with the difficult work of life. Through play comes peace, confidence, and self-esteem."
Anna Camazzola, program support teacher, St. Joseph Catholic School, Uxbridge, ON

The P.A.W. Room allows children to calm and refocus. I have seen the changes on their faces as they get involved in their chosen play activity. They are then able to return to participate in classroom activities.

Allowing children to make their own choices and accept responsibility for those choices shows respect for the child on the adult's part, and builds positive self-esteem for the child.

"I love this room. I wish I could come here every day!"
SK student

"He is so eager to go to the P.A.W. Room with you, and you know he has joined the cross country team!" (Grade seven teacher re: student who is very introverted)
Izabela Ballentine, educational assistant, St. James Catholic School, Ajax, ON

The value of our efforts was truly underscored when the innovation was nominated for the "Exemplary Practices in Integration" award. I have chosen to share the letters of support, so that you can see first-hand why I so strongly believe and support the endeavour of Play Therapy programs in the school setting.

Acknowledgements
I would like to thank my sons Ian and Sean for the opportunities we share, to experience our child within and have fun. They have shown me the joys of parenting. I would like to thank my husband Bruce for sharing the joys of parenting with me; and my mom, Georgina, for always being there when I needed her.

I am greatly appreciative of my many colleagues and especially to the Durham Region Roman Catholic Separate School Board, who have been overwhelmingly receptive and supportive of my initiative of introducing play therapy into their school community. They truly care.

I would like to say a great big "thank you" to my friends and colleagues, Eva Teresa Rhode and Maureen Hawkins. Their assistance in editing and typing this chapter has been invaluable.

I am forever grateful to the children I support who have inspired me. I have learned so much from children.

APPENDIX 10-A

Play Today

You say you love your children,
And are concerned they learn today?
So am I . . . that's why I'm providing
A variety of kinds of play.
You're asking me the value
Of blocks and other such play?
Your children are solving problems
They will use that skill everyday.

You're asking what's the value
Of having your children play?
Your daughter's creating a tower
She may be a builder someday.

You're saying you don't want your son
To play in that "sissy" way?
He's learning to cuddle a doll;
He may be a father someday.

You're questioning the value of toys.
They just look like useless play?
Your children are making choices;
They'll be on their own someday.

You're worried your children aren't learning;
And later they'll have to pay?
They're learning a pattern for learning
For they'll be learning always.

Author Unknown (Conference presentation, Texas, October 1994)

APPENDIX 10-B

Why Play/Art Therapy With Children?

Definition - Play/art therapy is the use of play/art to provide children an opportunity to express themselves verbally and non-verbally. Through play/art, children are able to explore problems, hopes, concerns, abilities, fears, and potentials.

1. Using play/art in therapy is a way to talk to children in their own language.
2. Children "talk"/learn through play. Play/art provides a "play-like atmosphere" in which children can learn.
3. Children communicate through non-verbal means: play, action. Children cannot always express their experience verbally. Children can communicate effectively through art and play.
4. Play/art therapy is fun. Children enjoy coming to sessions.
5. Play/art therapy is less threatening to children than just talking. Children relate to art and play and are not afraid of this type of format.
6. Children will reflect or act out their emotions through play. Observing a child at play allows me to get a glimpse of the child's world. What happens in the play/art therapy room is representative of what happens outside the play/art therapy room.
7. Children act out ideas or possibilities through play. The play/art therapy room is a safe place for children to test their abilities, ideas, and skills.
8. A great sense of accomplishment is felt when a child is successful in the play/art therapy room. This success enhances a child's belief in her abilities outside the play/art therapy room.
9. Over the course of therapy, a child learns that creativity/play is his ally. Play, fun, and art provide the child with an outlet for expression and teach the child about himself and others. This knowledge is learning that your child will take with him for the rest of his life. Art and play will continue to provide your child with a vehicle for self-understanding and awareness.
10. Play/art therapy teaches a child to identify and utilize her own creative abilities. Your child's unique creativity will be enhanced. Your child will ultimately develop self-nurturing abilities.

APPENDIX 10-C

Mary Birch, Art/Play Therapist, Nebraska
Counselling Intake Form

Name: Date referred:
D.O.B.: School:
Grade: Teacher:
Street Address:
Home Phone #: Work Phone #:
Mother's Name: Father's Name:
Siblings' Names: Age:
Age:
Age:

Strengths:

Likes/Interests/Hobbies:
Dislikes:

Fears/Worries:

Presenting Concern:

Goals:

Treatment Plan (Types of Initiatives/Strategies):

Is child presently seeing another counsellor or has in the past?
If so the counsellor's name is:
Time Frame:

Any additional comments:

APPENDIX 10-D

(Attachment to a covering letter explaining the school's play therapy program.)

Consent Form

Therefore, I feel that ___________________________would benefit from this support on a regular basis. Below is the related consent form. If you wish for your child to participate in the C.A.L.M. Room program, please sign it and return it to the school at your earliest convenience. Thank you for your support.

Sincerely,

(child's teacher)

I give ______________________________ permission to participate in the C.A.L.M. Room program on a regular basis.

Parent/Guardian signature:

APPENDIX 10-E

Confidential Teacher Referral For P.A.W./ C.A.L.M. Room Time
Student's name:
Teacher:
Preferred day:
Preferred time:
Reason for request:
Type of request: As needed: Regular Basis:

APPENDIX 10-F

Commercially Available Games

Ungame
A favourite non-competitive board game that provides choices, encourages self-expression and initiates discussion.
Kidsright: 1-800-892-KIDS

My Homes and Places
In this game feelings are expressed and experiences are shared. Thoughts, fears and wishes about family and self are exchanged.
Kidsright: 1-800-892-KIDS

Ups and Downs with Feelings Bag
There are seven games in one bag. Children will discover ways to identify feelings and gain more control of their lives. There are two versions, ages six years to adult and ages three to six years.
Kidsright: 1-800-892-KIDS

Capture a Feeling Card Game
There are many ways to express feelings in this pack of cards. Suggestions are included in the package.
Carole Gesme
4036 Kerey Court
Minnetonka, MN 55345
(612) 938-9163

Cooperative Games:
Mountaineering ages ten to adult
Deep Sea Diving ages ten to adult
Granny's House ages five to twelve years
Sleeping Grump ages five to twelve years
Funny Faces ages five to twelve years

Each of these cooperative games is great for experiencing problem solving and for the child to see positive results from good decision-making. Working cooperatively, players have to anticipate possible problems and decide how to either avoid the problem or to successfully deal with it. These games are great relationship builders and the child always feels a sense of being capable.

Playtoy Industries
29 Ingram Drive
Toronto, ON
M6M 2L7

APPENDIX 10-G

Commercially Available Books

Tracing Books
This popular activity helps children focus, controls pen to paper, and the child experiences a sense of control and mastery. Each page provides many choices. The child has to decide what head with what eyes, ears, nose, mouth, body, arms, legs, hair, etc. This activity is great for children who do not feel capable of drawing and often never finish a product. I let the child photocopy her finished picture to share with others.

Making Paper Airplanes
This is a great start to building a relationship. The child leafs through the book *Stunt Flying with Paper Airplanes,* by Bob Smith, and chooses the one she would like to make. The child chooses the size of paper, can ask for help if needed and can choose to decorate the plane. When the child flies the plane, she experiences the feeling of being capable as well as pride in having accomplished a finished product. This pride contributes to boosting self-esteem.

Doll-Making
Kids Can Easy Crafts: Dolls, by Judy Ann Sadler, contains ideas for doll-making. There are many dolls to choose from, including a worry doll. This is also a great relationship builder. The child talks while working and ends up with a product he wants to keep and cherish. Expressions on the child's face indicate to me that he is proud of his accomplishment.

Origami
There are many books with suggestions on origami. The child looks through the book and follows the pattern. He loves the end result. He is in control, has mastered a skill, and feels good about himself. He can also design his own and perhaps teach you. *Paper Tricks* and *Paper Ocean* are by Florence Temko and have many creative ideas. This is similar to origami.

Friendship Bracelets
These are the popular ankle or wrist bracelets you see children wearing, made out of embroidery floss. I have a variety of colours of floss for the child to choose from. They may choose a design from the book *Kids Can Crafts: Friendship Bracelets* by Camilla Gryski. I either hold the strands or tape them to the tabletop while the child weaves. This is usually an activity the child takes with her to complete, as it is time-consuming. Children love to show it off to their peers.

APPENDIX 10-H

Commercially Available Art and Craft Supplies

Goop
You need:
several plastic bottles with squeeze/squirt tips
4 cups flour
2 cups sugar
1 cup salt
2 1/2–3 cups of water mixed with 2 tbsp. paint

Mix dry ingredients to paint and water to a consistency able to flow through the tip of a squeeze bottle. Use a large piece of heavy paper and encourage the child to use goop freely by squeezing the bottle. Goop dries in about four hours. When squeezing goop from the bottle it produces a circular, shiny, dimensional tube. Children can use their hands to design anything they want. Kids love this. Warning! You go through a lot of goop.

Hand Painting
The child has his hand painted and makes a collage of handprints. Depending on how the child places his hands he can make a picture or animal (e.g., reindeer, turkey, bat, bunny, butterfly, etc.). This is a great product with amazing results.

Oogly
This is the best non-hardening clay I have found. This product lets you make an "Oogly" over and over, as you can construct and reconstruct with it. Using the Oogly is a great activity for stress release and being creative. The kit comes with tools that look like a garlic press, which is great for making hair. This activity is useful for starting a story or for sharing feelings. I have found this to be a no-fail experience. A complete kit comes with eight sticks of clay, two tools with two variably sized heads to make tubular hair-like pieces, an Oogly stick and simple instructions.

REFERENCES

Axline, V. (1964). *Dibs in search of self*. New York, NY: Ballantine Books.

Axline, V. (1969). *Play therapy*. New York, NY: Ballantine Books.

Barnes, M. (1991). *The magic of play therapy*. Paper presented at the conference of Mandala Therapeutic Services, Buffalo, NY.

Berger, J., Braun, K., & Task, A. (1994). *Wacky animals tracing fun*. New York, NY: Scholastic Inc.

Gryski, C. (1993). *Friendship bracelets*. Toronto, ON: Kids Can Press Ltd.

Kern, J. (1990). *Build the fort . . . today!* San Antonio, TX: The Desktop Publishing Service.

Landreth, G. (1991). *Play therapy: The art of the relationship*. Muncie, IN: Accelerated Development Inc.

Lubimiv, G. (1994). *Wings for our children*. Burnstown, ON: The General Store Publishing House.

Oaklander, V. (1969). *Windows to our children*. New York, NY: Real People Press.

Sadler, J. (1993). *Dolls*. Toronto, ON: Kids Can Press Ltd.

Smith, B. (1992). *Stunt flying with paper airplanes*. St. Petersburg, FL: Willowisp Press.

Sperling, A. (1990). *Silly monsters tracing fun book*. New York, NY: Scholastic Inc.

Temko, F. (1988). *Paper Tricks*. New York, NY: Scholastic Inc.

Temko, F. (1990). *Paper Tricks II*. New York, NY: Scholastic Inc.

SUGGESTED RESOURCES

A'Court, A., & Jackson, P. (1993). *The ultimate papercraft and origami book*. Toronto, ON: Read On Publications Inc.

Allan, J. (1991). *Inscapes of the child's world*. Dallas, TX: Spring Publications Inc.

Ammann, R. (1991). *Sandplay, healing and transformation*. Peru, IL: Open Court Publishing Company.

Annunziata, J., & Nemiroff, M. (1990). *A child's first book about play therapy*. Washington, DC: American Psychological Association.

Baillie, N. (Ed.). (1991). *Magical fun: Mystery potions: Card magic: Vanishing tricks: Plus puzzles, treats and much more*. Toronto, ON: Greey de Pencier.

Borba, M. (1990). *Esteem builders*. Rolling Hills Estates, CA: Jalmar Press.

Borba, M. (1982). *Self-esteem: A classroom affair*. San Francisco, CA: Harper and Row.

Brown, M., & Brown, L. (1986). *Dinosaurs divorce.* Boston, MA: Little Brown and Company.

Coloroso, B. (1994). *Kids are worth it.* Toronto, ON: Somerville House Publishing.

Firmin, G., & Petty, K., (1991). *Being bullied.* New York, NY: Barron's Educational Series Inc.

Gil, E. (1991). *The healing power of play.* New York, NY: The Guilford Press.

Gordon, M. (1992). *My brother's a world class pain: A sibling's guide to ADHD/hyperactivity.* New York, NY: GSI Publications.

Gryski, C. (1993). *Boondoggle: Making bracelets with plastic lace.* Toronto, ON: Kids Can Press Ltd.

Kates, B.J. (1992). *We're different, we're the same.* New York, NY: Random House.

Masson, A. (1989). *The magic of marionnettes.* Willowdale, ON: Firefly Books Ltd.

McGraw, S. (1994). *Gifts kids can make.* Willowdale, ON: Firefly Books Ltd.

Mills, J., & Crowley, R. (1986). *Therapeutic metaphors for children.* New York, NY: Brunner/Mazel Inc.

Piaget, J. (1962). *Play, dreams, and imitation in childhood.* New York: Rutledge.

Piper, W. (1989). *The little engine that could.* New York, NY: Platt and Munk.

Sanford, D. (1986). *Don't look at me: A child's book about feeling different.* Singapore: Multnomah Press.

Sanford, D. (1986). *I can't talk about it: A child's book about sexual abuse.* Hong Kong: Multnomah Press.

Sanford, D. (1985). *Please come home: A child's book about divorce.* Hong Kong: Multnomah Press.

Stinson, K. (1988). *Mom and Dad don't live together anymore.* Scarborough, ON: Firefly Books Ltd.

Walton, S., & Walton, S. (1994). *Make your own paper ocean.* North Vancouver, BC: Whitecap Books Ltd.

Webb, N.B. (1993). *Helping bereaved children: A handbook for practitioners.* New York, NY: The Guilford Press.

Weber, C., Behl, D., & Summers, M. (1994). Watch them play, watch them learn. *Teaching Exceptional Children, 27*, 30-35.

Wilson, K., Kendrick, P., & Ryan, V. (1992). *Play therapy: A non-directive approach for children and adolescents.* Great Britain: Bailliere Tindall.

CHAPTER ELEVEN

AN INDIVIDUAL PLAY/ART THERAPY ASSESSMENT MODEL

Judy Jones
Julie Regan
Barbara Jones Warrick

AN INDIVIDUAL PLAY/ART THERAPY ASSESSMENT MODEL

Introduction

In this chapter a hands-on play/art therapy assessment model will be presented. This model is a sequential, multi-faceted framework for working with children referred for individual treatment.

Clinicians recognize the value of play and art therapies when working with children. It is also common practice to spend some time assessing in the first few sessions. It is the goal of this chapter to combine assessment and play/art therapy in a practical, utilitarian model. Various contributors to the field of play/art therapy have identified the need for observing the child across a number of dimensions. Oaklander (1969, p. 165) was one of the first to identify the value of assessment, making observations about the child's "maturity, intelligence, imagination and creativity, cognitive organizations, reality orientation, style, attention span, problem solving abilities, contact skills, and so forth." Greenspan (1981, p. 15) maintains that active observation occurs on a variety of levels, involving the physical integrity of the child, his emotional tone, how he relates to the clinician, his specific affects and anxieties, and the way he uses the environment; also involved are thematic development of the child's play and the therapist's subjective feelings about the child. O'Connor (1991, p. 147) recognizes the value of assessment across a number of variables: "the child's choice of materials; the type of play in which she engages—its structure, organization, completeness; the symbols used; and so forth." These authors include assessment in their particular approach to working with children. However, there appears to be a need for a comprehensive play/art assessment model that may be implemented in a variety of settings across diverse child populations.

Rationale

Play and art therapy is a way of meeting and working with a child in her world. It is cross-cultural, requires neither that the child perform nor the therapist interpret, provides an enjoyable experience for the participants and serves as a pleasant introduction to therapy. The approach to assessment described in this chapter is designed for those working in private practice or agency settings where individual treatment of a child is being considered. It is also appropriate for use where group assessments are available but the child is not ready for group interaction, or where immediate treatment is not available (e.g., due to waiting lists). Implementing this model may provide interim treatment for a child awaiting more intensive, long-term therapy.

This model will provide the therapist with insight into the child's perception of his world. It is equally important to determine the context in which a child is situated by completing a child and family history and, where indicated, consulting with other treatment providers such as teachers, physicians, etc.

Goals

- To determine the most appropriate treatment approach (individual/family/group, art/play/other, directive/non-directive/combined, short/long term).
- To identify issues the child brings to therapy.
- To identify treatment goals.

Duration

This model consists of six to eight sessions. It is generally recommended that sessions be scheduled for one hour on a weekly basis. Flexibility in the length and frequency of sessions should take into consideration the age and stage of development of the child.

Population

This model has been developed for children aged three to twelve. Additional modifications to techniques outlined for each session may be required when working with children at either end of this age group or children with developmental delays, or physical or other disabilities. Other factors that might preclude individual treatment, such as ongoing or expected legal actions or parents' ability to pay for long-term therapy, should also be considered at the time of assessment. These factors will be addressed in the section entitled "Contra-indicators."

Structure

Over the course of the assessment the therapist will have the opportunity to observe and interact with the child in both directed and non-directed activities. Each session is organized around a specific theme and is designed to provide the therapist with information about various aspects of the child's life. Activities in each session are arranged to provide a natural flow within and between sessions. It has been our experience that this arrangement may need to be modified according to the child's needs, age, stage of development and attention span.

General format for all sessions:

- Free play portion (15–20 minutes)
- Story, snack and sharing portion (15–20 minutes)
- Directed art/play activity (15–20 minutes)

Depending on the age of the child, the time frames noted may need to be modified. Younger children have shorter attention spans and are generally less concerned with the outcome of their endeavours. Thus, the time spent on directed activities would be shortened while the free play period would be lengthened. The opposite is true for older children. Their need to give greater attention to detail and the more complex nature of the games they are able to participate in will require more time spent in directed activities and a free play period that is shorter. When working with older children the therapist may wish to shift the format, perhaps beginning with the directed art activity or game and ending with a brief period of free play. The table below outlines times for each of the activity periods for three age groupings.

Activity	Ages 4, 5, 6	Ages 7, 8, 9	Ages 10, 11, 12
Free play	30–40 min.	20–30 min.	10–15 min.
Story	10–15 min.	10–15 min.	10–15 min.
Art/Game	10–15 min.	15–20 min.	30–40 min.

The outline for each session includes:

- Organizing theme/objectives
- Activities for various ages/stages
- Materials for each activity
- Alternative themes/activities

Free Play: What To Look For

Free play provides the therapist with the opportunity to observe the child in unstructured, non-directed activities that facilitate open expression and sharing. In the assessment, interactions are limited to those initiated and directed by the child. During free play the therapist may wish to note the following:

Choice of materials/activities: type, repeated choice, single/varied, age appropriate, what is included/excluded, patterns.

Style of play: secretive, isolated, solo, parallel, interactive, directed (by child), symbolic, tactile, etc.

Themes: what they are and how they appear within and across sessions.

Interaction style: inclusive/exclusive, boundaries, age appropriateness.

Focus: ability to attend, duration, concentration, age appropriateness.

Affect: range, mode of expression, congruence with behaviours and verbalizations.

Verbalizations: speech and language skills, modulation, volume and intonation, silence, use of "baby talk" or other voices, other vocalizations.

Behaviour: patterns, extremes, age-inappropriate (too young/old) sexualized behaviour, violence, etc.

Motor skills: general mobility, ability to take physical risks, age appropriateness, fine and gross motor skill development, spatial awareness, spatial organization.

SESSION 1: GETTING ACQUAINTED

Free Play

Ages 4, 5, 6

Sand; water; play dough; dress-up clothes; guns; dolls; dollhouse (with figures and furniture); animals; cars; figures; army figures; crayons; markers and paper; puppets; rocking chair; rocking horse.

Ages 7, 8, 9

Sand; water; clay; dress-up clothes; dolls; dollhouse (with figures and furniture); cars; animals; crayons; markers and paper; puppets; simple board games; rocking horse; baseball bat and ball (nerf).

Ages 10, 11, 12

Sand; water; clay; dress-up clothes; dolls; dollhouse (with figures and furniture); cars; animals; crayons; markers and paper; puppets; board games; rocking horse; baseball bat and ball (nerf); pencil crayons; construction toys; face paint.

Story

Ages 4, 5, 6

The Paper Bag Princess, by Robert Munsch; *Gifts*, by Jo Ellen Bogart.

Ages 7 to 12

Erik the Viking Sheep, by Elizabeth Creith; *All I See*, by Cynthia Rylant.

Activity

Ages 4, 5, 6

Decorate art folder or envelope with picture of self.

Ages 7, 8, 9

Draw picture of self on art folder or envelope.

Ages 10, 11, 12

Make collage of self or symbols of self on art folder or envelope.

SESSION 2: SELF-CONCEPT

Free Play

Ages 4 to 12

Toys as before; mirror.

Story

Ages 4, 5, 6

Feelings, by Joan Murphy; *Rainbow Fish*, by Marcus Pfister; *The Very Quiet Cricket*, by Eric Carle.

Ages 7, 8, 9

Sticks and Stones, by Pierrette Dube; *I Know I'm Myself Because*, by Polly Greenburg.

Ages 10, 11, 12

The Girl Who Danced with Dolphins, by Frank De Saix; *The Short Tree and the Bird that Could Not Sing*, by Dennis Foon.

Activity

Ages 4, 5, 6

Paper plate me; body tracing; gingerbread body.

Ages 7, 8, 9

Paper bag puppet; picture of self as an animal; gift to self; mask of self.

Ages 10, 11, 12

Individual crest; self-portrait "the way I am"; self-portrait "the way I'd like to be"; gift to self; mask of self.

SESSION 3: THE FAMILY

Free Play

Ages 4 to 12

As in previous session; extra family figures.

Story

Ages 4, 5, 6

Let's Be Friends Again, by Hans Wilhelm; and *Alexander and the Terrible, Horrible, No Good, Very Bad Day*, by Judith Viorst.

Ages 7, 8, 9

Good Families Don't and *Love You Forever*, by Robert Munsch; *Alexander, Who Used To Be Rich last Sunday*, by Judith Viorst.

Ages 10, 11, 12

Love You Forever, by Robert Munsch; *Alexander, Who Used To Be Rich Last Sunday*, by Judith Viorst.

Activity

Ages 4, 5, 6

Family mobile; construction paper house and family members; picture of family.

Ages 7, 8, 9

Kinetic family drawing; family as animals; board games: Family Happenings, My Homes and Places.

Ages 10, 11, 12

Collage of family; family as symbols; family crest; board games: Family Happenings, My Homes and Places.

SESSION 4: SEXUAL ABUSE

Free Play

Ages 4 to 12

As in previous session.

Story

Ages 4, 5, 6

Secret of the Silver Horse, by Canadian Dept. of Justice; *No-No the Little Seal*, by Sheri Patterson..

Ages 7, 8, 9

Secret of the Silver Horse, by Canadian Dept. of Justice; *Am I the Only One?* by Dennis Foon.

Ages 10, 11, 12

Secret of the Silver Horse, by Canadian Dept. of Justice; *Am I the Only One?* by Dennis Foon; *Promise Not To Tell*, by Carolyn Polese.

Activity

Ages 4, 5, 6

Make a monster puppet; label body tracing with feelings; label gingerbread body with feelings.

Ages 7, 8, 9

Make a feelings booklet; draw a picture of something or someone that makes one feel scared; label gingerbread body with feelings.

Ages 10, 11, 12

Make a feelings booklet; draw a picture of a safe place; make a clay monster.

SESSION 5: ANGER/VIOLENCE

Free Play

Ages 4 to 12

As in previous session.

Story

Ages 4, 5, 6

Mommy and Daddy Are Fighting, by Susan Paris; *Land of Many Colours,* by Klamath County YMCA; *Temper Tantrum Book*, by E.M. Preston.

Ages 7, 8, 9

Mommy and Daddy Are Fighting, by Susan Paris; *Land of Many Colours*, by Klamath County YMCA; *Those Words*, by Frank Etherington.

Ages 10, 11, 12

Mommy and Daddy Are Fighting, by Susan Paris; *Something's Wrong at My House*, by Dianne Davis; *Never, No Matter What*, by Maryleah Otto.

Activity

Ages 4, 5, 6

My feelings book; draw picture of angry self; make an angry monster with clay.

Ages 7, 8, 9

Draw picture of anger in your house; the feelings booklet; shoebox "special" place.

Ages 10, 11, 12

Draw symbols of anger; shooting anger (self, parent, sibling); shoebox "special" place.

SESSION 6: LOSS

Free Play

Ages 4 to 12

As in previous sessions.

Story

Ages 4, 5, 6

I'll Always Love You, by Hans Wilhelm; *The Tenth Good Thing about Barney*, by Judith Viorst; *Moving Gives Me a Stomach Ache*, by Heather McKend.

Ages 7, 8, 9

I'll Always Love You, by Hans Wilhelm; *Moving Gives Me a Stomach Ache*, by Heather McKend; *Waiting for the Whales*, by Sheryl McFarlane.

Ages 10, 11, 12

Badger's Parting Gifts, by Susan Varley; *Waiting for the Whales*, by Sheryl McFarlane.

Activity

Ages 4, 5, 6

Puppet play of loss; draw a picture of yourself the day you lost___; draw a picture of the funeral of ___; draw a picture of yourself when you are sad.

Ages 7, 8, 9

Puppet play of loss; draw a picture of yourself the day you lost___; draw a picture of the funeral of___; draw a picture of your family before the loss and in the future.

Ages 10, 11, 12

Draw a picture of your family before the loss, now, and in the future; draw a picture of how it feels to lose something/someone; draw a picture of what happens after death.

SESSION 7: SUBSTANCE ABUSE

Free Play

Ages 4 to 12

As in previous sessions.

Story

Ages 4, 5, 6

I Wish Daddy Didn't Drink So Much, by Judy Vigna.

Ages 7, 8, 9

My Mom Drinks Too Much, by Kenny and Krull.

Ages 10, 11, 12

My Mom Drinks Too Much, by Kenny and Krull.

Activity

Ages 4, 5, 6

Puppet, sand or dollhouse play of a time when a parent was intoxicated.

Ages 7, 8, 9

Role play of child and adult in drinking setting; Scribble game; board game: Family Happenings; picture of family.

Ages 10, 11, 12

Role play of child and adult in drinking setting; adult/adult in drinking setting; Scribble game; board game: Family Happenings.

SESSION 8: SEPARATION & DIVORCE

Free Play

Ages 4 to 12

As in previous sessions; additional dollhouse (optional).

Story

Ages 4, 5, 6

Do I Have a Daddy, by Jean Warren Lindsay; *Now I Have a Step-parent*, by Janet Stenson; *Daddy Doesn't Live Here Anymore*, by Betty Boegehold.

Ages 7, 8, 9

Now I Have a Step-parent, by Janet Stenson; *Please Come Home*, by D. Sanford; *Two Homes To Live In*, by Barbara Hazen.

Ages 10, 11, 12

Now I Have a Step-parent, by Janet Stenson; *Two Homes To Live In*, by Barbara Hazen; *Jennifer Has Two Daddies*, by Patricia Galloway.

Activity

Ages 4, 5, 6

My family and my other family booklet; a two-sided construction house and family.

Ages 7, 8, 9

My family and my other family booklet; make a "Missing You" card; board game: My Homes and Places.

Ages 10, 11, 12

Make a "Missing You" card; board game: My Homes and Places; board game: The Divorce Game.

SESSION 9: PEER RELATIONSHIPS

Free Play

Ages 4 to 12

As in previous sessions.

Story

Ages 4, 5, 6

Brenda's Private Swing, by Bernice Chardiet; *Rainbow Fish*, by Marcus Pfister; *Sticks and Stones*, by Pierrette Dube.

Ages 7, 8, 9

No More Bullying, by Rosemary Stones; *Rainbow Fish*, by Marcus Pfister; *Sticks and Stones*, by Pierrette Dube.

Ages 10, 11, 12

The Very Best of Friends, by Margaret Wild and J. Vivas; *Martin and the Teacher's Pets*, by Bernice Chardiet and Grace Maccarone.

Activity

Ages 4, 5, 6

Make a best friend puppet; draw picture of favourite place to play; make a friend mobile.

Ages 7, 8, 9

Make a friend mobile; draw an imaginary friend; draw picture of self playing with friends; draw picture of self at school.

Ages 10, 11, 12

Make a friend mobile; draw picture of self and best friend; draw picture of self at school; draw picture of friends as animals.

SESSION 10: THE FUTURE

Free Play

Ages 4 to 12

As in previous sessions.

Story

Ages 4, 5, 6

Leo, the Late Bloomer, by Robert Kraus; *I'll Love You Forever*, by Robert Munsch.

Ages 7 to 12

Waiting for the Whales, by Shirley McFarlane; *The Girl Who Danced with Dolphins*, by Frank DeSaix.

Activity

Ages 4, 5, 6

Draw picture of self as grown up; role-play self as a teen; role-play self as an adult; make a time capsule.

Ages 7, 8, 9

Make a time capsule; booklet of self as baby, now, and as an adult; draw picture of your three wishes.

Ages 10, 11, 12

Make a time capsule; picture of self now and in the future; draw picture of your three wishes; imagine you won a million dollars and role-play what you would do.

* * *

Story, Snack and Sharing

The sharing of story and snack is a way to transit the gap between non-directive and directive activities. The therapist chooses a story determined by the topic accorded to the session. The child is invited to share a snack provided by the therapist. The therapist encourages discussion and asks questions to further explore the topic. A comfortable atmosphere of eating, reading and dialogue is created.

During story, snack and sharing the therapist may better note the following:

- Additional theme exploration
- Child's world view
- Child's ability to give and receive nurturing
- Communication skills/style, receptive and expressive
- Language
- Cognitive development
- Relational capacity skills
- Attention span, listening
- Social skills
- Personal boundaries

Directed Art/Play Activities

Directed activities provide the therapist with information about how the child responds to structure, direction, specific topics and types of activities. The art projects and games are selected by the therapist and may be activities the child is neither familiar with nor friendly towards. Activities are success oriented and are structured to provide the child with new information and experiences. Directed activities will assist in the assessment of the following:

Ego strength

- Familiarity with and response to rules, direction and structure
- Topic exploration and response to specific cues
- Communications skills
- Interpersonal and cooperative skills
- Motor skills
- Flexibility, risk-taking, trust and ability to predict
- Task completion
- Identification of emotional/psychological triggers
- Determination of child's experience of trauma/stress

Directed Activities

Some of the activities given below have been used in the sample sessions provided.

Paper plate me

Using a paper plate and a variety of graphic and construction materials, children create a face/mask of themselves. Children may talk about or from the mask.

Body tracing

The child lies on a large sheet of paper and is traced by the therapist. The child then paints or colours his body. Feeling labels may be attached in a later session.

Gingerbread body

The child traces a gingerbread body shape onto construction paper and decorates it to look like herself. Feeling labels may be attached in a later session.

Paper bag puppets

Using paper bags with square bottoms, and a variety of graphic and construction materials, the child creates a puppet of himself or a friend.

Collage of self
Using pictures from magazines, posters, etc. children create a collage that tells about themselves—their likes, dislikes.

Collage of family
Children cut pictures from magazines, posters etc. to create a family collage.

Kinetic family drawing
Children are asked to draw a picture of their family, including themselves. May use pencils, crayons or markers and the paper should be relatively large.

My family as animals
After the child draws each family member as an animal, the therapist asks the child to talk about her perceptions of the animals.

My friends as animals
After the child draws each of his friends as an animal, the therapist asks the him to talk about his perceptions of the animals.

Family mobile
Children can draw and cut out family members from tag board or construction paper. They can then decorate each person and suspend them all from a coat hanger to form a mobile. Younger children will find tracers of various sizes and shapes helpful.

Individual crest
The child is asked to think about and draw symbols of himself. This can be directive if the therapist focuses the child on past, present or future symbols.

Family crest
As above, with family symbols.

Gift to self
The child is asked to make a box, decorate it, and put symbols of good things about herself inside.

Mask of self
The child forms a mask out of plaster of Paris, using a balloon or pre-formed mask base. He then paints and decorates the mask symbolically.

Construction paper house and family
Using construction paper of various colours and shapes, children construct a house. They then choose pre-cut figures of family members and place appropriate "feeling faces" on them. It is important to have a variety of sizes and shapes of figures available, as well as a large variety of "feeling faces."

Two-sided construction paper house and family
As above, with each side representing a parental home.

Shoebox special place
Using a shoebox and a variety of constructive materials, child creates a fantasy special place. The therapist encourages child to talk about what makes it special.

Shooting anger picture
In the centre of a large piece of paper, the children draw an angry person (self, parent etc.). The child is then asked to draw anger radiating out from the centre. Around the outside, the child draws the person whom the anger affects.

Time capsule
The child is asked to make a small box and fill it with descriptors of himself, symbols of himself, favourite things.

Scribble game
The child and therapist take turns starting a scribble that they then take turns completing. The person who starts the scribble then guesses what the completed drawing is.

Contra-indicators
There are times when a child's involvement in individual assessment and therapy are contra-indicated. It is the responsibility of the assessing therapist to determine, either in consultation with the members of a multi-disciplinary team, family members or other involved professionals, which, if any, of the factors listed below apply. Generally the existence of multiple factors would suggest that involvement with the child be deferred until such time as her situation has improved. However, the presence of any single factor may also indicate the need to re-examine the appropriateness and timing of the referral and to consider excluding certain, related topics/sessions:

- Custody has not been decided and one or more parent views the assessment as a source of support for their "side."
- The child is involved in an on-going abuse investigation.
- The child continues to live with an untreated perpetrator of abuse.
- The parents or others hope to find a label for the child.
- The parents or others attempt to address larger systems issues (family, social, etc.) by identifying the child as the problem.
- The parents hope to improve their own mental health through the child's therapy.
- The parents or others have an agenda other than assessment and treatment.
- The child is at risk of self-harm and a risk assessment has not been completed.
- The parents are unwilling or unable to respect the confidentiality of the therapeutic relationship.
- The parents are unwilling or unable to guarantee the child's regular attendance.

Summary

This individual play/art therapy assessment model is a flexible framework that covers a broad age range of clientele. The activities and games outlined in the model may be modified and new activities may be substituted. The model may be implemented in a variety of therapeutic settings. This model provides the therapist with an effective assessment tool while meeting the developmental and psychological needs of the child.

BIBLIOGRAPHY

Boegehold, B. (1985). *Daddy doesn't live here anymore*. New York: Western Publishing Company, Inc.

Bogart, J. (1994). *Gifts*. Richmond Hill: North Winds Press.

Bourgois, P. (1993). *Franklin and the dark*. Toronto: Kids Can Press.

Bourgois, P. (1993). *Franklin gets bossy*. Toronto: Kids Can Press.

Bourgois, P. (1993). *Franklin plays the game*. Toronto: Kids Can Press.

Brett, J. (1989). *The mitten*. New York: Scholastic.

Canadian Department of Justice. (1989). *The secret of the silver horse*. Ottawa: Communications and Public Affairs.

Carle, E. (1997). *The very quiet cricket*. New York: Philomel Books.

Chardiet, B. (1991). *Brenda's private swing*. New York: Scholastic.

Chardiet, B. & Maccarone, G. (1991). *Martin and the teacher's pets*. Toronto: Scholastic.

Creith, E. (1997). *Erik the Viking sheep*. Toronto: Scholastic Canada Ltd.

Davis, D. (1989). *Something is wrong at my house*. Seattle: Parenting Press.

De Saix, F. (1990). *The girl who danced with dolphins*. New York: Farrar, Straus & Giroux, Inc.

Dube, P. (1993). *Sticks and stones*. Toronto: Scholastic Canada Ltd.

Etherington, F. (1982). *Those words*. Toronto: Annick Press.

Fernandes, E. (1987). *The difficult day*. Toronto: Kids Can Press.

Foon, D. (1985). *Am I the only one?* Vancouver: Douglas & McIntyre.

Foon, D. (1986). *The short tree and the bird that could not sing*. Toronto: Meadow Mouse Paperback.

Galloway, P. (1985). *Jennifer has two daddies*. Toronto: The Women's Press.

Gilmore, R. (1988). *My mother is weird*. Charlottetown: Ragweed Press.

Greenburg, P. (1986). *I know myself because*. New York: Human Sciences Press.

Greenspan, S. (1981). *The challenging child*. Boulder, CO: Perseus Publishing.

Hazen, B. (1983). *Two homes to live in*. New York: Human Sciences Press.

Kenny, K. & Krull, H. (1992). *My mom drinks too much*. Austin: Raintree Sech-Vaugh Publishing.

Klamath County YMCA. (1993). *The land of many colours*. New York: Scholastic.

Kraus, R. (1981). *Leo, the late bloomer*. Southold, NY: Windmill Books.

Mayer, M. (1983). *I was so mad*. New York: Western Pub. Co.

Mayer, M. (1983). *Just go to bed*. New York: Western Pub. Co.

Mayer, M. (1983). *What a bad dream*. New York: Western Pub. Co.

Mayer, M. (1988). *I just forgot*. New York: Western Pub. Co.

McFarlane, S. (1991). *Waiting for the whales*. Victoria: Orca Book Publishers.

McKend, H. (1988). *Moving gives me a stomach ache.* Windsor: Black Moss Press.

Munsch, R. (1980). *The paper bag princess.* Toronto: Annick Press.

Munsch, R. (1990). *Good families don't.* Toronto: Doubleday Canada Ltd.

Munsch, R. (1995). *From far away.* Toronto: Annick Press.

Munsch, R. (2000). *Love you forever.* Buffalo, NY: Firefly Books Ltd.

Munsch, R., & Kusugak, M. (1988). *A promise is a promise.* Toronto: Annick Press.

Murphy, J. (1988). *Feelings.* Windsor: Black Moss Press.

Oaklander, V. (1969). *Windows to our children.* Highland, NY: Gestalt Journal Press.

O'Connor, K. (1991). *The play therapy primer.* New York: John Wiley & Sons Inc.

Otto, M. (1988). *Never, no matter what.* Toronto: The Women's Press.

Paris, S. (1986). *Mommy and Daddy are fighting.* Seattle: Seal Press.

Patterson, S. (1982). *No-no the little seal.* New York: Random House.

Pfister, M. (1992). *Rainbow fish.* New York: North-South Books.

Polese, C. (1985). *Promise not to tell.* New York: Human Sciences Press, Inc.

Preston, E. (1976). *The temper tantrum book.* New York: Puffin Books.

Rylant, C. (1988). *All I see.* New York: Orchard Books.

Sanford, D. (1985). *Please come home.* Portland: Multnomah Press.

Slater, T. (1988). *Molly's monsters.* New York: Grosset & Dunlap.

Stenson, J. (1979). *Now I have a step-parent.* New York: Avon.

Stones, R. (1992). *No more bullying.* London: Harper Collins.

Varley, S. (1985). *Badger's parting gifts.* London: Harper Collins.

Vigna, J. (1988). *I wish daddy didn't drink so much.* Morton Grove, IL: Albert Whitman & Co.

Viorst, J. (1971). *The tenth good thing about Barney.* New York: Aladdin Paperbacks.

Viorst, J. (1972). *Alexander and the terrible horrible no good very bad day.* New York: Aladdin Paperbacks.

Viorst, J. (1978). *Alexander, who used to be rich last Sunday.* New York: Atheneum.

Warren Lindsay, J. (1982). *Do I have a daddy.* Buena Park, CA: Morning Glory Press.

Wild, M. & Vivas, J. (1989). *The very best of friends.* Toronto: Kids Can Press.

Wilhelm, H. (1986). *Let's be friends again.* Toronto: Scholastic.

Wilhelm, H. (1990). *I'll always love you.* Toronto: Scholastic.

Wise Brown, M. (1947). *Goodnight moon.* Mexico: Harper& Row.

CHAPTER TWELVE

USING PLAY AND ART THERAPY TO WORK WITH FAMILIES

Bridget Revell

USING PLAY AND ART THERAPY TO WORK WITH FAMILIES

Play and art therapy have demonstrated the benefits of using play and art to encourage communication, explore issues and facilitate growth and healing in individual clients. Family therapy has shown us how the family group influences and affects each and every member of a family, including the children. For years the two fields of play therapy and family therapy remained distinct, each with their own proponents, theories, guidelines and followers. Thankfully, in recent years, therapists have begun moving between these two camps and attempts are being made to marry their approaches. The purpose of this chapter is to provide practical suggestions for how therapists can further develop the relationship between play therapy and family therapy through using play and art in their work with families.

It is essential for therapists using play and art with families to have a grasp of basic play therapy theory and family systems theory. However, providing that background is beyond the scope of this chapter. Readers are encouraged to review standard texts in both fields and familiarize themselves with the underlying theories (Axline, 1969; Gil, 1991; Gil, 1994; Minuchin, 1974; Landreth, 1991; O'Connor, 1991; Satir, 1983; Schaefer & O'Connor, 1983; Wachtel, 1994). The purpose of this chapter is not to argue the relative merits of child vs. family therapy or individual vs. systems therapy but to provide suggestions for linking these approaches.

This chapter will explore four main questions:

1) When should we work with families?
2) Why should we use play and art to work with families?
3) How can we use play and art to work with families?
4) What challenges will we face when we use play and art with families?

At the end of the chapter, a case example will illustrate how play and art were used to meet the therapeutic goals of one particular family.

When Should We Work with Families?

"Problematic behaviour in children expresses individual concerns and defence mechanisms on the one hand and family systems issues and family defence operations on the other." (Wachtel, 1994, p. 18).

The children that we meet in therapy settings are children and they are individuals. Given that they are children, we must greet them and work with them using the language and interventions that they can understand: play. Given that they are individuals we must recognize that they have their own personal thoughts, feelings, ideas and concerns. These must be listened to. For these reasons, many therapists choose to work individually with children using play therapy.

However, the children that we meet are also part of a family. The family children are born into, live with, and interact with on a day-to-day basis has a profound impact on who children are, how they express themselves, what feelings they communicate and how they behave. We cannot ignore the importance of what the child's family has taught him about life, relationships and behaviour. As a result, many therapists choose to work with children and families together.

As therapists, using our assessment of the situation and our therapeutic goals, we must decide to work with a given child individually or with her family. Many therapists balance these approaches, providing a combination of individual and family sessions. Family sessions may involve a variety of groupings of family members. The entire family may be seen together, children may be seen with one parent, with both parents or with siblings. Separate sessions may be held that include only the child's parents.

Working with Issues that are Important to the Family as a Whole

We can work with issues that are important to the family as a whole, since families go through many experiences together. At times, these experiences prove stressful for the entire family, and therapy can be used as a way of working through the issues associated with the stressful event. For example, family work may be beneficial when parents have separated or divorced, when a significant family member or friend has died, when family members are locked into conflict with each other or when the family has undergone trauma together (e.g., earthquake or house fire).

Working with Individual Issues that Affect the Family

Many issues that have a primary effect on an individual also affect that person's family. For example, when a woman loses her job this can be a significant issue for her, but it also has an impact on her partner and children. Similarly, if a child is paralyzed in an accident, the child will have many individual adjustments to make, but the family will also struggle to accommodate the new situation. In such situations, individual therapy may be beneficial to assist the affected individual in coming to terms with his experience, while working with the family allows for an exploration of the impact of the situation on all family members and their relationship with each other.

Relationship Building

Family members interact and relate to each other on a daily basis. Many families that we work with experience difficulty in communicating with each other and enjoying each other's company. Frequently, individuals have reached a point where they feel that they do not know or understand the other person in their family. Family sessions can be effective tools for re-acquainting family members with each other and for facilitating the development of relationships among them. Such sessions can also be used when new members join the family through marriage, fostering or adoption.

When Should Other Interventions Be Considered?

Family sessions should be avoided in any situation where they will do more harm than good for any member of the family. The safety of all family members should be considered when undertaking family sessions. Family sessions should never be pursued if family members would be at risk of physical or emotional abuse as a result of the feelings they shared, questions they asked or statements they made during the session. In cases where family members may be at risk of physical or emotional abuse as a result of participation in family sessions, individual work and work with subgroups within the family is recommended until the risk is no longer present.

Family sessions can pose a risk for children if the children are consistently and repeatedly exposed to information pertaining to the intimate relationships among the adults in their lives. For example, children should not be given details about, drawn into or asked to take sides in the conflicts between their caregivers. Similarly, it is inappropriate for a child to be provided with details regarding the sexual relationships between their caregivers and others. In some situations, family sessions can be structured through the use of play so that such issues are not raised. However, if repeated discussion of these issues cannot be avoided, family sessions are contraindicated.

Family sessions will be most effective when family members perceive a need to change and are committed to working towards that change. If an impasse is reached, where the therapist is continually justifying and explaining the rationale behind family work and little else is being accomplished, consideration should be given to working with individuals or subgroups within the family.

A therapist who undertakes work with a family must recognize that the family is made up of unique individuals. Family work may not provide the opportunity that a child or adult in the family needs to explore his or her own personal questions and issues. Individual work may need to be pursued in conjunction with family-based interventions to provide these opportunities.

Why Should We Use Play and Art To Work with Families?

The healing properties of play have been outlined in *The Therapeutic Powers of Play* (Schaefer, 1993). It is noted that play enables us to: deal with resistance, facilitate communication, develop a sense of mastery and control, promote creativity, express and release emotions, try out new ways of being through role-play, establish and enhance relationships, explore fantasy, make use of metaphoric teaching, and have fun. Therapists who welcome play into family sessions are able to make use of each of these therapeutic characteristics of play. A brief overview is provided below of some of the most powerful uses of play in family sessions.

As play therapists have discovered, the language that children best speak is the language of play (Axline, 1969; Gil, 1974; Landreth, 1991; Schaefer, 1993). Children can say through play and artwork things that they could never articulate using spoken words. Work with adults using art and sand play has shown that they can also use play to explore complex concepts and issues that they may be unable to verbalize (Bradway *et al*, 1990; Furth, 1988; Mitchell & Friedman, 1994). The ability of play to facilitate communication quickly on many levels is one of its greatest advantages in family sessions (Gil, 1994).

In order to ensure the involvement of all family members in sessions, interventions must be planned at the level of the lowest common denominator, a level that allows everyone in the family to understand and participate. When children are present in session, restricting interventions to verbal interactions may exclude them or limit their involvement. When play- or art-based interventions are introduced, children are able to comfortably participate on an equal basis with others in the family. By using play, therapists "treat children as equally important family members, with valuable information to provide and assimilate" (Gil, 1994. p.41).

When a family plays games they haven't played before, in a way and place they haven't played them before, they learn things about themselves that they haven't learned before (Gil, 1994; Kobak & Waters, 1984). Working with families using play and art allows them to look at, see and understand things differently. This in turn allows them to change, grow and develop.

Through introducing play or art activities and observing how family members respond to them, therapists are able to assess many different dimensions of family functioning. For example, when a family is asked to complete a task as a group, the therapist can consider:

> Who takes charge of organizing the activity?
> Do others listen to this person?
> What happens when family members disagree?
> How do they show their disagreement?
> Is someone left out?
> Who talks to whom?
> Who listens to whom?
> When do problems arise?
> How do family members handle these problems?

Based on their observations, the therapist will be able to develop hypotheses about the family's communication patterns, roles, hierarchies, alliances, boundaries and negotiation skills (Gil, 1994; Wachtel, 1994). Similarly, if family members are asked to work on a task individually, the therapist can assess how family members handle parallel but separate activities, when family members seek each other out and how family members respond to interruptions (Wachtel, 1994).

When a therapist introduces play or art into sessions, the family is less likely to know what to expect. This allows the therapist to assess how family members handle unexpected situations. Furthermore, the family will not be able to prepare in advance or manipulate the session to create a particular impression for the therapist.

Art and play can be used to structure family sessions and to meet specific therapeutic goals. For example, in families where a great deal of verbal conflict is present, the therapist may ask that they complete a play activity in silence. If the therapist has established a goal to further develop the relationship between a girl and her mother, they may be asked to work on a puppet play together while the father and other children observe. When working with families who continually interrupt and speak on top of each other, a rule can be established that only the person holding a particular ball, stuffed animal or rock may speak. Rules of interaction are changed if play, art and discussion are used together in family sessions. The therapist has an opportunity to structure these rules in a way that meets the needs of the family.

Play is something that everyone has done and everyone can do. When play is introduced as a way of helping the family, it can be empowering for caregivers who feel that they have the skills required by the therapist to help their child.

Interventions involving play and art allow the family to have fun. Many families that participate in therapy have been under stress and experiencing difficulty for some time. They have often forgotten how to experience joy in each other's company (Wachtel, 1994, p. 47). Through the use of play, opportunities can be provided for family members to laugh and enjoy time together. Generating this laughter may prove to be the most therapeutic aspect of our work with families.

How Can We Use Play and Art To Work with Families?

Play and art can be used in two main ways during family sessions:

> Play and art activities may be used to provide a description of family events (e.g., the family is instructed to use the dollhouse to demonstrate the fight they had).
>
> Play and art can be used to create metaphors that allow symbolic exploration of the family's underlying issues (e.g., a couple is asked to draw a road that represents their relationship).

When play and art are introduced into family sessions, the therapist may choose to have the family work together on a single task or may suggest that each family member pursue the task individually and later share it with the group. The instructions given by the therapist will be determined by the established treatment goals.

Play- and art-based interventions can be designed to meet many of the goals of therapists who work with families. Some common goals of therapeutic work with families are listed below with ideas for play- and art-based interventions that can be used to pursue that goal. The list is designed to suggest ideas and promote creativity. It is in no way exhaustive or definitive. Many other goals and activities may be pursued by therapists working with families and the activities listed below can be structured in different ways to meet other treatment goals.

Assessment

Formalized ways of using art, puppetry and sand play have been outlined in detail by writers in the fields of play and art therapy and will not be reviewed here (Burns & Kaufman, 1970; Gil, 1994; Mitchell & Friedman, 1994; Ross, 1991; Rubin & Magnussen, 1979).

During an initial session, non-directive play can provide detailed information about the family. For example, a therapist can invite a family into the playroom and ask them to play for half an hour. The family's play can be observed through a one-way mirror or the therapist may sit to one side in the playroom. By paying attention to what family members play with, whom they play with, how they play, and what themes are present in their play, the therapist will learn about the family.

The tools of sand play, a small sandbox and many miniature items (see Mitchell & Friedman, 1994), can also be used for obtaining information about family interactions. The family can be presented with the sandbox and toys and asked to create a picture or a story. A wealth of information is available through watching how the family proceeds with this task. Is the sandbox divided so that each family member can work individually in a designated space? Does one particular person direct the process of creating the scene? Are items that are placed into the sandbox by one person removed by another? Is this done with or without the other person's consent? Consideration of these and other questions will allow the therapist to use the family's sand play as an assessment tool.

When a family is struggling with a particular issue (e.g., a child not completing his chores), role-play, work in the sandbox or puppetry can be used to have families illustrate the difficulties they are facing (Ross, 1991). Potential solutions and alternative ways of approaching the problem can be incorporated into the family's work. For example, a sandbox could be divided into two and a mother and son could each be instructed to set up a scene in the sandbox that illustrates what it was like when the mother asked the son to clean up his room. These two scenes can be used as a way of understanding each person's perspective and of generating potential solutions.

Storytelling can also provide insight into family situations. Family members can be asked individually or as a group to tell a story about a particular event (e.g., "when our house burned down") or to focus on a particular theme (e.g., "our family having fun"). The opening line of a story can be given to the family, such as "Once upon a time there was a squiggle . . ." or "Once upon a time there was an egg . . ." and they can be asked to finish the story with each family member contributing a line as they go around the circle. By examining the themes, conflicts, problems and solutions found in the story, the therapist will come to better understand the family.

Nurturing

In many families the skills of nurturing each other have been forgotten or were never learned. Troubled children and troubled adults often crave nurturing. Play-based interventions can be used to meet some of these needs while developing and reinforcing the skills that make it possible for family members to nurture each other in a safe way outside of therapy sessions.

Theraplay, a therapy based on the "intimacy and physical interplay that characterize normal relationships between mother and child" (Jernberg, 1979, front cover), places emphasis on nurturing activities. "The purpose of Nurturing activities is to communicate to the child that he can get what he needs without always having to work for it, deny the existence of the need for it, or be rejected for expressing the need" (Jernberg, 1979, p. 47). A wide variety of nurturing activities is part of Theraplay, including feeding, back and tummy rubs, applying lotion and baby powder, singing and cuddling (Jernberg, 1979). Another nurturing activity that has been used by parents and children for generations and can be brought into family sessions is reading and storytelling.

Nurturing activities can be made part of any family session. Ending sessions with nurturing activities allows the family members to leave the session with positive feelings and with the understanding that they can meet each other's needs and feel good about each other.

In some families, where caregivers have not had their needs met, the children may assume responsibility for nurturing their caregivers. If this situation arises, the therapist should structure the use of nurturing activities so that this pattern is not reinforced in session. For example, the therapist can teach the nurturing activity to the caregiver and then have the caregiver repeat the technique with the child. Therapists may also choose to nurture everyone in the family through reading or telling a story to them.

Individuality

It is important that family members recognize and respect others in the family as unique individuals with their own thoughts and feelings. Assigning individual art tasks (e.g., "Draw three things that make you happy" or "Draw your wishes for the next year") that are later discussed as a group allows the therapist to emphasize the separateness of family members. Family members can be directed to individually complete creative visualization exercises that have been outlined by several writers (Allan, 1988; Barnes & Revell, 1995; Oaklander, 1978). When this work is completed individually and then shared with the group, similarities and differences among family members are highlighted.

When family members recognize and value each other's uniqueness, this can help with the development of self-esteem and facilitate nurturing. Family members may be asked to end a session by talking about one thing they like about others in the family or one thing they feel other family members do well. Barnes and Revell (1995) outline a number of "joining" activities that are designed to "help people connect with, relate to and enjoy each other" (p. 83). These include development of a secret handshake, touching fingers while sharing positive attributes, and sharing positive memories. These activities can become a useful addition to family sessions.

Other play and art activities that can be used to emphasize individuality are described below:

1) Room sides.
The therapist calls out a few characteristics (e.g., brown hair, plays hockey, male, child) and asks all people that meet the characteristics to go to one side of the room and all the people who do not meet the characteristics to go to the other side of the room. The therapist can structure this activity to emphasize the difference between two enmeshed individuals or to point out similarities between two people who maintain a distant relationship.

2) First word
The family is shown a picture and each person is asked to call out or write down the first word that comes into their minds. Often one image will arouse different associations for different people. This allows the therapist to point out their client's individuality.

3) Typical day interview
Eliana Gil (1994) describes in detail the use of "typical day interview." Clients are asked to select a day of the week. They are next asked to select dollhouse figures to represent the people they live with. The therapist then leads the client through a re-enactment of his day using the dollhouse figures. This can provide a great deal of information about family members while emphasizing differences in their days.

Feelings Expression
Many different activities designed to explore feelings have been documented in the play and art therapy literature (Allan, 1988; Oaklander, 1978; Schaefer & O'Connor, 1983). Many of these activities can be successfully used in family groups. Examples of specific activities are provided below. In each instance, family members may be asked to work individually or together.

1) Feelings pictures
Family members are asked to draw a picture reflecting how they felt at a certain time, e.g., "Can you each take a piece of paper and draw me a picture of how you felt when Gramma died?"

2) Colours as feelings
Family members are asked to depict their feelings using scribbles of different colours, e.g., "I would like to know how everyone is feeling today. Can you each take a piece of paper and some crayons and scribble with the colours that show me how you are feeling?"

3) Feelings graphs
Family members are asked to make a list of all the feelings they had at a particular time (e.g., when the house burned down). These feelings are then written along the bottom of a piece of paper. At this point, family members are asked to make a line showing how big each feeling is.

4) Feelings masks
As a group, family members are asked to make a list of all the feelings they have and are then instructed to make paper plate masks to represent these feelings. After the masks have been made, they can be used in role-plays to explore when feelings are experienced by family members and how they are expressed: e.g., "I would like each of you to pick a mask to work with today. I want you to hold the mask in front of your face, tell me what you are feeling and why you are feeling that way." Or, " I want everyone to have a chance with the sad mask. Hold it in front of your face and show me what you do when you are sad." Masks and role-play can also be used to help family members develop more appropriate ways of expressing emotions.

5) What I need
Family members are asked to draw pictures depicting what they need when they are experiencing a certain emotion; e.g., "Please draw pictures of what would help you feel better when you are feeling sad."

6) Letting people know
For this exercise, family members are asked to draw a picture illustrating how they show that they are feeling a certain emotion (love, anger, sadness etc.). "Can you all draw me a picture of how you tell your family that you love them?" Completing this exercise can be instructive. Family members may learn that something they saw as an everyday action, Dad bringing ice cream home, is really his way of saying "I love you."

Family identity
Sometimes therapists may wish to help families understand who they are as a family and what it means for them to be a family. This work will involve exploring who is in the family and then developing a sense of the family members as a unit.

Who is the family?
A number of art tasks can provide therapists with an understanding of who is considered to be part of the family. Individually, family members may be asked to draw a picture of their family or a picture of their family doing something (Burns and Kaufman, 1970; Gil, 1994). A good understanding of family members can be obtained by asking the family members to depict their family as animals (Oaklander, 1978). Family sculpture has been outlined by a number of writers as a valuable technique for exploring family relationships (Gil 1994; Holman, 1983; Satir, 1972). As a homework task, the family could be asked to keep a journal detailing family activities.

Family tree and family history.
The therapist can direct the creation of a family tree or genogram including grandparents, aunts, uncles, cousins etc. (Holman, 1983). The family may be asked to work on a book depicting the history of their family, including where family members were born, where they have travelled to, how they met, the things they did, etc. Through these tasks, the family will learn more about who they are and where they have come from, while the therapist can obtain valuable information about significant figures and supportive resources in the extended family.

Then and now pictures.
Individually or as a group, family members are asked to draw a picture of their family at two different times (e.g., before and after a divorce, before and after the death of a significant family member). This task can be used at the end of therapy to emphasize the changes the family has experienced as a result of the therapeutic process.

Wishes for the family.
Each family member can be given the opportunity to make a wish for the family. This may be done verbally, as a drawing or through role-play. The therapist can structure this task by asking the family to draw a picture representing something that they would like the family to start doing, stop doing, do more of, or change.

Family coat of arms or family song.
As a group, the family is asked to create a product that reflects who they are and what is unique and valuable about them as a family.

Family supports

One of our therapeutic goals, when working with individuals and families, is to help clients become more aware of the personal resources and supports that are available to them on a day-to-day basis. This goal can be pursued with family groups in a number of different ways.

Our community.

A family could be asked to make a map of their community and to use coloured dots to mark the resources and supports that are available. This could be done by using one dot colour for the family; or each individual could be given his or her own colour. If each individual is given a colour, it is expected that everyone would mark some places on the map (e.g., family doctor, police station). This will emphasize that the family shares some resources, while others are specific to a particular individual. This exercise could also be conducted in the sandbox, with miniature items being used to represent resources in the community.

Family ecomap.

Holman (1983) describes in detail the use of a family ecomap. A circle is placed in the centre of a paper to represent the family. Family members can be drawn or their names written in the circle. Supports or resources available to the family are drawn or depicted around the edge of the paper. Some of these resources will support the entire family, while others will be used by individual family members. Lines can be drawn from the family circle or from the individual family members to the various resources in order to depict the relationship between them.

Having fun as a family

As mentioned earlier, many family members need a chance to have fun together and to enjoy each other's company. Family sessions involving play and art are a wonderful opportunity to create this experience. The therapist can provide music and ask the family to dance together or provide instruments and ask the family to make music together. Active games such as Charades, Twister or Pictionary are another way to promote fun. Art activities that can meet the goal of "having fun" may include finger painting to music, slapping handprints on paper, or drawing a picture piece by piece as a family with each person contributing his or her piece while blindfolded. When the therapist is designing activities to provide the family with a "fun" experience, the activity in and of itself is therapeutic and follow-up discussion is usually kept to a minimum, since it would detract from the fun moment.

Working together
In situations where significant conflict or competition has arisen between family members, activities can be designed to foster cooperation and working together. Any time that a therapist instructs a family to work as a group, opportunities for cooperation are generated. If the facilities are available, the therapist could ask the family to bake together. Other examples of joint tasks include painting a mural (Rubin & Magnussen, 1979), joint finger-painting, or creating a board game. Family members could each be given a set of blocks and challenged as a group to make a tower that reaches to the ceiling.

The ways that play and art can be used in family sessions are endless. The only limitation is the creativity of the therapist.

The Challenges of Using Play when Working with Families

This family won't play
Many therapists express concerns about using play and art with families, fearing that the family will not be willing to play. While this may initially be true, many families come to recognize the value of the play activities over time. The therapist can encourage the family to play in a number of different ways:

1) Explain the process.
Family members will be more willing to play if they can recognize the value of the activities being suggested by the therapist. Many parents are willing to pursue play and art activities in order to help their child, once they understand how and why "just playing" is helpful.

2) Start simply.
Many individuals are reluctant to pursue activities if they feel they will not succeed. As a result, initial tasks assigned to family members should guarantee success; these tasks should be easy and should not require an explicit finished product. In addition, if the family members are asked to work as a group or in pairs, they may feel less conscious of

their own contribution. Examples of initial tasks include scribbling colours on paper, building towers out of blocks, finger-painting to music or dancing.

3) Show them what you mean.
In order for family members to be comfortable playing, they must know that they are in the presence of a therapist who is also comfortable playing. The therapist must be willing to energetically demonstrate, participate and encourage family members in their play. If a therapist wants a family to dance to music, the therapist should be found in the middle of the room demonstrating silly dance steps and asking others to join in.

4) Make sure the family can do what you ask.
If family members do not have the skills required to complete the play or art activity suggested, significant difficulty may arise. For example, asking a family to represent their feelings as colours will not work if one family member is colour blind. Tasks involving reading or writing should be avoided, if literacy is a concern. Similarly, having family members release energy by shouting may be overwhelming if one family member is sensitive to loud noises.

As much as possible, make sure that the activities designed fit the family style, values and strengths (Wachtel, 1994). Therapists must always be ready to adjust their plan if family members are unable to complete the suggested task. If family members have concern about their ability to finish a task "successfully," some pressure can be taken off them by asking them not to work "too hard" or by giving them a limited time to work in.

"I don't know what to do"
When working with a family using play and art, therapists can struggle, looking for ideas and feeling unsure of which activities to use. When a therapist feels stuck it is important that there is a clear understanding of the goals for the family sessions. Once this understanding is established, the best source of ideas for family sessions is the therapist's own childhood, and books about children's games. By reviewing games that children play, the therapist will often be able to generate ideas for family sessions. If the therapist wants to

have "fun as a family," she should think about things that she enjoyed and that made her laugh when she was young. If the established goal is to have families cooperate, the therapist can review group games. The benefit of using activities from the therapist's childhood is that the therapist will know how the activity works and what the rules are. This in turn will make it easier for the therapist to confidently present the idea to the family.

The session is out of control!

When many people are involved actively in a therapy session, things may feel out of control. The therapist's interventions and instructions can structure the session so that things proceed more smoothly. For example, if family members are constantly interrupting, directing, or insulting each other, the therapist can assign a task that must be completed in silence. Any family discussion can involve the use of a "talking stick" so that only the person holding the stick is allowed to speak. If family members invariably engage in conflict when they work together, individual tasks may be assigned. If toys or art materials are to be used in the session, it may be beneficial if the therapist keeps these out of reach until the activity has been introduced to the family. The structure that is provided by using games and play can be manipulated by the therapist to provide safety and control in the session.

Who sets the limits?

Therapists providing therapy in family sessions are often faced with inappropriate behaviours. Both the therapist and the family members need a clear understanding of who is responsible for setting limits with the children in the therapy room. This should be discussed and agreed upon by the caregivers and therapist prior to the first family session.

If caregivers are given responsibility for limit setting from the first session, this reinforces their responsibility as caregivers. However, caregivers are often experiencing difficulty with limit setting prior to beginning therapy, and may not have the skills required. In addition, caregivers may be more stringent than therapists and place many limits on behaviours that are not a concern for the therapist. If the therapist initially assumes responsibility for limit setting in family therapy sessions, this will allow him to model techniques for the caregivers and to clearly establish the rules of the therapy room. When the therapist has agreed to initially assume control of limit setting, this removes pressure from caregivers who are otherwise anxious about appearing to do a "good job." In situations where a therapist begins by assuming responsibility for limit setting, this duty should be slowly transferred back to caregivers as they develop skills and strength.

Can I do individual and family therapy?
Many therapists who are using play and art therapy in family sessions also provide individual play or art therapy for children and adults. If a therapist is providing individual therapy for someone who is also participating in family therapy, care must be taken to maintain a strict boundary between the two therapeutic relationships. If this proves too difficult, it may be beneficial to have separate therapists provide individual and family therapy.

Bringing play and art into family therapy sessions can be very challenging. However, with patience and creativity, therapists will experience the benefits of this approach.

Case Example
A case example will illustrate some uses of play in family sessions. A brief description of the family will be provided. Following this, some of the goals of the work with this family will be listed and examples of the use of play and art directed towards meeting these goals will be provided.

The family
Mary was an eight-year-old girl who was living in a foster home with her brother Brian, aged six. Both children had been physically abused and had witnessed their biological mother, Jane, being assaulted by her partner. The children had regular contact with their biological mother and it was hoped that they would be able to return to live with her in the near future. Jane, who had been abused and neglected as a child, stated that she never felt her parents loved her. As an adult, it appeared that Jane was searching for nurturance in her relationships with men and through her children. Family sessions were suggested as a way of helping Mary and Brian get to know their mother better and further develop their relationship.

Assessment
The therapist held an initial meeting with Jane, in which she obtained background information regarding Jane and the children. In addition, time was spent discussing Jane's goals for family work. The

therapist spoke with Jane about upcoming family sessions and the use of play and art in this work. It was agreed that the therapist would initially take responsibility for limiting the children in session. Throughout this meeting Jane appeared timid and quiet.

A non-directive play session was used to obtain information about family interactions and communication. After greeting Brian, Mary and Jane, the therapist provided them with a variety of play and art materials and asked them to play together.

Brian and Mary got down on the floor and began looking through the toys. While Jane watched her children she spoke with the therapist about her day and a recent doctor's appointment. Mary quickly found a doll to play with and began feeding it. Brian continued to look through toys and then began drawing a picture. As soon as Brian began to draw, Mary went over and began to tickle him and asked Brian to chase her. Brian got up and began chasing Mary around the room. When he was unable to catch her he returned to his drawing. As Brian drew, Mary danced around him making faces and taunting him. Brian looked up occasionally but did not chase Mary again. Mary then got some crayons and began drawing on Brian's paper. At this point, Brian responded by shouting at Mary and pushing her away. Jane continued to sit on the chair and watch the children.

Later during the session, the therapist repeated her invitation to Jane to join the children in playing. Jane got down on the floor and began to colour. Jane asked Mary what she would like her to draw and Mary asked her mother to draw a cat. Jane became absorbed in her drawing. Brian and Mary watched their mother closely and tried to speak with her, but she did not respond. Then Brian tried to climb on his mother's lap. Jane gently pushed Brian away, stating that she was busy,

Brian found a doctor's kit that he began to play with. Mary moved away from her mother and began taking items out of the doctor's kit. When Brian protested, Mary threw the toy syringe and pill bottles to the other side of the room.

Therapeutic goals

Based on the assessment session and referral information, a number of therapeutic goals were established. Four of these goals will be explored here:

1) To promote positive, involved interactions among family members.
2) To assist Jane in responding to and nurturing her children.
3) To develop Mary and Brian's ability to play individually without interrupting each other.
4) To develop the self-esteem of family members.

1) Promoting interaction.
Puppet plays were used to promote interaction among family members. The therapist would instruct either Mary or Brian to put on a puppet show. Jane and the other child would watch the show. At the end of the show, each of the observers would ask the puppets three questions about the show. On other occasions, Jane and the child watching the play would be asked to choose a puppet and to go, one at a time, and talk to the puppets that had been in the story. Having the one child put on the show alone reinforced the message that at times they could play individually. Initially the family had difficulty with this task. Jane would direct her questions about the play to the therapist and Mary would try to intervene in Brian's story, suggesting different plot lines. However, with encouragement and modeling by the therapist, these behaviours slowly changed.

The family was asked to work on several other tasks together (finger-painting, building a tower out of blocks, and tracing each other's hands). In addition, joint scribble drawings were used to encourage interactions among family members. The therapist would start a picture with a scribble. Going around the circle, each family member would add to the picture until everyone decided that the picture was finished. Since Mary had a tendency to correct Brian or to tell him how to work on the picture, a rule was established that no one could talk while scribble drawings were being created.

2) Nurturing.
Each session was ended with a nurturing activity. It was felt that this allowed Jane, Mary and Brian to leave the session with a positive image of nurturing or being nurtured. Given Jane's pattern of seeking nurturing from her children, tasks were initially structured so that Jane was giving the nurturing.

In one session the therapist taught the family how to draw pictures on each other's backs by gently using a finger. The family was asked to sit in a line with Brian in front of Mary and Mary in front of Jane. Jane was asked to draw a picture on Mary's back and Mary was asked to try and copy her mother's picture on Brian's back. Brian and Mary then changed places and the process was repeated.

In another session, Jane was taught how to gently spread baby powder in her children's hands and tell their fortunes in the lines that emerged from their hands (Jernberg, 1979).

Jane was musical and stated that she enjoyed singing. She was encouraged to end some sessions by singing lullabies to her children. At times she was asked to sing one lullaby for both children and in other sessions she was asked to sing to Mary and Brian individually. Initially the children were invited to get a teddy bear to hold while they listened to their mother. As the weeks progressed, the children would lean against Jane while she was singing and eventually she was able to put her arm around them and cuddle them as she sang.

When Jane's ability to nurture and give to her children appeared to have improved, other activities were introduced that allowed everyone in the family to nurture each other. Mary, Brian and Jane were asked to sit in a circle and the therapist gave them each a pile of animal crackers. A set of all the animals in the box was set up in the centre of the circle. Family members took turns asking each other if they had a particular animal (e.g., "Mom, do you have a lion?"). If the person had the animal that was requested, the cracker was fed by hand to the person who had asked the question. Brian initially had difficulty being fed by his mother. He would attempt to take the cracker out of her hand and feed it to himself. With reminders, he was able to gently nibble the cracker out of her fingers.

3) Playing individually.
It was noted in the family's initial session that Mary tended to interrupt Brian when he became absorbed in an activity. As a result, a number of tasks were planned where family members would work individually and then share their work.

In one session, the family members were asked to individually create and draw imaginary communities on the moon (Barnes & Revell, 1995). Mary, Brian and Jane started working at the same table. However, Mary and Brian began fighting over crayons and criticizing each other's work. As a result they were each given their own drawing materials and asked to go to different areas of the room to work. After Christmas, family members were asked individually to draw three things they liked about their holiday. When they had finished they came back and shared their work with each other.

4) Developing self-esteem.
Attempts to meet this goal were not made until family members had experienced several positive sessions together. The therapist then asked family members to draw a picture of one thing they enjoyed about coming to their family sessions. In drawing and discussing these pictures, Mary, Brian and Jane were able to begin acknowledging what they enjoyed about spending time with each other.

In one session, Brian, Mary and Jane were each given two chocolates.They were asked to feed one chocolate to each of the other people in their family after they had talked about one thing that they liked about that person. Brian said to his mother, "I like it when you sing," and fed her the chocolate. He then told his sister, "You give me good hugs," and fed her. Mary and Jane then took their turns.

A summary of the interventions to meet four specific treatment goals with Jane, Brian and Mary has been provided. Additional goals and activities were introduced as family work proceeded.

Conclusion
This chapter has provided an overview of the ways that play and art can be used in therapeutic interventions with families. The reasons for working with families and for using play and art as a part of this work were explored. Ways of structuring play- and art-based interventions to meet specific treatment goals were discussed. In addition, some common concerns about using play and art in family therapy were considered. Finally, a brief case example was used to illustrate the use of play and art to meet some of the treatment goals of one particular family. It is hoped that this chapter will challenge other therapists and allow them to experience the rewards of bringing play and art into family sessions.

REFERENCES

Allan, J. (1988). *Inscapes of the child's world: Jungian counselling in schools and clinics.* Dallas, Texas: Spring Publications Inc.

Axline, V. (1969). *Play therapy.* (2nd ed.). New York: Ballantine Books.

Barnes, M., & Revell, B. (1995). *Self discovery through inner play: A manual of guidelines for going inward with creative imagery exercises and experiential world exploration.* Ottawa: Viktoria, Fermoyle and Berrigan Publishing House.

Bradway, K., Signell, K.A., Spare, G.H., Stewart, C.T., Stewart, L.H., & Thompson, C. (1990). *Sandplay studies: Origins, theory and practice.* (Rev. ed.). Boston: Sigo Press.

Burns, R.C. & Kaufman, S.H. (1970). *Kinetic family drawings (K-F-D): Research and application.* New York: Brunner/Mazel.

Furth, G.M. (1988). *The secret world of drawings: Healing through art.* Boston: Sigo Press.

Gil, E. (1991). *The healing power of play: working with abused children.* New York: The Guilford Press.

Gil, E. (1994). *Play in family therapy.* New York: The Guilford Press.

Holman, A.M. (1983). *Family assessment: Tools for understanding and intervention.* Beverly Hills: Sage Publications

Jernberg, A.M. (1979). *Theraplay: A new treatment using structured play for problem children and their families.* San Francisco: Jossey-Bass Publishers.

Kobak, R.R. & Waters, D.B. (1984). Family therapy as a rite of passage: Play's the thing. *Family Process, 23,* 89-100.

Landreth, G.L. (1991). *Play therapy: The art of relationship.* Muncie, Indiana: Accelerated Development Inc., Publishers.

Minuchin, S. (1974). *Families and family therapy.* Cambridge, Massachusetts: Harvard University Press.

Mitchell, R.R. & Friedman, H.S. (1994). *Sandplay: Past, present and future.* New York: Routledge.

Oaklander, V. (1978). *Windows to our children: A Gestalt therapy approach to children and adolescents.* Moab, Utah: Real People Press.

O'Connor, J.K. (1991). *The play therapy primer: An integration of theories and techniques.* New York: John Wiley & Sons, Inc.

Ross, P. (1991). The family puppet technique: For assessing parent-child and family interaction patterns. In C.E. Schaefer, K.Gitlin & A.Sandgrund (Eds.), *Play diagnosis and assessment.* Toronto, ON: Wiley-Interscience.

Satir, V. (1972). *Peoplemaking*. Palo Alto, CA: Science and Behaviour Books, Inc.

Satir, V. (1983). *Conjoint family therapy*. (Rev. ed.). Palo Alto, CA: Science and Behaviour Books, Inc.

Schaefer, C.E. (1993). *The therapeutic powers of play.* Northvale, NJ: Jason Aronson.

Schaefer, C.E. & O'Connor, K.J. (Eds.) (1983). *Handbook of play therapy*. New York: John Wiley & Sons.

Wachtel, E.F. (1994). *Treating troubled children and their families*. New York: The Guilford Press.

CHAPTER THIRTEEN

CHILDREN & DEATH: UNDERSTANDING, GRIEF PROCESS, AND COUNSELLING

Suzanne Lister

CHILDREN & DEATH: UNDERSTANDING, GRIEF PROCESS, AND COUNSELLING

Should you shield the canyons from the windstorms
You would never see the beauty of their carvings
Native American saying

As a culture, North America tries valiantly to defy and avoid death and the discussion of it. This avoidance begins early in life, from the rare inclusion of death education in school, to euthanasia, to costly life-saving machines, and finally cryogenics. So is it any wonder that as adults we pass our fears onto our children? And yet, except for birth, death is the only experience that every living being will experience. Therefore, if we could come to accept and even embrace death as an inevitable part of life (or as Kübler-Ross [1975] calls death: "the final stage of growth"), then could we not embrace living more thoroughly and completely? Could we teach our children that death is not taboo and teach them to live thoroughly and completely? Can we give someone who is grieving the time, space, nurturance, and support that he needs?

These are big questions and not ones that can be answered easily or succinctly. However, as counsellors dealing with grieving children these are questions that must be addressed both personally and with children experiencing loss. This chapter will outline children's understanding of death in a developmental framework, describe children's grief process, and describe ways in which we, as therapists, can help children work through the loss, keeping the first two points in mind. Each of these facets must be understood in order to effectively deal with grieving children.

There is a popular misconception that children, particularly young children, do not understand death and therefore should be shielded from it or excluded from death rituals such as funerals, burials, etc. Children have a natural curiosity about death and if we do not help to educate them, our omission can fuel misconceptions and fears that can manifest over the years.

Euphemisms are a common and unintentional way of speaking that leaves the child confused and consequently frightened. One parent discussed with his child a funeral of an uncle that he was going to attend. He told the child that he was going to "visit Uncle Charlie."

Upon return from the funeral, the child was very distressed. Fortunately the parent persisted in eliciting the reason for the child's distress. The child's understanding was that the parent was going to heaven to visit Uncle Charlie and therefore he was afraid that his father would not return. It is very important to be clear when discussing death with children. It can be helpful to ask the child to reiterate what you have just told him so that you know what his comprehension has been. This can save him from unnecessary distress and feelings of abandonment, loss, and insecurity. It is also important to use clear terminology such as "die" or "dead," and not ambiguous phrases such as "passed away" or "gone to sleep." These terms are confusing to the child and will have to be addressed later only after the confusion has manifested. It is not only important to use clear terms but it is also important to have an understanding of the child's concept of death.

From 1934 to the present, there have been over 100 studies of children's understanding of death (Speece, 1995). When do children begin to understand what it means to be dead? As a result, an increasing body of research has gone into what it means to be dead. The mature concept of death is complex and has relatively distinct components. The most commonly explored components are: irreversibility, nonfunctionality, and universality (Speece, 1984). However, more recently (Speece, 1995) additional components have been added to the mature concept of death. These are: causality, noncorporeal continuation, death animism, and decomposition.

Universality means that all living things must eventually die. Irreversibility means the body will never come alive again once it has died. Nonfunctionality means that once a living thing has died, all the typical life-defining functions of the physical body stop. Causality suggests a realistic understanding of the external and internal events that cause death. Noncorporeal continuation addresses the various beliefs a person has about what happens after the physical body dies, such as the afterlife. Death animism reflects the understanding that only animate things die. Disposition involves the knowledge of body disposition methods and funeral practices. And finally, decomposition means an understanding of what happens to the body organically. Clearly death is a complex concept and we come to understand it only gradually. And yet as we will see, the understanding of death is not clear-cut and may need to be revised.

Children's understanding of death seems to follow Piaget's theory of cognitive growth (Wass, 1991). Until the age of five, children have a fairly immature understanding of death. Death is viewed as temporary, reversible, sleeping, and a loss of functions such as mobility. At this age, there are degrees of death (Nagy, 1948). Death is seen as living somewhere else and it only comes to the aged and it usually strikes at night (Lonetto, 1985). These beliefs are in keeping with Piaget's preoperational stage. The child's thinking is animistic, magical, and psychologically causal, in that there is a psychological motive for everything (such as being given a needle because the child is bad), and finally, artificialistic such that everything is made for the benefit of people (so that when people are broken they can be repaired) (Wass, 1991).

Therefore, there is clearly no room for death in the child's thinking. The causes of death at this age are usually external such as being stabbed, shot, burned in a fire, or eaten by an animal. Children rely on magic and significant adults to protect them. They feel that they can reverse death by helping the dead person get up or by taking them to the hospital. Encounters with death at this age are usually nonexistent to minimal. Wass (1991) suggests creating situations that address death by obtaining a pet animal with a short life expectancy such as a fish or gerbil; or by reading *Charlotte's Web* (White, 1952) or *The Tenth Good Thing About Barney* (Viorst, 1971). These "small deaths" allow the parent or adult to discuss the concept of death and to help grasp the child's understanding of death.

Between the ages of four and six years, the child believes that dead things have diminished capabilities such as being able to hear but not talk. Children often see death as a result of some wrongdoing (Stehbens, 1988).

After the age of six, children begin to grasp the concept of universality. Prior to this understanding, children believe that certain actions could be taken to avoid death, such as being clever or lucky (Speece, 1984). These children are interested in the post-mortem and the concept of rigor mortis. While adults may view these interests as morbid, it is a natural curiosity and it is therefore important that we answer their questions honestly. Children in the age range of seven to nine years still engage in some magical thinking to assuage their fears, like holding their breath when they pass a cemetery. They often imagine what it is like to be dying, and they usually accept their parents' beliefs about death. By the age of eight or nine, almost all children have a mature understanding of death (Lansdown & Benjamin, 1985). Lansdown and Benjamin (1985) also found that approximately 60% of six-year-olds who were verbally competent had a complete or almost complete understanding of death. Therefore, children's understanding of death develops in a stage-based progression such that by the age of nine they will have a mature concept of death; however, if the child is verbally competent, she may well have a grasp by the age of five or six.

However, recent research by Brent and Speece (1993, in prep.) is challenging the current definition of "dead." When addressing the question of irreversibility: "Can a dead person become alive again?" 93% of children responded "no" and only 55% of adults responded in the presumed correct direction (Brent & Speece, 1993). The recent interest in near-death experience research and developments in medical technology have challenged the inclusion or definition of irreversibility and noncorporeal continuation.

When children experience a death, it is imperative to be open and honest with them. It is important to bear in mind the above-mentioned stages when discussing death with a child. The child may have a limited grasp of what death means and as a result his grief process will be quite different from that of an adult's. The signs and symptoms of childhood grief are often short and intense, but various symptoms may manifest for many years. Segal (1984) found that bereaved children may demonstrate one or more of the following behaviours: denial of the trauma, guilt and blame for the event, internalization or acting out of anger, repressed feelings, obsession with fear of loss of remaining family members, and search for immediate ways of regaining control over their lives. Children do not grieve in a stage-like way. It is not like the stages of dying. There is a general consensus that children who are under the age of four do not have the capacity of achieving complete mourning, but they do react to loss (Zambelli, Johns Clark, & Heegaard, 1989). Because children use more primitive defences such as denial and regression, it is more difficult to understand that the child is grieving. The behaviour is often less obvious than an adult's, and thus it appears that the child has resolved the loss. Unfortunately, the child's way of responding results in a heightened psychological risk.

When assessing the impact of a death of a sibling in childhood, Davies (1991) found long-term implications. Up to three years after the death at least 50% of the children exhibited nervousness, preferred to be alone, and were unhappy, sad or depressed. In addition, 30% of the children also had psychosomatic complaints such as headaches, stomachaches, and sleeping problems such as nightmares and sleepwalking. Other behaviours that continued included poor eating habits, feelings of anxiety, loneliness and poor school performance. This study also found that with time, scores for internalizing behaviours increased and social competency decreased. Therefore, these children gradually turned inward, felt sad and lonely, and became socially withdrawn. Seven to nine years after the death of a sibling the loneliness and sorrow persisted; however, many of the children experienced growth, a heightened maturity and increase in self-concept. Thoughts of the sibling continued, with the majority of children thinking of the deceased at least once a day. Adults who lost a sibling in childhood continued to feel the impact. These adults felt more comfortable with death and developed a positive outlook on life. And while the early maturity in adolescence may have initially been beneficial it was also accompanied by a seriousness that left little room for normal childhood antics; and thus the adults often withdrew from socializing, causing them to feel lonely.

This study quite clearly demonstrates the impact of significant death in childhood. Therefore, as therapists it is imperative to be aware of the tendency of bereaved children to begin to internalize and withdraw from social situations, so that when a child comes in for therapy these issues can be addressed both with the child and with the parents. And as Martinson and Papadatou (1994) state, children often require lengthy bereavement supports, particularly after a sibling dies. When working with these families it is important to know the family dynamics and coping patterns that were utilized throughout the illness and death. This will help the therapist understand the current coping mechanisms so that if the parents excluded the sibling during the illness and death, chances are that the child continues to feel outside the family system, and thus has no one with whom to talk and share her feelings of grief.

Wolfelt (1990) outlines differences between normal grief and clinically depressed children. Normal grief responses in children include the ability to respond to comfort and support; they are able to use play to work out their feelings of grief; they can openly display anger; they can still experience times of joy; they may experience some guilt or have transient physical complaints; and they may experience a temporary decrease in self-esteem. Coping responses that may suggest clinical depression include rejecting support and resistance to the use of play; and the child may openly express anger, experience chronic physical problems, exhibit generalized feelings of guilt, and experience a greater intensity of low self-esteem. Therefore, one needs to be aware of the intensity and the duration of the child's response, whether the child is experiencing a normal grief or something more pathological.

In the last twenty years there has been a growing body of research and literature that outlines suggestions for working with bereaved children. Because children are experiencing so much cognitive and psychological change during the first 13 years it is important to bear in mind their ability to process the death.

A child who is five years of age and has lost an older brother will undoubtedly experience different emotions than an eleven-year-old whose father has died. The therapist needs to be aware of the child's understanding of death and how children tend to grieve. Typically children have difficulty verbalizing their emotions and thoughts, and it is for that reason that techniques that employ art and play are often less threatening to the child because they do not require him to discuss this taboo topic. Art and play therapy are also very natural ways in which the child communicates. In this way he can project onto the art or play his feelings of sorrow, loss, grief, anger, and guilt.

The following section will outline, in general terms, guidelines for working with bereaved children, and then will focus on some specific techniques utilizing art and play.

Guidelines

Grollman (1991) describes 11 guidelines for working with bereaved children. These guidelines are useful for the therapist and also for the parent, and when meeting with the parent it can be helpful to discuss these suggestions. Obviously a pro-active approach is the best so that if the parent knows that the child will be experiencing a death through illness of parent, grandparent, sibling, pet, etc., then it is most helpful to initiate these suggestions before the death. However, as suggested earlier, the parent can also include the topic of death when it is a less significant loss such as a goldfish or distant family friend. By bringing up the topic of death at this time, children learn that it is all right to discuss death and that the parents will be receptive when there is a more significant loss. This leads to Grollman's first suggestion:

1) Do not avoid the subject of death in the home, or at the school or religious centre. There is a misconception that children are too fragile to cope with death. Grollman states, "good mental health is not the denial of tragedy but frank acknowledgement of painful separation" (p. 4).

2) Do not discourage emotions of grief. Grief is as natural an emotion as happiness and anger and while it is painful to experience or to watch, it is imperative that it be experienced as a natural course of mourning.

3) Do not tell children something that they will later need to unlearn. This was addressed earlier and bears mentioning again. Children need to learn the truth and they need to know that they can trust the adult to give them honest answers. If the adult offers an explanation that the child later learns was false, then the child has no reason to expect that the adult will be truthful again in a similarly emotionally charged situation. It is also important to tell the child when you don't know the answer. It is all right to say, "I don't know," or "Let's go to the library and look it up," or "Let's ask the religious leader and find out." Children will accept that sort of response over a fabrication that saves the adult from appearing fallible. It also models to the child that there are some questions that do not have clear answers and that ambiguity is a part of life.

4) Do not alter the role of the child. The surviving child cannot replace the deceased child, father or mother. Also, requesting that the child "be brave" makes grieving difficult, so that she puts on a front that satisfies the needs of other family members at the expense of her own. The child needs to know how special and unique the deceased person was, but also how important and individual she is as well.

5) Do not speak beyond the child's level of comprehension. Once again bearing in mind the child's developmental level and the aforementioned understanding of death, the adult should try to use terms that are easily understood by the child. To say to the four-year-old child, "Your grandfather passed away of leukemia and he is going to be cremated" makes no sense to the child. Instead, use a statement such as, "Your grandfather's blood was sick and so he died. That

means his body stopped working and we won't be able to visit him anymore." Children ask many questions and it is important to answer them simply and truthfully.

6) Allow children to go through their own phases of grief. As mentioned before, there is no preset course for grief. Each child's course is unique; however, one must also be aware of the child's subtle responses or prolonged intense responses that may need further help. It is important to allow for tears but also to be aware of the child who is *not* crying. One parent remarked at his daughter's funeral that he felt his son was coping well; he hadn't shed a tear. This assumption is false; there must be time for tears. If the death is of a parent, oftentimes the child may feel very afraid that the other parent is going to die as well. It is helpful for the surviving parent to discuss this issue and to say that if something did happen then the child would be living with a prearranged relative or friend of the family. It is also important to be aware if the child feels guilty about the death. It is not uncommon for children to say to one another, "I wish you were dead!" Then when the sibling dies, the surviving sibling may believe that he caused the death through his wish. Once again, an awareness of the child's cognitive level helps to alleviate potential problems before they arise; so that when talking to the surviving sibling, the parent or therapist can discuss with him the cause of death and reassure him that he had nothing to do with the death.

7) Make referrals to other supportive people. This suggestion refers to the potential for prolonged, unresolved grief. If as a therapist there has been little movement in the child's grieving, it may be helpful to refer her to a bereavement group. As will be discussed later, one of the biggest advantages to a group is that other bereaved children are available to normalize the grieving process.

8) Notify the child's school or daycare about the death. As mentioned earlier, oftentimes schoolwork and behaviour can be affected, and so it is important that the teacher know what has caused the changes.

9) Encourage children to participate in family sorrow. Children need to know that they can be part of the funeral arrangements and that they can attend whatever parts they feel comfortable with, so that they, too have an opportunity to say goodbye. In working with one girl who lost her older brother to cancer, she said that she was not

permitted to go to the hospital near the time of death nor was she allowed to be part of the funeral arrangements. The parents felt that they should protect her from these things; however, the child clearly demonstrated anger and confusion as to why she was excluded from something as important as her brother's death. Conversely, another family whose daughter died of cancer offered their surviving children the opportunity to participate in the funeral. The children decided to read from the scriptures and to read a story they had written about their older sister's illness. The impact of each of these families' decisions had far-reaching consequences. The first child learned early on that death was taboo and that she could not discuss the brother with her parents, while the second family learned that this was a family experience and one that was shared uniquely and yet together.

The final two suggestions are to consider grief support groups for children, and to give continued assurance of love and support. It is important that children be allowed to talk or to draw or to play out their grief, and as adults it is our job to be available to them as they work out their grief in their own way.

Excell (1991) suggests that there are a number of ways in which we can be available to a child once she has been informed of the death. Firstly, allow for an open and honest non-judgmental environment so that the child feels she can ask questions or display emotions. Body language is very helpful in demonstrating acceptance of the child's emotional response. For example, sitting in a comfortable setting in an open position indicates receptivity. Opening statements are important for establishing the relationship. Statements such as, "This must be a very sad/scary time for you," or "When someone dies we sometimes feel confused, frightened, angry. Why don't we talk and you can tell me about [the person who died]." All of these approaches help to build rapport with the child.

Because of the developmental differences in the understanding of death, children come with their own ideas of what death is. It is helpful to ask the child direct questions pertaining to death, such as, "What happened when [the deceased] died?" or, "What do you think you will see when [viewing the body]?" or, "What questions do you have at this time?"

An art technique that can be helpful is to ask the child to draw what they think death is. This technique can help the therapist understand some of the child's ideas or misconceptions. It can also elucidate the degree of grief that the child is experiencing. For example, if the child has drawn himself very small it may mean that he is feeling overwhelmed by grief; and conversely, if he draws himself very large, it could suggest that he is feeling immense grief. Art and play allow the child to access his intuitive awareness and to ease his fear of abandonment and sense of aloneness (Baker, 1991).

Once again, Excell (1991) emphasizes the need to provide correct and factual information. If the therapist is working with the child immediately after the death and before the funeral, it is helpful to describe for her what she will see at the funeral; and if the child wishes to touch the deceased, to tell her that the deceased will feel cold and hard. Whether the therapist sees the child before or after the funeral, it can be helpful to ask her to draw the funeral and/or visitation. This will help give a sense of the family's dynamics and coping. This time is often overwhelming to the family and results in varied responses, from happy socializing with friends and family who come to pay their respects, to intense crying and grieving. The therapist can get a clearer picture of whether the child was involved or excluded from these important rituals.

It is helpful for the child to have his feelings normalized so a discussion of the varying responses to death can be very beneficial. Art techniques such as drawing the family before the death and after the death or drawing faces that represent the child's varied and complex feelings, often give a better representation of the family environment and his emotional state than can words. The therapist can give the child a blank drawing of a human figure with the introduction that we all have lots of feelings inside, and sometimes we share them and sometimes we keep them inside. Describe various feelings like happiness, anger, sadness, guilt, depression, and fear and ask the child to take a colour to represent each feeling and colour where he feel that feeling in his body. It is also helpful to find if the child has any psychosomatic complaints and if so, what emotion is related to that area of the body.

If the death is the result of a lengthy illness, the grieving process starts well before the death. Additional art techniques include drawing the self/family before the illness, during the illness now, and what the child imagines for the future. Play techniques include doing puppetry whereby the puppets talk about their feelings when someone they loved died, and using the dollhouse to show the home before and during the illness and at present. The availability of sand is very beneficial as it allows the child to engage in burying objects. Often the child will try to bury himself in the sand. The child needs to resolve the burial aspect of the death.

The child needs to be made aware of the various ways in which to say goodbye. If the child chose not to be part of the funeral or was excluded from the funeral, then she can say goodbye in other ways. She may wish to have a memento placed in the casket, or she may wish to draw a picture of the deceased or write a poem, or engage in a game or activity that was special between herself and the deceased. A useful technique is Junge's (1985) memory book. This is a book created by the child or by the whole family about the person who died. The child can include things that remind her of the deceased, such as photographs, objects, drawings, stories, poems, pieces of clothing, and so on. When the child is feeling sad she can bring out the memory book to reconnect with the person who has died. Often children are afraid that they will forget what the deceased looked like, sounded like, or smelled like and this book can help stimulate those senses.

As mentioned previously, individual therapy can be very helpful in allowing the child to work through his grief; but some children may need additional support through peer activities and relationships. Understandably, with the risk of increased social isolation that these children may experience, group therapy can help minimize that risk. Bereavement groups help to normalize the children's feelings and to help them feel connected to other children.

Typically, goals of the group include developing rapport among group members, providing grief education, discussion of beliefs about death and the hereafter, identification and acceptance of the new family system, memorialization of the deceased, discussion of coping and communication patterns in self and family, identification of support systems, and description of future expectations (Peterson, 1994; Zambelli et al, 1989). Bereaved Families of Ontario has developed a model program for bereaved children (Fleming & Balmer, 1991).

Children attending this group are between the ages of six and twelve years and have experienced the death of either a sibling or a parent.

Communication with the parent before, during and after the group is included in the seven-week program. There is a minimum of five participants and a maximum of ten, with siblings being in different groups when at all possible. One of the outstanding features of this program is their inclusion of a bereaved child co-leader. This child has already been through the group and has completed an eight-week training program.

The themes of the seven weeks are: 1) getting acquainted; 2) relationship with the deceased; 3) the funeral; 4) feelings; 5) changes; 6) looking to the future; and 7) saying goodbye. In the first session the children become acquainted with one another and are given the opportunity to tell their stories. The bereaved child co-leader can be the first to tell his story. The leaders can then discuss similarities and differences in the children's experiences, which process helps the children empathize with others and also to bring the topic of death to the forefront. The second session requires the child to bring something associated with the deceased such as a photograph or object. The third meeting includes an educational component about the funeral so as to correct any misconceptions and misunderstandings. A technique they use is the question box, whereby children can drop questions into the box that they feel uncomfortable asking. Each member can then select a question and lead the discussion. Another suggested technique is the "weather inside." Ask the child to draw a picture of the weather on the day of the funeral and then ask him to draw a picture of the weather on his "inside" on the day of the funeral.

The fourth meeting includes storytelling. The leader reads a story that reflects the situation of the majority of the members. The children then discuss what feelings the children in the story may be experiencing. This technique allows the child to displace her feelings onto the story characters in a non-threatening way. The second technique uses a mandala. Children are given the emotions of sad, angry, scared, shocked, relieved, guilty, and lonely, and one blank card for an emotion that the child would like to add. Each child is given a piece of paper with a blank circle and is asked to colour the circle using various colours to represent his emotions and their intensity.

The fifth group discusses the many changes that have resulted from the death such as change of residence, finances, family roles, school etc. The art technique used in this group is to draw the family before and after the death. The sixth and seventh sessions involve discussing the future and saying goodbye. The group shares their thoughts and feelings of the past weeks and how they can relate it to the future. Members are asked to share activities that they liked or disliked, to reflect on specific group memories, and to make suggestions for future groups.

When children experience a significant death, their world has turned upside down. Children often do not understand what it means to be dead, they often may feel responsible for some aspect of the death, and they are oftentimes left to grieve alone. Parents may have difficulty offering support to the child because they too are grieving. As therapists it is our job to help the child grieve and to help the parents accept and be aware of the way in which children grieve. The therapist needs to be aware of what the child's understanding of death is, how the child and family cope with death, how grief can manifest itself in children, and how as therapists we can help children grieve. The approach can be directive as described above, but also nondirective. Nondirective art and play therapy allow the child to process at her own rate and in her own way. In either approach, the therapist must be receptive to the child's unique communications. Bereavement therapy has been proven to have long-lasting effects (Black, 1991); therefore, the therapist is not only helping the child through the short term of intense grief, but also providing a framework and grounding from which the child can draw for future losses.

REFERENCES

Baker, S.R. (1991). Utilizing art and imagery in death and dying counselling. In Papadatou, P. and Papadatos, C. (Eds.), *Children and Death* (pp.135–143). New York: Hemisphere Publishing Corporation.

Black, D. (1991). Family intervention with families bereaved or about to be bereaved. In Papadatou, P. and Papadatos, C. (Eds.), *Children and Death* (pp.161–175). New York: Hemisphere Publishing Corporation.

Brent, S.B., & Speece, M.W. (1993). The "adult" conceptualization of irreversibility: Implications for the development of concept of death. *Death Studies, 17*, 203–224.

Brent, S.B., & Speece, M.W. (1996). The development of the concept of death among Chinese and U.S. children 3–17 years of age: From binary to "fuzzy" concepts. *Omega: Journal of Death and Dying, 33*, 67-83.

Davies, B. (1991). Responses of children to the death of a sibling. In Papadatou, P. and Papadatos, C. (Eds.), *Children and Death* (pp. 125–133). New York: Hemisphere Publishing Corporation.

Excell, J.A. (1991). A child's perception of death. In Papadatou, P. and Papadatos, C. (Eds.), *Children and Death* (pp.87–103). New York: Hemisphere Publishing Corporation.

Fleming, S., & Balmer, L. (1991). Group intervention with bereaved children. In Papadatou, P. and Papadatos, C. (Eds.), *Children and Death* (pp. 105–124). New York: Hemisphere Publishing Corporation.

Grollman, E.A. (1991). Explaining death to children and to ourselves. In Papadatou, P. and Papadatos, C. (Eds.), *Children and Death* (pp. 3–8). New York: Hemisphere Publishing Corporation.

Junge, M. (1985). The book about Daddy dying: A preventive art therapy technique to help families deal with the death of a family member. *Art Therapy, 2*, 410.

Kübler-Ross, E. (1975). *Death: The final stage of growth*. Inglewood Cliffs, NJ: Prentice Hall.

Lansdown, R., & Benjamin, G. (1985). The development of the concept of death in children aged 5–9 years. *Child Care, Health and Development, 11*, 13–20.

Lonetto, R. (1985). Children's concepts of death. In G.H. Paterson (Ed.), *Children and Death*. Proceedings of the King's College Conference, Helping Children Cope with Death. London, Ontario, Canada (pp.43–70).

Martinson, I.M. & Papadatou, D. (1994). Care of the dying child and the bereaved. In D.J. Bearison & R.K. Mulhern (Eds.), *Pediatric Psycooncology: Psychological Perspectives on Children with Cancer* (pp. 193–214). New York: Oxford University Press.

Nagy, M. (1948). The child's theories concerning death. *Journal of Genetic Psychology, 73*, 3–27.

Peterson, L.W. (1994). A therapeutic program for bereaved children. *Archives of Family Medicine, 3,* 76–82.

Segal, R.M. (1984). Helping children express grief through symbolic communication: Social casework. *The Journal of Contemporary Social Work, 65,* 590–599.

Speece, M.W. (1995). *The search for the mature concept of death.* Paper presented at the meeting of The Seventeenth Annual Association for Death Education and Counselling, Miami, Fl.

Stehbens, J.A. (1988). Childhood cancer. In D.K. Routh (Ed.), *Handbook of Pediatric Psychology* (pp. 135–61). New York: Guilford.

Viorst, J. (1971). *The tenth good thing about Barney*. New York: Atheneum.

Wass, H. (1991). Helping children cope with death. In Papadatou, P. and Papadatos, C. (Eds.), *Children and Death* (pp. 11–32). New York: Hemisphere Publishing Corporation.

White, E.B. (1952). *Charlotte's web*. New York: Harper Row.

Wolfelt, A. (1990). Suggestions for assessing depression in grieving children. *Bereavement.*

Zambelli, G.C., Johns Clark, E., & Heegaard, M. (1989). Art therapy for bereaved children. In H. Wadeson, J. Durkin, & D. Perach (Eds.), *Advances in art therapy* (pp. 60–80). NewYork: John Wiley & Sons.

CHAPTER FOURTEEN

ETHICS AND PROFESSIONAL PRACTICE

Sharron Zweig

ETHICS AND PROFESSIONAL PRACTICE

Introduction

To begin this chapter, I would like each reader to ask himself how often he feels that the issues of ethics and professional practice impinge on his daily work routines. Do these issues emerge as isolated and rare events or are they inherent in the therapeutic relationship—as in how to manage power differentials? Are they strictly law, code and textbook issues, or are they generated by values and personal principles, as in dealing with racism, sexism or religious or cultural beliefs? The answers that I would give are irrelevant. What is critical for the reading of this chapter is that each individual begin the process of recognizing, struggling with and finally coming to some decision on these and other questions. In fact, this chapter will be more about raising questions and providing background information than providing answers.

Given the material at hand and the nature of our subject, it is the rule rather than the exception that more questions are raised than definitive answers found. The practice of ethics is often a struggle, a process that usually involves weighing conflicting rights. The goal of this chapter is to identify some of the issues, some possible responses, and ultimately help the reader become comfortable with less-than-perfect solutions. Often, the most we can hope for at the end of our struggles is a morally substantial solution rather than a morally perfect one. That is, after carefully weighing all the relevant information, we will be able to offer a response not only to our clients, but to our agency team and peers as well.

Throughout this chapter, reference to the various principles given below will be in italics.

COMMON ETHICAL PRINCIPLES, RELEVANT LAWS AND USEFUL QUESTIONS

Duty to Client/Consumer

Beneficence/non-maleficence (do good/do no harm)
Confidentiality: client comes first
Full disclosure of: fees, status, limits of confidentiality, roles, boundaries and expectations, dual relationship
Respect for: autonomy, self-determination, avoidance of dependency
Privacy
No dual relationships
No benefits to the therapist at the disadvantage to the client
Respect for persons

No discrimination
Sensitivity to social or cultural risk factors
Integrity
Competence and knowledge
Sensitivity to power imbalance
Diligence and availability
Notation and just the facts and keep for at least seven years
Inform other professionals
Termination and Referrals
Accept liability
Impartiality (third party)
Right to read record
Staying current
Knowing protocols

Artwork
Respect and dignity
Owned by client
Specific releases
Anonymity
High-risk material

Duty to Profession
Derogatory acts: inducing to use services, sexual relations, false reporting, counselling fraudulent acts, failure to report incompetence, violations
Diagnosing without credentials

Duty as Professional
Practicing while impaired
Taking care of self: burnout, stress, compassion fatigue
Counter-transference
Boundaries: physical, emotional, social

The Law
Duty to report
Duty to protect and warn
Counselling under 12
Access to records
Laws and regulations specific to populations

Useful Questions
Who is the client?
Whose needs are being met?
Who can help me with this?

FIGURE 1

DOMAINS OF ETHICAL DECISION-MAKING

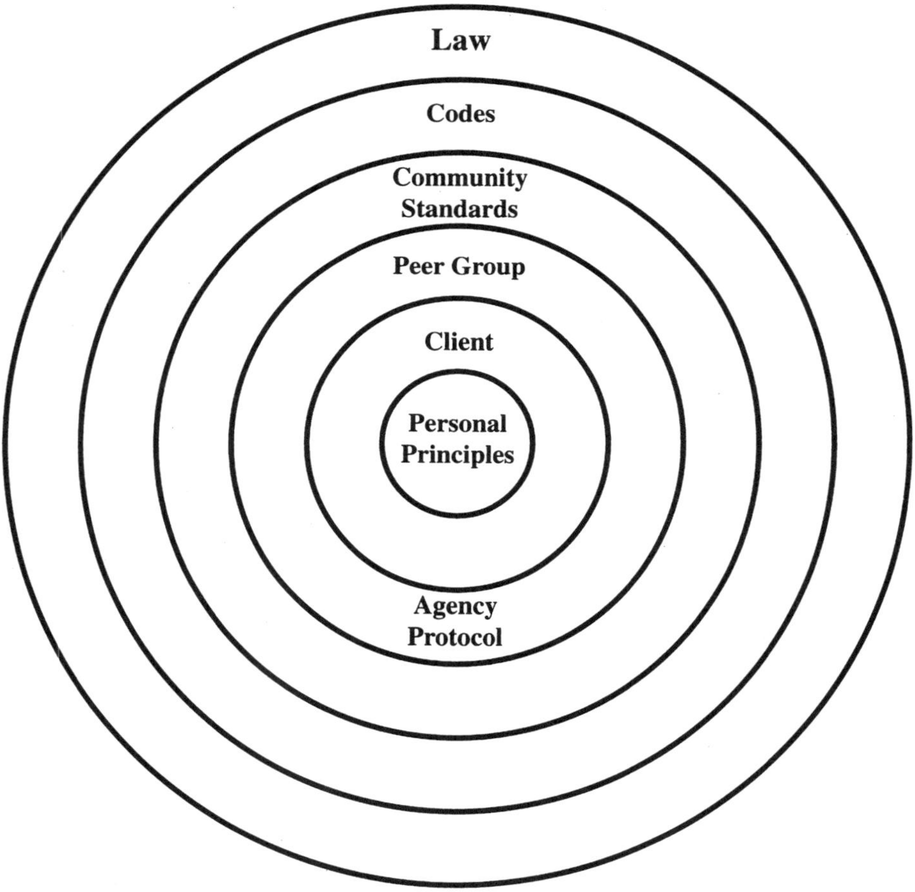

In struggling with ethical issues, it is imperative that we have all the relevant information, to make a substantial response. By substantial, I mean that we should be able to identify the issues arising from the pertinent domains, as well as articulate the reasons that were persuasive to us, in coming to our conclusion. In addition, we should be aware of the impact of our decision on our client and set out a plan to mediate those effects, to the best of our ability. Again, I must repeat, that we rarely encounter a situation that is black or white. We are usually working with shades of grey, attempting to balance on a very fine line between two hues. Whether we work on a team where our opinion matters or is never called upon, or whether we work alone, it is important that we begin to develop our own sense of ethical boundaries.

As a starting point, we will review the various domains in which we will find that information. They are the following: personal principles and values; the client; peer and agency protocols; community standards; the code; and the law.

Personal Principles

When dealing with ethical dilemmas, most practitioners are very clear that *the client comes first.* But, in reality, decision-making is often influenced by less obvious domains. The personal values and principles of the therapist often are masked or not recognized. For example, the therapist who enjoys the hour spent with the client and ignores the signs that *termination* is in order because no further work is possible or necessary, may believe that the therapeutic relationship should be characterized by friendship. Or on a case management level, there is the therapist who believes that anyone could or should complete college, and constantly raises the issue with a client who is struggling to find housing, despite every sign of resistance. Here the *respect for the person or autonomy* may be compromised. Another common example in our multicultural environment is the worker who encourages a pre-adolescent to use her newly trained assertiveness skills in confronting a potentially violent parent who is from a culture where authoritarian rule by father is the norm. Here basic safety is the issue. All these examples arise from the interplay of personal principles and values on the decision-making process. These principles and values need not negatively impact if they are clearly recognized and accounted for in the decision-making process. Self-awareness is a critical factor in the application of values in ethical decision-making.

The first step is to know what is important to you. When these beliefs are engaged, as they often are, we can then make choices about how to respond. For example, if children's rights are important to you, a primary value, you may choose not to work in an environment where children's rights are ignored. Or you may choose to refer a client whose belief system is offensive to you, or discuss the problem with the client at intake, allowing him to decide if, knowing your values, he would be comfortable working with you.

Whether you choose not to work with this client, or he makes the decision, it is important to know whom you cannot work with. Which population, because of personal principles or *counter-transference* issues, could you not provide professional level service to? Knowing what personal principle, value or experience might compromise effective service delivery is an important piece of self-awareness. If, for example, it is a past experience that triggers *counter-transference*, then options for dealing with that experience may be in order. In short, "making the invisible visible" allows us to make clear choices and better decisions as professionals.

The Client

As stated earlier, the client does come first. Doing no harm (*non-maleficence*) and doing good (*beneficence*) are fundamental principles of every code of ethics. If doing only good were simple, there would be no need for detailed codes. If by simply following the codes, we were assured of only doing good, ethics would be simple. In fact, there exist, within most codes, potentially conflicting statements. Two common examples are the injunctions to *respect confidentiality* and *obey the law*—e.g., report disclosures. The family in treatment may not feel that you have respected confidentiality if you report that a child is currently being "abused" by a parent who is using harsh disciplinary methods. Not only will you be breaking confidentiality, but you will be compromising the therapeutic relationship. Knowing your codes is essential, but they are only guidelines. In addition, they are often minimal standards for professional behaviour. As we shall see, the codes are basic components in the decision-making process, in which the goal is to meet the needs of the client.

To help meet this goal, I would like to propose a set of **useful questions**. In determining how best to meet the needs of the client, it is often productive to ask, *who is the client?* It is surprising how often this step is overlooked. For example, a therapist might give a detailed report of her session with an eleven-year-old child to the parent without ever considering to whom that information belongs. Who is the client? It is the child, regardless of who is paying. By disclosing unnecessary information, are you breaching the client's confidentiality? A mature eleven-year-old could have some voice in what is conveyed and to whom, unless safety is an issue. If there is material that the child chooses to report to parents, he could be encouraged or supported in delivering that information himself. If the child is not comfortable talking to the parent about an issue and no amount of role-playing, letter-writing or support will facilitate communication, then the therapist might choose to make a contract with the child, listing the specifics of what should be disclosed and to whom. Do you think an eleven-year-old should write his own contracts? Which contracts should the child sign—consent for service, consent for supervision, releases to obtain information? At what age do you think a child could participate in this kind of decision-making? Or more specifically, at what age does the principle of *confidentiality* become important? In fact, a child over 12 can sign his own contract for service, with qualifications (see Law section). Another aspect of this question is how the therapist's discussions with the child's caregiver impact on the therapeutic relationship (specifically the issue of trust).

Another useful question in case management, ethics and professional practice, is *whose needs are being met?* In the earlier case where the therapist should have terminated because the client was not making further gains, this question would have been productive. I would guess that the therapist's need for friendship became more important than the client's needs for professional service. There might be times when one chooses to put agency, legal or professional obligations before the client's needs, but this needs to be a careful and deliberate choice, taken only after weighing all the possibilities and recognizing that the client's needs have been compromised. In these cases, part of the solution will involve organizing a therapeutic response to mediate the effects of your decision on your client.

A final question, in your deliberations on behalf of the client is, *who can help me with this?* Obviously students can and should access their supervisors, both agency and art or play. In addition, agency teams, peer support and even lawyers should be consulted, if necessary. Today, not only are the questions complex, but the repercussions can be profound for both therapist and client. Students are especially vulnerable, given the autonomy and responsibility of practicum situations. There can be a sense that they should be able to handle any situation without asking for help. But students are not the only practitioners that fail to access resources in the decision-making process. Mature practitioners may also try to solve every dilemma on their own, mindful of issues of confidentiality. It is because confidentiality is so relevant that it helps to know how it can be worked with. For example, students should have releases for supervision from the start; agencies usually have intra-agency releases for the team, but here it is necessary to know who is on the team and who is not. For example, if you are working in the school system as a counsellor, do you share information with the teachers, principal or school psychologist? The issue of who is covered by releases and who is not should be determined at the outset. Mature practitioners can, under carefully controlled circumstances, where the anonymity of the client is maintained, consult other professionals like lawyers, psychiatrists, etc. Consents, releases, contracts and notification at intake of the limits of confidentiality are some of the essentials of professional practice. You never know in which case you will have to consult. For this reason, all these paperwork details are critical to protect your client and yourself and to effectively meet your client's needs.

A final point. The primary goal of every counsellor could be stated as delivering the best quality services, within your mandate to the client. The issue of remaining within your mandate is central to case management. If, for example, you are working in a shelter where residents can remain for only six weeks, is it good professional practice to undertake sexual abuse treatment with the residents? Can you complete the course of therapy in that time? If you cannot, then probably you should not start. Does it meet your formal mandate? If not, then you should not start. This does not mean you should not undertake safety training (home, school or street-proofing) or even sexual abuse pro-active training in a shelter. These may be within your mandate and time limitations. There is a difference between providing support and resources and therapy. It is important to know where and when to draw the line. These are all issues for case management.

If delivering the best quality services to meet your client's needs, while remaining within your mandate, is the primary goal, then it follows that if you have done your job you will become redundant. You will have avoided client *dependency*, by teaching her how to meet her own needs through training and resource development. Thus, making yourself redundant, though not formalized in any code, could be considered a valid goal or outcome of successful therapy.

Peer and Agency Protocols

Both students and mature practitioners should be familiar with how their agency chooses to respond to particular situations. Most agencies have a handbook of protocols available for their workers. It is too late to guess how the agency handles suicidal clients, when you have one in front of you. It is too late to wonder what happened, when you find that a child client will not be seeing you because he is in the hospital, victim of a caregiver who went too far—this time. (You thought that your agency supervisor had reported your suspicion of abuse.) It is too late to discover when you are facing a lawsuit by parents who were told by the agency that physical restraints were never used, but you did not know because it never came up. These are just a few examples of what can go wrong, when you are not *familiar with agency procedures*.

Another area for consideration is how your peers—other art or play therapists—in your locality carry out therapeutic interventions. That is not to say that you should pattern yourself automatically on other practitioners, but that you should be aware of how individuals working in your field generally respond to situations. If you choose to carry out your responsibilities in a way that is not congruent with conventional peer practice, then it is extremely important that you be able to substantiate your choices. This is one situation where accountability is somewhat more enhanced, but in general one needs to be able to discuss the rationale or theory behind any intervention.

Peers and their activities become important in responding to various principles embedded in the codes. For example, most codes insist that the practitioner *remain current*. To do that, we need to know what our peers are doing and writing. We need to attend conferences and workshops and stay connected in whatever way we can. Another aspect of peer involvement is knowing who in your area specializes in what populations. *Knowing your local resources* is important in the referral process that is often a central part of case management. Can you identify a practitioner in your area who deals with AIDs clients or where some of the services you offer are available at no cost? Or if you work in a no-fee agency, where they can get the same service for a fee. These are all relevant components of professional practice and are frequently part of the ethical decision-making process.

Community Standards

Community standards is an overlapping category that it includes both peer practice and the combined standards set out by various codes. I use the term to describe those common ethical principles that are expected by the community of mental health service providers. In the **Common Ethical Principles** section, I list some of the common principles that deal with duty to client or consumer, responsibility for artwork, duty to profession and duty as professional, which are relevant to art and play therapy practice. Please note that this short review of common principles is not meant to replace a careful scrutiny of your own relevant code, e.g., the Art or Play Therapy Codes. You must know your own code, but in court, for example, you may be judged on community standards of practice.

Duty to client/consumer

Under "*Full disclosure of . . .*" there are features that should be part of every intake session (they will be discussed in detail in the Intake section). The two aspects of this section that are most often forgotten are failure to disclose to clients one's *status as an intern or student*, and the open discussion of *conflict or dual relationship situations* and the resulting written contract of understanding. Another critical area that is often overlooked at intake is disclosure of the *limits of confidentiality,* e.g., *duty to report* [child abuse], *duty to protect and warn* (not mandated in law but an issue for potential litigation), *access to records* (they could be subpoenaed and a play therapist may be compelled to *breach confidentiality* if under investigation by the ethics committee). These are the basic limits to confidentiality and every client should be notified at intake. With children, I would focus on *duty to report* and *duty to protect and warn* (if a child is being hurt or threatens to hurt herself or others). A young child may need to be reminded in the first session as well. More will be said about this in the Intake section.

How would you explain the limits of confidentiality to a five-year-old? Under what circumstances would you notify a client that another agency client, his lover, has now been confirmed as HIV positive (*duty to warn*)? Would you notify him? How would you notify him? How would you come to that decision? Whose input would you seek? Do you think an eight-year-old needs to know about *duty to protect*? Do you believe that eight-year-old children could commit suicide? (They can and they do.) These are just a few of the questions that emerge out of the *limits of confidentiality*. Depending on the populations you work with, there will be a multitude of questions that are worth thinking about before the situation occurs. One final note: *duty to protect* usually from harm to self or suicide, is a responsibility most agencies take seriously. Thus, there will be formal procedures to handle high-risk clients. Every practitioner should know not only the procedures, but the counselling response (signs, questions to ask, and local resources) to deal with this situation, and how to monitor the client when the crisis seems past. This all falls under the principles of *diligence and competence*.

Another area where practitioners tend to display deficits is in the area of *notation*. Given that the client has the right to read her records (unless it would negatively impact on therapeutic goals), it is critical that records be written in a neutral and professional manner. Here, *just the facts* are called for. Quotes are useful if they serve a purpose, but diagnosing, unless you are certified to do that or are using a previous diagnosis, or setting out a sequence of hypotheses can compromise your credibility, if the records are used in court. It is not that we never work with hypotheses, but too many of them, in print, make us look like amateur sleuths. It is better to track your hunches elsewhere and only write what can be substantiated by behavioural, verbal or graphic evidence. *Just the facts* will help to keep you and your clients safe.

Also, take care with your language. There are certain words that should be used only after some careful consideration. For example, the word enmeshed. From a feminist viewpoint, the word is loaded with unfair negative connotations. If children are dependent on a mother, as of course they are, then how does this relationship automatically become negative? That is the question they might ask. And how is it we do not refer to "trauma bonding" between a child and a perpetrator in the same "gendered" way? These are interesting questions that underline the care we must take in language use. Meanwhile, our reports will be more useful, if instead of using labels like "enmeshed," we note the specific maladaptive behaviours displayed by the caregiver or client.

Another way in which language is abused in report writing is in the use of empty subjective terms like "beautiful." What information do we get from reading that a drawing is "beautiful"? It would be better to address comments to the specifics of the drawing, like the display of advanced skill in the rendering, or the carefully drawn figures, or the use of bright colour, etc. Another use of subjective terms that should be avoided is the characterization of an individual as "good" or "bad." For example, one should avoid referring to "a good mother." Instead one could note the mother's "strengths" as specific skills.

These are all fine points, but they could affect the response to the records, ultimately compromising your reputation, credibility and your therapeutic goals.

A final word on *notation*: most codes call for keeping the records for a reasonable amount of time. To be safe, records should be kept for a minimum of seven years. In some government-funded programs, records should be kept for 20 years. It's important to know which time span is appropriate for your practice.

Artwork

The use and dispensation of artwork is a somewhat ambiguous area. That is, although some codes (Quebec Art Therapy Code) suggest that ownership of artwork is a treatment issue or designated by the agency, we must always treat it *as if it belongs to the client*. That is, for use in supervision, display, or education, we must always have *consents* and protect the *anonymity of the client*. These should be arranged at intake and any discussion of ownership should occur at that point. If the client is willing to sign consents, but uncomfortable with the idea of handing over his work, a photograph or a facsimile drawing by the therapist could be presented at supervision (with consents). One situation where the therapist might consider *not* releasing the artwork can occur where taking the artwork home might put the child at risk—for example, if the child is living with domestic violence and the drawing, a rendering of a violent situation, could be viewed by the perpetrator. This would call for some negotiation with the client.

All codes call for treating client artwork with the same *respect and the dignity due to the client*. This principle invites some intriguing questions. For example, would you allow a client to crumple, tear and otherwise destroy a drawing? How would allowing a client to do that affect his self-esteem? Would it encourage him to think that his productivity or creativity is worthless? Would you handle it as a treatment issue? What do you think? Where would you draw your lines and why?

Another interesting set of questions emerges from the very question of ownership. If, for example, you wrote a brilliant paper in college or university, could your teacher rationalize her ownership of the product? If I went to a workshop on storytelling and wrote a wonderful children's story, would I let the facilitator keep it, or would I take it home and try to publish it? What if I had painted a picture, or made a puppet? Would that change the "ownership" question? How do these questions relate to ownership of the art; do they relate to the ownership of the art generated in an art therapy session? How will you resolve the ownership question in your practice?

Duty to Profession

Here we find some of the most serious infractions. Many codes explicitly stipulate that engaging in *sexual relations* is a *derogatory act*. This is one of the few principles that is nearly absolute. Some codes suggest that a period of two years or more should elapse before intimate relations between a therapist and an ex-client would be acceptable. Most writers consider these relationships as minimally *dual relationships*, but more generally an abuse of power, even between adults. What do you think? How long after the professional relationship has ended before a "friendship" could be initiated?

Consider the idea of friendship within the therapeutic relationship. Do you think it is a valid component of therapy? Would you invite your client to your home or attend her birthday parties? To answer these questions, refer to the injunctions against *dual relationships* in your Code. Here is where the *Whose needs are being met?* question is valuable. By encouraging friendship, are we encouraging *dependency* in our clients? Would it not be preferable to support them in developing their own social network, even as a treatment goal? What about the treatment goal of making yourself redundant? Does it show *integrity* when you are a paid friend? These are all interesting questions. According to law professor Connie Conniglio (verbally transmitted), the therapeutic relationship should be marked by "friendliness but not friends." This could be especially important when working with children, whose understanding of the boundaries of a professional relationship may be lacking. To insert ourselves in their lives, under the guise of being there permanently, could be setting them up for abandonment issues. How friendly you become with your clients is a matter of style, but there is a line that probably should not be crossed. Where would you draw that line?

Duty as Professional

There is a variety of injunctions to be found in the codes around *practicing while impaired* or under the influence of drugs and alcohol. Some codes even recognize stress-related impairments as limits to effective functioning. These are the kinds of events that many of you may recognize as warrants for mental health days. Unfortunately, I know of no code or professional organization that officially subscribes to systematic mental health days. Instead, we are expected to self-monitor and *take care of ourselves*. In our current economic environment, where resources seem scarce, and front-line workers are overworked and under-supported, *stress, burnout or compassion fatigue* is a reality.

As such, it is critical that every professional have available a mental health kit. This could include his best friend, a respected colleague, a good therapist, a stalwart supervisor, a hobby that he is passionate about, massage or bodywork or an escape plan (lake, cottage, tree, garden, fill in your own) that is reasonably accessible. Other professionals have relied on peer support groups, a sport they love, romance and detective novels, etc. My favourite is the flannel zone, which includes an ancient pair of flannel pajamas with bucking broncos all over, a vast goose-down comforter, and four pillows and a sheet—all flannel-covered. Obviously humour and escape work for me. The best inoculation against burnout I have heard was offered by a student. I apologize for not remembering her name, but she concluded a class discussion on front-line stress by saying, "Get a life." Today we often confuse a profession with a life. Do you think that they should be one and the same?

Another strategy for de-stressing is finding ways to leave work in the office. That may include finding a particular landmark on the route home and mentally unloading all your work-related concerns there. Just unload, divest and pick them up on your way back to work the next day. If you choose a mall, you can have the added satisfaction of leaving something behind other than your money, especially if you don't go in. Or, before leaving the office, you could make a quick list of all the unresolved issues of the day—all the questions and concerns. After reviewing them, you can file them wherever. If it is possible, a long, hot shower or bath, as soon as you get home, can be helpful to some. Let the water take it all down the drain. Whatever you choose to do to take care of yourself, do it with as much seriousness as you display with your case management of clients' stressors. Personal management and case management are both legitimate professional issues.

Another area that can cause problems for therapists is *counter-transference* issues. These emerge when the client triggers a past experience, issue, or pattern of relating in the therapist. The resulting feelings are projected onto the client or the relationship. This is not always easily recognizable. Sometimes the feelings are the result of a positive identification that we don't expect. For example, we may begin to notice that the child described at intake by mother as non-compliant is actually angelic or better. Is the child really problematic and some counter-transference is going on, or is the mother and her report the problem? It is in situations like these, when the team and good supervision are important. In addition, knowing your own issues and responses can be critical. For example, when my emotional response or temperature goes into the acute range, I might question if counter-transference is implicated. A hint for me might be the use of the word angelic. It's not that I cannot conceive of a truly angelic child, only that I have never met one in therapy. It is rare for a child from a dysfunctional family coming into therapy not to have some areas that need development.

Everyone has different signals for when the therapeutic process might be clouded by counter-transference issues. It is the task of the mature professional to become self-aware and to deal with them. There is a variety of ways to work with or take responsibility for those intrusions. Supervision, peer support, and counselling are a few of the conventional ways. Finding the way that works for you is imperative. Otherwise, you will be facing yourself across the sand box or table, instead of the client, and never see the client at all.

Finally, there is the issue of *boundaries*. Boundaries can be professional (the question of friendship), social (how you respond when meeting your client in public) or physical (touching clients). Since we have dealt with a professional boundary, we will move on to a common experience for counsellors and therapists, especially those who work in smaller cities. How do you deal with your clients when you meet them in the supermarket, mall or on the street? If you greet them and politely enquire how they are, are you respecting their *privacy*? Many clients, especially children, will be happy to see you in public, but what if they are on week-end visitation, and in the company of the non-custodial violent parent? Do you want her to know your face, your license number? Would you be compromising your client's safety? Because of the potential risk to all parties and to respect the principle of privacy, I let my clients know at intake that if I see them on the street, I will ignore them, unless they choose to approach and initiate a conversation with me. Any public interaction will of necessity be brief.

The issue of *physical boundaries* has become extremely controversial, especially when working with children. Today, with victims of sexual abuse and sexual abuse allegations a prominent part of our practice, we need to exercise due caution. Children and adults who have been abused, sexually or physically, have (at the very least) suffered from boundary intrusions. This child or adult may have been socialized by the trauma to expect boundary intrusions. Often, educating the client about appropriate boundaries and body rights can be an important therapeutic goal. Given this scenario, what does it say about the child's body rights to appropriate boundaries, when the therapist can hug the child or pat the child or move into his space at will? How does it feel to a new client, who has experienced physical abuse, when she sees your hand coming up towards her head? How will she know you just want to pat her? Will her socialization or her very real life experience make her cringe for just a moment, before your intent becomes clear?

We are not speaking about a long-standing therapeutic relationship, where issues of boundaries have been worked out and the child has real choices. We are speaking of the short-term client that we want to comfort and nurture. After all, that is why we are here—we care. But again, the question must be asked: *whose needs are being met?* Keep in mind, that even when the child knows that he has to ask for a hug, if he has been sexually abused, he may already use his body to neutralize any potentially threatening adult—you. A child or adult who is not aware of boundaries may ask for hugs. Before you give one, would you consider using the invitation as a therapeutic opportunity to begin a discussion of boundaries?

There are no hard-and-fast rules about physical boundaries. It is a grey area dependent on many contingencies: stage of therapy, issues being worked on, style, comfort level with physical contact, and so on. Some therapists never touch their clients. One way to gain some control of the issue is to make rules (with children) about touching. This can be done at intake or in the first session. My rule (from Greg Lubimiv, in discussions) is that no one can touch the other without asking. The rule is for everyone in the playroom/studio, myself included. Another small point to keep in mind when working with sexually abused children or adolescents is never to work with them while alone in a building or entirely isolated. Some therapists will even keep the door a little open. This is a minor consideration, but given the allegations of abuse against therapists, we need to be cautious of not only what we do, but of how it may be perceived.

The Codes

In this section, I would expect you to insert your own professional code, whether it be the social work code, the psychotherapists' code or the art or play therapy code. Read them and know them. They are your profession's minimal standards for practice. Of course knowing them is just a beginning. In reality, codes cannot keep up with practice. Most codes are revised, but not every year. In addition, codes are largely reactionary; that is, they were a response to some widespread or public issue that has now been resolved. A current example of codes being slow to react is the new legislation regarding records being subpoenaed and the whole question of the use of therapeutic records in court. Currently most codes add little to the discussion, but future codes will no doubt reflect the struggle to *maintain adequate records*, while protecting our client's trust in *confidentiality*. Have you or your agency considered how they will handle the request for records from the court? Will your records stand up to professional standards?

The Law

This section is not intended to be an exhaustive discussion of all the relevant laws, for all the populations we serve. As a practitioner, you are expected to know not only agency protocols, e.g., to restrain or not restrain, but also the relevant laws, if you are working with a specific population; an example is The Young Offenders Act. In this section, I briefly review some relevant laws for working with children in Ontario.

Duty to report

The Child and Family Service Act 1990 (see Appendix 14-A) defines "a child in need of protection" as one who has suffered the "sins of commission"—e.g., physical or sexual abuse, or the "sins of omission"—e.g., failure to provide supervision, care, medical services, psychological services, etc. In addition, the Act stipulates that a child of twelve and over can consent to treatment (28). A guardian's signature would be welcome but not necessary. Finally, the twelve-year-old can read his or her records, unless doing so would cause harm (184 and 185).

The details and fine print of The Child and Family Service Act are basic knowledge for every practitioner working with children. If you have never read the Act, this is your opportunity to do so. One interesting detail that is sometimes missed is the **actual duty to report.** The law insists that each individual having a reasonable belief that a child is in need of protection **must notify the authorities**. Most agencies have a chain of command and protocols about by whom and how those calls are made. The individual who first heard the disclosure may not be the person to make the call. The problem is that the Act says "the individual who believes . . ." should report. Does that mean that even if your supervisor is responsible for making the call, you have to call as well? I do. As a professional, I read this to mean that even if I am with the guardian as support, while he is making the call, I will still take a moment to make my own call after having notified the guardian that I would. How does your agency handle this question? Are you comfortable with their position? Whom could you access to discuss your concerns?

What can you do if you are not sure that you have reasonable grounds for a call to children's services? You can do a run-by. A run-by is when you call, without disclosing any identifying information other than your own identity, and give the intake worker all the information you have. Then you ask if he is interested in pursuing the matter. It is helpful to your notation to write the worker's name, the date and time of the call, and his response. If he says he is interested, then you can tell him you will call back. After you hang up, you can initiate whatever procedures your agency has set out, which may or may not include notifying the caregivers. Whether you notify them and make them part of the formal call or not will depend on whether the child will be placed at risk by her caregiver's knowing. Handling disclosures is one of the most delicate and heart-wrenching experiences a therapist can have. Two common problems are the child's lack of gratitude and sense of betrayal and the Child Protection Service's inability to respond in the way that we would hope. In the first problem, the child may be attached or loyal to the perpetrator and feel that you have betrayed her confidence. Although it is a small comfort, one can begin the ensuing discussion with, "Remember at our first meeting when I told you that it is not okay for children to be hurt, and that if I knew that you were being hurt I would tell someone?"

The frustration expressed by many therapists against the child protection system is probably matched by the frustration felt by the workers within that system. Cutbacks, human resource shortages, escalating crises, and so on have all managed to limit their effectiveness and their ability to do the kind of job that they want to do. There is no question that we will have to become more creative and open in trying to meet our goals. But the goals of the therapist or counsellor are not always the same as those of the child protection workers.

One place where they diverge dramatically is the appropriate professional response to a disclosure of abuse by a child. Here the role of the therapist is primarily to support the child and pass on the information. It is the role of the child protection worker to receive the information and interview the child. These are two different roles. The therapist should not be interviewing the child. To begin with, any information will be second-hand and not useful in court. Without explicit training in the interview process, leading questions may be asked inadvertently, thus contaminating the evidence. It is simply not the place of the therapist to gather this information. And finally, it would be very unwise to lead a child into thinking that you will never tell Mom or Dad, just to keep him talking. That would be a deliberate lie, to no avail, since your information would be hearsay (unless you are a designated child protection worker). If the child begins to talk then we listen; we let him know that we believe him and pass the information on. From the beginning and beyond the disclosure, it is our role to support the child.

Duty to protect and warn

Duty to protect and warn refers to our obligation to act to protect those who threaten harm to themselves (suicide) or others (homicide, assault, the spread of AIDS). Unlike the *duty to report* (child abuse), these duties are not codified in law, but if you fail to act, you may be open to civil litigation. Duty to protect is more commonly respected and may be found in professional codes such as the nursing code. In fact, most agencies have protocols around dealing with high-risk clients. As stated earlier, not only do you need to be familiar with the protocols, you should know the signs in your client population. For example, children will present differently than adults. They might display inordinate interest in toxins and flammables, they may be accident-prone, they will be more spontaneous in their attempts, and so on. In addition, children under the age of ten may believe that death is not permanent. What is common for most populations is depression, helplessness or hopelessness, loss, and alienation. Knowing the signs, the appropriate interview and counselling goals—within and post-crisis—as well as community resources, are crucial to dealing with this issue.

Duty to warn is currently a very controversial topic, with no easy, available answers. The focus today is often on how we handle HIV-positive clients, if we know that their partners (who may also be our clients) are unaware of the situation. *Confidentiality, privacy, autonomy, and respect for persons* may all come into play here, as well as agency, peer and community standards. Do we warn the partner? This is one scenario where supervisors and legal consults may be necessary. Just a point to keep in mind: none of these legal obligations replaces our need to provide counselling, therapy, or otherwise fulfil our mandate. Certainly the legal aspects can confound case management, but it does not release us from our contract to provide service, if the client chooses to remain with us. Even if our legal interventions ultimately destroy our relationship, it is important to try to schedule a termination session, to allow the client to get closure and give you an opportunity to offer at least two referral possibilities. Unfortunately, the legal ramifications of our duty may make the client unwilling to deal with us, or even forbid contact because of litigation. Ideally, we should attempt to provide the final step, if possible.

A somewhat less complex scenario arises from a client who threatens to harm someone. For example, you are working with a young adult male who is depressed and tells you that he will kill his girlfriend if she tries to leave him. He has assaulted her twice in the past. One assault landed her in the hospital. Would you warn her? How would you come to that decision? Whom would you invite into your deliberations? I would hope that you would include legal advice, before you act. Again, these decisions are so complicated that they are probably beyond the capacity of most therapists to decide without legal advice. Can you think of any other interventions you might utilize before you took the last step?

In this section we have made a cursory review of the domains of ethical decision-making. As we moved through, we have encountered many of the common ethical principles formalized in professional codes. This discussion is not intended to be exhaustive, nor to replace an ethics course or shared discussion, consultation or supervision. As I stated at the outset, this chapter is intended as an introduction to ethics and professional practice; it is an opportunity to scan the field to see the parameters, to gather some information and help the reader become comfortable with issues. Having introduced you to the raw material of ethics, we will now move on to the Ethical Decision-making Format, derived from the work of Connie Coniglio, Ph.D.

Ethical Decision-making Format

This is a useful sequence of steps to work through almost any dilemma. What is especially important is steps 5-7, simply because they are most frequently omitted. Try using it on a current issue in your own practice, or apply it to one of the questions in the previous section. It can be a productive way to organize your thinking and allow the systematic working through of complex situations.

ETHICAL DECISION-MAKING FORMAT

1. Identify ethically relevant issues and practices in all domains i.e. the client, peer or agency, standards and protocols, community standards, personal principles and the law. (May include supervisor, team/professional consultation or legal advice.)

2. Develop alternative courses of action.

3. Analyze short-term, ongoing and long-term risks and benefits of each course of action on the individual, groups involved or likely to be affected—clients, client's family or employees, institution, colleagues, profession, society and self. Keep in mind the identified client.

4. Choose a course of action after conscientious application of existing principles, values, standards and protocols.

5. Carry out action plan with a commitment to assume responsibility for consequences of the action.
6. Evaluate the course of action.
7. Assume responsibility for the consequences of action, including correction of negative consequences, if any, or re-engaging in decision-making process if ethical decision not resolved.

Intake Process

Throughout this chapter, I have been suggesting that intake is the appropriate time to carry out certain tasks. Many of you have probably been thinking that my intakes must take hours. They do. But if I do an intake correctly, without missing any pieces, then my future sessions are immeasurably easier. In reality, there is nothing you can do to guarantee a successful course of therapy; there is nothing you can do to guarantee that the client will be safe or that you will be safe (from lawsuits). There are simply no guarantees in life or in counselling. Short of guarantees, a complete intake is the next best thing, and so I have included this checklist of what I do and when:

1. *Prior to intake meeting, mail out:*

   Information on services, fees, service provider, training or background status (interim)
   Information on confidentiality and limits of confidentiality (duty to warn, protect, subpoenas, right to review record, breach confidentiality if investigation)

   Information on expectations (therapist and clients, e.g. 24-hour notice of missed appointment)

   Intake, including question about what the client wishes to focus on or change in therapy, goals of therapy

Instruct client to bring forms to first meeting (including copy of custody form).

2. *First meeting—review and discuss, sign where applicable:*

   Approach, training, and status of service provider

   Confidentiality, limits and right to read records

   Fees, how and when paid, scheduling

Consultations, notifying other therapists

Informed consent: obtain and release information, to treatment, use of materials for supervision, education, display, or recording

Client will not be required to do anything not willing to do (unless mandated): the therapeutic alliance

Process and conditions that will cause renegotiations of contract

Dual relationship and social contact (public acknowledgment)

Substance abuse and safety contracts

3. *Contract:*
   Goals (set together)
   Fees, number of sessions
   Scheduling of sessions

4. *First session with child—review:*
   Limits to confidentiality
   Threat to harm or being hurt
   Rules of session
   Child doesn't harm self, other person, toys or room
   Child doesn't leave session before therapy session is completed
   Everything stays private
   No touching without permission
   Materials stay in room
   Rules are for everyone
   Clean up at end

Because my intakes are comprehensive, whenever possible I try to mail out a package to the prospective client. Usually the package consists of my brochure listing status, training, and services offered. Fees are usually negotiated over the phone at first contact, before the package goes out. With the package goes a form called Procedures and Guidelines for Counselling, which sets out the limits of confidentiality, expectations (24 hours' notice of missed appointments, etc.), a requisition for a copy of custody papers (if applicable), substance abuse contract (if applicable), and the actual intake form. The client is asked to review the package and bring it to the intake meeting. This preliminary review allows the client to become comfortable with the process. It mediates the usual sense of being overwhelmed that would occur if I blitzed her with paperwork in the first session. It also provides her with some time and privacy to consider her goals in therapy before I ask her.

The next step is the actual meeting, in which I review and answer any questions the client may have. One area that is easily missed is checking out his expectations of therapy, especially when working with his children. This is an opportunity to clarify my probable inability to fix the child in five sessions or less.

I also will check whether the client is currently working with another professional. If so, I will ask for a specific release to notify the other professional that I will also be working with the client. If the other professional is or may be working on similar issues with the client, then I may, after discussing it with the professional and client or caregiver, choose not to take on the case. There are several reasons to do so. For example, if the client is working with another art therapist and wants to do similar work with me, I will decline the contract. If the client is working with a psychiatrist and simply wants to use art therapy as an adjunct, with the full knowledge and support of the primary therapist (the psychiatrist), I will work with the client, but remain in contact with the primary worker to integrate our services so that we are not working at cross-purposes. The same may be said of other service providers. If the client is working in a group of sexual abuse survivors, then I would still want a release to stay in touch with the group leaders to avoid putting the client at risk by assigning tasks when she is already in crisis. Again, there are no hard and fast rules here. Each case is different. But it is a good idea to check for other services and get a release to facilitate good case management. This release should be specific and negotiated with the client in terms of duration or time frame for sharing information and precisely what information and for what purpose this contact should be maintained. In general, all releases should be specific and thoroughly discussed with the client. If you knew a client was working with another professional, but she was unwilling to sign a release allowing you to contact that professional, would you work with her?

Not only consents to obtain and release information are prepared at intake. Consents to use and present information for supervision are signed. I have children sign their own consent forms if they are mature enough to comprehend. Although the codes do not specify these actions, I feel they encourage *autonomy and respect*. To date, I have only had one child refuse to sign consents for supervision. It was a decision that I could live with, simply because I was working on a discrete and limited issue.

If you are taking on a client where *role conflict* or *dual relationship* is an unavoidable issue, and (for whatever reason) you are choosing to work with this client, a thorough discussion of the issues and boundaries of the relationship should occur. A written contract outlining the agreed-upon stipulations should be drawn up and signed by both the client and therapist. If you are a play therapist, it is a code violation if you fail to do it. Even if you are not a play therapist, if you must become involved in dual relationships (I would advise against it), then a written agreement is valuable.

Finally, on the list is the contract for services. To be effective it should include the fees, the name of the therapist, and the number of sessions; and it should be the result of a complete discussion of the client's goals. If you are working with a child, it is important to know why they think they are there, how they feel about being there and who you are and what you do. Also, a discussion of confidentiality and the limits of confidentiality should occur here.

In your first session with the child, especially if you are using a playroom, negotiating the rules and consequences is a useful start. According to Greg Lubimiv (in discussions), children enjoy practicing breaking the rules. My experience bears this out. Not only do they become more invested in the rules that they have co-created, they get to send you to the time-out chair!

Conclusion

In this chapter I have tried to give you a sense of the challenge and the shape of ethics and professional practice today. One chapter does not replace a book or experience or a whole course. I trust by now that you recognize not only the complexity, but the everyday nature of these questions. For those of you for whom a course is not feasible, I strongly encourage you to read, attend workshops, access senior practitioners in your own field and begin to develop your own personal principles, positions and questions.

APPENDIX 14-A

CHILD AND FAMILY SERVICE ACT

Revisions to the Ontario Child and Family Services Act came into effect in the year 2000. The revisions noted in this chapter are important and have been highlighted for this specific chapter on Ethics. The information is from a brochure put out by the Ontario government, the Ministry of Community and Social Services. The brochure is called "Reporting Child Abuse and Neglect."

The Act defines the term "child in need of protection" and sets out what must be reported (CFSA S. 72(1)). It includes physical, sexual and emotional abuse, neglect and risk of harm.

Responsibility to report a child in need of protection CFSA S. 72 (1)
If a person has reasonable grounds to suspect that a child is or may be in need of protection, the person must promptly report the suspicion and the information upon which it is based to a children's aid society.
(Note the explanation of CFSA S. 72 (1) at the end of this outline)

Ongoing duty to report CFSA S. 72 (2)
The duty to report is an ongoing obligation. If a person has made a previous report about a child, and has additional grounds to suspect that a child is or may be in need protection, that person must make a further report to a children's aid society.

Persons must report directly CFSA S. 72 (3)
The person who has the reasonable grounds to suspect that a child is or may be in need of protection must make the report directly to a children's aid society. The person must not rely on anyone else to report on his or her behalf.

"Reasonable grounds" are what an average person, given his or her training, background and experience, exercising normal and honest judgement, would suspect.

Special responsibilities of professionals and officials, and penalty for failure to report CFSA S. 72 (4), (6.2)
Professional persons and officials have the same duty as any

member of the public to report a suspicion that a child is in need of protection. The Act recognizes, however, that persons working closely with children have a special awareness of the signs of child abuse and neglect, and a particular responsibility to report their suspicions, and so makes it an offence to fail to report.

Any professional or official who fails to report a suspicion that a child is or may be in need of protection, where the information on which that suspicion is based was obtained in the course of his or her professional of official duties, is liable on conviction to a fine of up to $1,000.00.

Professionals affected CFSA S. 72 (5)

- Persons who perform professional or official duties with respect to children include the following:
- health care professionals, including physicians, nurses, dentists, pharmacists and psychologists;
- teachers, and school principals;
- social workers and family counsellors;
- priests, rabbis and other members of the clergy;
- operators or employees of day nurseries;
- youth and recreation workers (not volunteers);
- peace officers and coroners;
- solicitors;
- service providers and employees of service providers; and
- any other person who performs professional or official duties with respect to a child.

This list sets out examples only. If your work involves children but is not listed above, you may still be considered to be a professional for purposes of the duty to report. If you are not sure whether you may be considered to be a professional for purpose of the duty to report, you should contact your local children's aid society, professional association or regulatory body.

Professional confidentiality CFSA S. 72 (7), (8)

The professional's duty to report overrides the provisions of any other provincial statue, specifically, those provisions that would otherwise prohibit disclosure by the professional or official.

That is, the professional must report that a child is or may be in need of protection even when the information is supposed to be confidential or privileged. (The only exception for "privileged" information is in the relationship between a solicitor and a client.)

Protection from liability CFSA S. 72 (7)
If a civil action is brought against a person who made a report, that person will be protected unless he or she acted maliciously or without reasonable grounds for his or her suspicion.

CHILD and FAMILY SERVICES ACT CFSA S. 72 (1)
Despite the provisions of any other Act, if a person, including a person who performs professional or official duties with respect with children, has responsible grounds to suspect one of the following, the person shall forthwith report the suspicion and the information on which it is based to a society.

1. The child has suffered physical harm, inflicted by the person having charge of the child or caused by or resulting from the person's

   a) failure to adequately care for, provide for, supervise or protect the child or

   b) pattern of neglect in caring for, providing for, supervising or protecting the child.

2. There is a risk that the child is likely to suffer physical harm inflicted by the person having charge of the child or caused by or resulting from that person's

   a) failure to adequately care for, provide for, supervise or protect the child, or

   b) pattern of neglect in caring for, providing for supervising or protecting the child.

3. The child has been sexually molested or sexually exploited by the person having charge of the child or by another person where the person having charge of the child known or should know of the possibility of sexual molestation or sexual exploitation and fails to protect the child.

4. There is a risk that the child is likely to be sexually molested or sexually exploited as described in paragraph 8.

5. The child requires medical treatment to cure, prevent or alleviate physical harm or suffering and the child's parent or the person having charge of the child does not provide, or refuses or is unavailable or unable to consent to, the treatment.

6. The child has suffered emotional harm, demonstrated by serious,

   I. anxiety

   II. depression

   III. withdrawal

   IV. self-destructive or aggressive behaviour, or

   V. delayed development.

   and there are reasonable grounds to believe that the emotional harm suffered by the child results from the actions, failure to act or pattern of neglect on the part of the child's parent or the person having charge of the child.

7. The child has suffered emotional harm of the kind described in subparagraph I, II, III, IV or V of paragraph 6 and the child's parent or the person having charge of the child does not provide, or refuses or is unavailable or unable to consent to, services or treatment to remedy or alleviate the harm.

8. There is a risk that the child is likely to suffer emotional harm of the kind described in paragraph I, II, III, IV, and V or paragraph 6 resulting from the actions, failure to act or pattern of neglect on the part of the child's parent or the person having charge of the child.

9. There is a risk that child is likely to suffer emotional harm of the kind described in subparagraph I, II, III, IV, and V of paragraph 6 and that the child's parent or the person having charge of the child does not provide, or refuses or is unavailable or unable to consent to services or treatment to prevent harm.

10. The child suffers from mental, emotional or developmental condition that, if not remedied could seriously impair the child's development and the child's parent or the person having charge of the child does not provide, or refuses or is unavailable or unable to consent to, treatment to remedy or relieve the condition.

11. The child has been a abandoned, the child's parent has died, or is unavailable to exercise his or her custodial rights over the child and has not made adequate provision, for the child's care and custody or the child is in residential placement and the parent refuses or is unable or unwilling to resume the child's care and custody.

12. The child is less then 12 years old and has killed or seriously injured another person or cause serious damage to another's person's property, services or treatment are necessary to prevent reoccurrence and the child's parent or the person having charge of the child does not provide, or refuses or is unavailable or unable to consent to those services or treatment.

13. This child is less then 12 years old and has on more the one occasion injured another person or caused loss or damage to another person's property, with the encouragement of the having charge of the child or because that person's failure or inability to supervise the child adequately.

OTHER LEGAL RESPONSIBILITIES OF THERAPISTS

Duty to Protect and Warn

If client discloses intent to hurt self or others, the therapist has a duty to protect the client from self-harm and must warn others if threat seems reasonable. In these instances, supervision, consultation (both professional and legal) and due diligence are necessary to avoid loss of life and lawsuits.

LEGAL RESOURCES TO ORDER

Titles from the Ministry of the Attorney General, 720 Bay St., Toronto, Ontario, M5G 2K1:

Where do I stand? A child's legal guide to separation and divorce.
What women and men should know about family law.
What's my job in court? Victim/witness assistance program.

Titles from the Centre for Children and Families in the Justice System of the London Family Court Clinic, 254 Pall Mall St., Suite 200, London, Ontario, N6A 5P6 (useful for preparing children for court, etc.):

Reducing the system induced trauma for child sexual abuse victims through court preparation assessment and follow-up. (1991).
Three years after the verdict. (1993).
What you should know after the verdict.
Tipping the balance of the secret.

Betty Bedard Bidwell

CONTRIBUTORS

BETTY BEDARD BIDWELL

Betty is a certified play therapist and trainer/supervisor for both the Canadian and American Play Therapy Associations. As well, she is a registered art therapist with the Ontario Art Therapy Association and the American Art Therapy Association. Betty was the first internationally certified therapist with her Art and Play Therapy Certification. She has presented at conferences and workshops in Canada and the United States.

Ms. Bidwell is the founder and coordinator of the Play Therapy Diploma Program and is one of the co-founders of the Art Therapy Program at the University of Western Ontario. She continues to be an instructor for the Art Therapy Program and is now the coordinator for the CACPT Certificate Play Therapy Program. Betty is a supervisor for both art and play therapy students/interns.

Betty is the owner/operator of a children's private residential treatment program called Betamarsh Inc. Her facility has two licensed group homes, foster care program and after care. Betmarsh Inc. is licensed for forty children/youth with a wide range of presenting difficulties.

Ms. Bidwell has a small private practice for children, youth, adults, couples and families. Betty is very involved in her community, and she recently received the distinguished Premier's Award in recognition of her many years of dedication and commitment to children and their families. Betty has been involved in numerous roles in her community as well as within the Canadian Play Therapy Association.

Ms. Bidwell is the mother of two girls, Jessica and Alisha. She says that her husband has given her unconditional support and understanding of her work. Her hobbies are raising cocker spaniel puppies, her four horses, and her small hobby farm with goats, sheep and chickens. Betty also loves decorating and art.

DONNA CUTHBERTSON

Donna Cuthbertson has been a child and youth counsellor for the past twenty years, working with children with varying special needs in various settings. Her counselling has always utilized play.

Donna is a certified child psychotherapist and play therapist, with training and experience through the International Play Therapy Association, as well as the Canadian Association for Child and Play Therapy.

Donna is professionally affiliated with the International Association for Play Therapy as well as the Council for Exceptional Children. Donna had served on the executive committee of CEC-Durham Chapter 584 since 1993. Donna is a past board member with the Canadian Association for Child and Play Therapy.

In addition to working with the Durham Region Roman Catholic Separate School Board, Donna is setting up private practice in the Durham region.

BARB DORRINGTON

Barb has been a social worker in the London community since 1977, receiving her art therapy registration status from the Ontario Art Therapy Association in 1984. Barb has always worked with children and their families in counselling and for the past ten years has also enjoyed supervising practicum placements of art therapy students from the University of Western Ontario.

Presently Barb works as a social worker for the London and Middlesex Catholic School Board where she is able to use her art therapy skills as well as supervise students on placement. Barb also has her registration with the American Art Therapy Association.

JUDY JONES

Judy works in the Early Intervention Program and Early Years' Assessment Program at Madame Vanier Children's Services in London, Ontario.

Judy has many years of valuable play therapy experience, which she utilizes in her daily work with children.

SUZANNE LISTER

Suzanne is the coordinator of Pediatric Oncology Art Therapy at Children's Hospital of Western Ontario in London. In addition to working with children diagnosed with cancer, Ms. Lister also works with bereaved siblings. Ms. Lister's research interests include the assessment of drawings of children on and off treatment for cancer, for which she received the Research Award from the American Art Therapy Association in 1993. Ms. Lister is past president of the Ontario Art Therapy Association and past ethics chair of the Canadian Association for Child and Play Therapy.

GREG LUBIMIV

Gregory P. Lubimiv, M.S.W., is executive director of the Phoenix Centre for Children and Families, a children's mental health centre in southeastern Ontario. He also operates Transitions, a private practice that provides training and consultation services across the continent. Greg is a certified child psychotherapist and play therapist as well as a certified supervisor with the Canadian Association of Child and Play Therapy. He is an experienced clinician and a dynamic teacher, who has written numerous articles on play and other forms of therapy. His recent book *Wings for Our Children* is a "must read" for anyone embarking on the journey to use play and art therapy with children.

MARG McBRIDE

Marg McBride has worked as a child psychotherapist, play therapist and child life specialist with hospitalized children.

She currently provides care for geriatric and palliative patients. She is also self-employed as a reflexologist.

Marg lives in St. Mary's, Ontario with her husband and two sons.

DR. EVANGELINE MUNNS

Dr. Munns is the clinical director of Play Therapy Services at Blue Hills Child and Family Centre in Aurora, Ontario, which currently has the largest Theraplay training school in Canada. She has studied experimental and clinical psychology at the University of Alberta, University of Toronto, and York University, graduating with a Ph.D. from the latter. She is a certified psychologist and has had extensive experience in working with troubled children and their families as well as being a consultant to various mental health agencies in Ontario. She is a certified therapist and trainer in both non-directive play therapy and Theraplay. Dr. Munns is a popular presenter, has given workshops across Canada and has presented at several international conferences.

JULIE REGAN

Julie is a social worker at Madame Vanier Children's Services in London, Ontario, and is presently on a sabbatical from this agency.

Julie is a certified play therapist who utilizes her play therapy experience in her practice with families, particularly sibling groups. She is the CACPT president for 2000-2001

BRIDGET REVELL

Bridget is recognized as a play therapist and supervisor with the Canadian Association of Child and Play Therapy, the Association for Play Therapy (based in the United States), and the International Board of Examiners of Certified Play Therapists.

Bridget has her M.S.W. from Wilfred Laurier and has worked in a number of children's mental health agencies in Ontario, Canada. A portion of her therapeutic practice focuses on providing play therapy to child victims of sexual abuse. In 1994, Bridget received the Monica Herbert award presented by the Canadian Association for Child and Play Therapy in appreciation of outstanding contribution to play therapy and the community. She has also been president and a board member of the Canadian Association of Play Therapy.

MARGOT SIPPEL

Margot Sippel is a registered art therapist with the Ontario Art Therapy Association and the American Art Therapy Association. She is a certified child psychotherapist and play therapist with the Canadian Association for Child and Play Therapy. She has been certified by the International Board of Examiners in Play Therapy as a play therapist and supervisor. Margot teaches in the Child and Youth Worker Program at Fanshawe College in London, Ontario. Her work has been influenced by Virginia Axline, Clarke Moustakis, Betty Bedard Bidwell, and her main mentor, Irene Dewdney. More recently, the work of Susan Bach has played an important role in her development. Margot is presently involved in a research project funded by the C.G. Jung Foundation, which investigates art created by children with cancer.

BARBARA JONES-WARRICK

Barbara Jones-Warrick is a social worker at Madame Vanier Children's Services in London, Ontario. She is a certified play therapist who specializes in work with families, individuals and groups.

SHARRON ZWEIG, OATR

Sharron Zweig is a graduate of The University of Western Ontario, with a degree in anthropology and a diploma in art therapy. She received her play therapy training through a CACPT accredited training program. She is a lecturer in the Art Therapy and Play Therapy Programs at the University of Western Ontario, and currently sits on the board of directors of The Ontario Art Therapy Association. She is the mother of one social worker, two lawyers, and the best friend of two boisterous Bouviers.

ABOUT THE ARTIST

GWEN KIAR

A graduate of the Mohawk College Art Program, Gwen worked as a graphic designer in Waterloo County for ten years before moving with her husband Christian to Ontario's "west coast." Now university graduates, their children Deanna and Paul were raised in the small port of Goderich on Lake Huron.

Gwen's art studio/gallery, "The Gallery in the Garden," was opened in November 1988. Her watercolour paintings have hung in solo exhibitions and public art galleries in and around Ontario. She finds it an inspiration to paint in "plein-air," and also enjoys teaching her young, energetic art students.